Fry the Party!

The Best Recipes to Enjoy During Birthdays, Celebrations and Anniversaries

By
Sean Foster

Table of Contents

The Complete Air Fryer Cookbook with Pictures

Air Fryer Cookbook for Two

Vegan Air Fryer Cookbook

The Complete Air Fryer Cookbook with Pictures

70+ Perfectly Portioned Air Fryer Recipes for Busy People on a Budget

By

Sean Foster

Table of Contents

INTRODUCTION:

The aim of this cookbook is to provide the easiness for those who are professional or doing job somewhere. But with earning, it is also quite necessary to cook food easily & timely instead of ordering hygienic or costly junk food. As we know, after doing office work, no one can cook food with the great effort. For the ease of such people, there are a lot of latest advancements in kitchen accessories. The most popular kitchen appliances usually helps to make foods or dishes like chicken, mutton, beef, potato chips and many other items in less time and budget. There are a lot of things that should be considered when baking with an air fryer. One of the most important tips is to make sure you have all of your equipment ready for the bake. It is best to be prepared ahead of time and this includes having pans, utensils, baking bags, the air fryer itself, and the recipe book instead of using stove or oven. With the help of an air fryer, you can make various dishes for a single person as well as the entire family timely and effortlessly. As there is a famous proverb that "Nothing can be done on its own", it indicates that every task takes time for completion. Some tasks take more time and effort and some requires less time and effort for their completion. Therefore, with the huge range of advancements that come to us are just for our ease. By using appliances like an air fryer comes for the comfort of professional people who are busy in earning their livelihood. In this book, you can follow the latest, delicious, and quick, about 70 recipes that will save your time and provide you healthy food without any great effort.

Chapter # 1:
An Overview & Benefits of an Air Fryer

Introduction:

The most popular kitchen appliance that usually helps to make foods or dishes like chicken, mutton, beef, potato chips and many other items in less time and budget.

Today, everything is materialistic, every person is busy to earn great livelihood. Due to a huge burden of responsibilities, they have no time to cook food on stove after doing hard work. Because, traditionally cooking food on the stove takes more time and effort. Therefore, there are a vast variety of Kitchen appliances. The kitchen appliances are so much helpful in making or cooking food in few minutes and in less budget. You come to home from job, and got too much tired. So, you can cook delicious food in an Air Fryer efficiently and timely as compared to stove. You can really enjoy the food without great effort and getting so much tired.

The Air Fryer Usability:

Be prepared to explore all about frying foods that you learned. To crisp, golden brown excellence (yes, French-fried potatoes and potato chips!), air fryers will fry your favourite foods using minimum or no oil. You can not only make commonly fried foods such as chips and French fries of potatoes, however it is also ideal for proteins, vegetables such as drummettes and chicken wings, coquettes & feta triangles as well as appetizers. And cookies are perfectly cooked in an air fryer, such as brownies and blondies.

The Air Fryer Works as:

- Around 350-375°F (176-190°C) is the ideal temperature of an Air Fryer
- To cook the surface of the food, pour over a food oil at the temperature mentioned above. The oil can't penetrate because it forms a type of seal.
- Simultaneously, the humidity within the food turns into steam that helps to actually cook the food from the inside. It is cleared that the steam helps to maintain the oil out of the food.
- The oil flows into the food at a low temperature, rendering it greasy.
- It oxidizes the oil and, at high temperatures, food will dry out.

On the other hand, an air fryer is similar to a convection oven, but in a diverse outfit, food preparation done at very high temperatures whereas, inside it, dry air circulates around the food at the same time, while making it crisp without putting additional fat, it makes it possible for cooking food faster.

What necessary to Search for in an Air Fryer?

As we know, several different sizes and models of air fryers are available now. If you're cooking for a gathering, try the extra-large air fryer, that can prepare or fry a whole chicken, other steaks or six servings of French fries.

Suppose, you've a fixed counter space, try the Large Air Fryer that uses patented machinery to circulate hot air for sufficient, crispy results. The latest air fryer offers an extra compact size with identical capacity! and tar equipment, which ensures that food is cooking evenly (no further worries of build-ups). You will be able to try all the fried foods you enjoy, with no embarrassment.

To increase the functionality of an air fryer, much more, you can also purchase a wide range of different accessories, including a stand, roasting pan, muffin cups, and mesh baskets. Check out the ingredients of our air fryer we created, starting from buttermilk with black pepper seasoning to fry chicken or Sichuan garlic seasoning suitable for Chinese cuisine.

We will read about the deep fryer, with tips and our favourite recipes like burgers, chicken wings, and many more.

Most Common - Five Guidelines for an Air Fryer usage:

1. Shake the food.

Open the air fryer and shake the foods efficiently because the food is to "fry" in the machine's basket—Light dishes like Sweet French fries and Garlic chips will compress. Give Rotation to the food every 5-10 mins for better performance

2. Do not overload.

Leave enough space for the food so that the air circulates efficiently; so that's gives you crunchy effects. Our kitchen testing cooks trust that the snacks and small batches can fry in air fryer.

3. Slightly spray to food.

Gently spray on food by a cooking spray bottle and apply a touch of oil on food to make sure the food doesn't stick to the basket.

4. Retain an Air fry dry.

Beat food to dry before start cooking (even when marinated, e.g.) to prevent splashing & excessive smoke. Likewise, preparing high-fat foods such as chicken steaks or wings, be assured to remove the grease from the lower part of machine regularly.

5. Other Most Dominant cooking techniques.

The air fryer is not just for deep frying; It is also perfect for further safe methods of cooking like baking, grilling, roasting and many more. Our kitchen testing really loves using the unit for cooking salmon in air fryer!

An Air Fryer Helps to reduce fat content

Generally, food cooked in deep fryer contains higher fat level than preparing food in other cooking appliances. For Example; a fried chicken breast contains about 30% more fat just like a fat level in roasted chicken

Many Manufacturers claimed, an Air fryer can reduce fat from fried food items up-to 75%. So, an air fryer requires less amount of fat than a deep fryer. As, many dishes cooked in deep fryer consume 75% oil (equal to 3 cups) and an air fryer prepare food by applying the oil in just about 1 tablespoon (equal to 15ml).

One research tested the potato chips prepared in air fryer characteristics then observed: the air frying method produces a final product with slightly lower fat but same moisture content and color. So, there is a major impact on anyone's health, an excessive risk of illnesses such as inflammation, infection and heart disease has been linked to a greater fat intake from vegetable oils.

Air Fryer provides an Aid in Weight Loss

The dishes prepared deep fryer are not just having much fat but also more in calories that causes severe increase in weight. Another research of 33,542 Spanish grown-ups indicates that a greater usage of fried food linked with a higher occurrence of obesity. Dietetic fat has about twice like many calories per gram while other macro-nutrients such as carbohydrates, vitamins and proteins, averaging in at 9 calories throughout each and every gram of oil or fat.

By substituting to air fryer is an easy way to endorse in losing weight and to reduce calories and it will be done only by taking food prepared in air fryer.

Air Fried food may reduce the potentially harmful chemicals

Frying foods can produce potentially hazardous compounds such as acrylamide, in contrast to being higher in fat and calories. An acrylamide is a compound that is formed in carbohydrate- rich dishes or foods during highly-heated cooking methods such as frying. Acrylamide is known as a "probable carcinogen" which indicates as some research suggests that it could be associated with the development of cancer. Although the findings are conflicting, the link between dietary acrylamide and a greater risk of kidney, endometrial and ovarian cancers has been identified in some reports. Instead of cooking food in a deep fryer, air frying your food may aid the acrylamide content. Some researches indicates that air-frying method may cut the acrylamide by 90% by comparing deep frying method. All other extremely harmful chemicals produced by high-heat cooking are polycyclic aromatic hydrocarbons, heterocyclic amines and aldehydes and may be associated with a greater risk of cancer. That's why, the air fried food may help to reduce the chance of extremely dangerous chemicals or compounds and maintain your health.

Chapter # 2:

70 Perfectly Portioned Air Fryer Recipes for Busy People in Minimum Budget

1. Air fried corn, zucchini and haloumi fritters

Ingredients

- Coarsely grated block haloumi - 225g
- Coarsely grated Zucchini - 2 medium sized
- Frozen corn kernels - 150g (1 cup)
- Lightly whisked eggs - 2
- Self-raising flour - 100g
- Extra virgin olive oil - to drizzle
- Freshly chopped oregano leaves - 3 tablespoons
- Fresh oregano extra sprigs - to serve
- Yoghurt - to serve

Method

1. Use your palms to squeeze out the extra liquid from the zucchini and place them in a bowl. Add the corn and haloumi and stir for combining them. Then add the eggs, oregano and flour. Add seasoning and stir until fully mixed.
2. Set the temperature of an air fryer to 200 C. Put spoonsful of the mixture of zucchini on an air fryer. Cook until golden and crisp, for 8 minutes. Transfer to a dish that is clean. Again repeat this step by adding the remaining mixture in 2 more batches.

3. Take a serving plate and arrange soft fritters on it. Take yoghurt in a small serving bowl. Add seasoning of black pepper on the top of yoghurt. Drizzle with olive oil. At the end, serve this dish with extra oregano.

2. Air fryer fried rice

Ingredients

- Microwave long grain rice - 450g packet
- Chicken tenderloins - 300g
- Rindless bacons - 4 ranchers
- Light Soy sauce - 2 tablespoons
- Oyster sauce - 2 tablespoons
- Sesame oil - 1 tablespoon
- Fresh finely grated ginger - 3 tablespoons
- Frozen peas - 120g (3/4 cup)
- Lightly whisked eggs - 2
- Sliced green shallots - 2
- Thin sliced red chilli - 1
- Oyster sauce - to drizzle

Method
1. Set the 180°C temperature of an air fryer. Bacon and chicken is placed on the rack of an air fryer. Cook them until fully cooked for 8-10 minutes. Shift it to a clean plate and set this plate aside to cool. Then, slice and chop the bacon and chicken.
2. In the meantime, separate the rice grains in the packet by using your fingers. Heat the rice for 60 seconds in a microwave. Shift to a 20cm ovenproof, round high-sided pan or dish. Apply the sesame oil, soy sauce, ginger, oyster sauce and 10ml water and mix well.

3. Put a pan/dish in an air fryer. Cook the rice for 5 minutes till them soft. Then whisk the chicken, half of bacon and peas in the eggs. Completely cook the eggs in 3 minutes. Mix and season the top of half shallot with white pepper and salt.
4. Serve with the seasoning of chilli, remaining bacon and shallot and oyster sauce.

3. Air fried banana muffins

Ingredients
- Ripe bananas - 2
- Brown sugar - 60g (1/3 cup)
- Olive oil - 60ml (1/4 cup)
- Buttermilk - 60ml (1/4 cup)
- Self-raising flour - 150g (1 cup)
- Egg - 1
- Maple syrup - to brush or to serve

Method
1. Mash the bananas in a small bowl using a fork. Until needed, set aside.
2. In a medium cup, whisk the flour and sugar using a balloon whisk. In the middle, make a well. Add the buttermilk, oil and egg. Break up the egg with the help of a whisk. Stir by using wooden spoon until the mixture is mixed. Stir the banana through it.
3. Set the temperature of an air fryer at 180C. Splits half of the mixture into 9 cases of patties. Remove the rack from the air fryer and pass the cases to the rack carefully. Switch the rack back to the fryer. Bake the muffins completely by cooking them for 10 minutes. Move to the wire rack. Repeat this step on remaining mixture to produce 18 muffins.
4. Brush the muffin tops with maple syrup while they're still warm. Serve, if you like, with extra maple syrup.

4. Air fried Nutella brownies

Ingredients
- Plain flour - 150g (1 cup)
- Castor white sugar - 225g (1 cup)
- Lightly whisked eggs - 3
- Nutella - 300g (1 cup)
- Cocoa powder - to dust

Method
1. Apply butter in a 20cm circular cake pan. Cover the base by using baking paper.
2. Whisk the flour and sugar together in a bowl by using balloon whisk. In the middle, make a well. Add the Nutella and egg in the middle of bowl by making a well. Stir with a large metal spoon until mixed. Move this mixture to the previously prepared pan and smooth the surface of the mixture by using metal spoon.
3. Pre - heat an air fryer to 160C. Bake the brownie about 40 minutes or until a few crumbs stick out of a skewer inserted in the middle. Fully set aside to cool.
4. Garnish the top of the cake by dusting them with cocoa powder, and cut them into pieces. Brownies are ready to be served.

5. Air fried celebration bites

Ingredients
- Frozen shortcrust partially thawed pastry - 4 sheets
- Lightly whisked eggs - 1
- Unrapped Mars Celebration chocolates - 24
- Icing sugar - to dust
- Cinnamon sugar - to dust
- Whipped cream - to serve

Method

1. Slice each pastry sheet into 6 rectangles. Brush the egg gently. One chocolate is placed in the middle of each rectangular piece of pastry. Fold the pastry over to cover the chocolate completely. Trim the pastry, press and seal the sides. Place it on a tray containing baking paper. Brush the egg on each pastry and sprinkle cinnamon sugar liberally.

2. In the air-fryer basket, put a sheet of baking paper, making sure that the paper is 1 cm smaller than the basket to allow airflow. Put six pockets in the basket by taking care not to overlap. Cook for 8-9 minutes at 190°C until pastries are completely cooked with golden color. Shift to a dish. Free pockets are then used again.

3. Sprinkle Icing sugar on the top of tasty bites. Serve them with a whipped cream to intensify its flavor.

6. Air fried nuts and bolts

Ingredients

- Dried farfalle pasta - 2 cups
- Extra virgin olive oil - 60ml (1/4th cup)
- Brown sugar - 2 tablespoons
- Onion powder - 1 tablespoon
- Smoked paprika - 2 tablespoons
- Chili powder - 1/2 tablespoon
- Garlic powder - 1/2 tablespoon
- Pretzels - 1 cup
- Raw macadamias - 80g (1/2 cup)
- Raw cashews - 80g (1/2 cup)
- Kellog's Nutri-grain cereal - 1 cup
- Sea salt - 1 tablespoon

Method

1. Take a big saucepan of boiling salted water, cook the pasta until just ready and soft. Drain thoroughly. Shift pasta to a tray and pat with a paper towel to dry. Move the dried pasta to a wide pot.

2. Mix the sugar, oil, onion, paprika, chili and garlic powders together in a clean bowl. Add half of this mixture in the bowl containing pasta. Toss this bowl slightly for the proper coating of mixture over pasta.

3. Set the temperature at 200C of an Air Fryer. Put the pasta in air fryer's pot. After cooking for 5 minutes, shake the pot and cook for more 5-7 minutes, until they look golden and crispy. Shift to a wide bowl.

4. Take the pretzels in a bowl with the nuts and apply the remaining mixture of spices. Toss this bowl for the proper coating. Put in air fryer's pot and cook at 180C for 3-4 minutes. Shake this pot and cook for more 2-3 minutes until it's golden in color. First add pasta and then add the cereal. Sprinkle salt on it and toss to mix properly. Serve this dish after proper cooling.

7. Air fried coconut shrimps

Ingredients

- Plain flour - 1/2 cup
- Eggs - 2
- Bread crumbs - 1/2 cup
- Black pepper powder - 1.5 teaspoons
- Sweetless flaked coconut - 3/4 cup
- Uncooked, deveined and peeled shrimp - 12 ounces
- Salt - 1/2 teaspoon
- Honey - 1/4 cup
- Lime juice - 1/4 cup
- Finely sliced serrano chili - 1

- Chopped cilantro - 2 teaspoons
- Cooking spray

Method
1. Stir the pepper and flour in a clean bowl together. Whisk the eggs in another bowl and h panko and coconut in separate bowl.   Coat the shrimps with flour mixture by holding each shrimp by tail and shake off the extra flour.   Then coat the floured shrimp with egg and allow it to drip off excess. Give them the final coat of coconut mixture and press them to stick. Shift on a clean plate. Spray shrimp with cooking oil.
2. Set the temperature of the air-fryer to 200C. In an air fryer, cook half of the shrimp for 3 minutes. Turn the shrimp and cook further for more 3 minutes until color changes in golden. Use 1/4 teaspoon of salt for seasoning.   Repeat this step for the rest of shrimps.
3. In the meantime, prepare a dip by stirring lime juice, serrano chili and honey in a clean bowl.
4. Serve fried shrimps with sprinkled cilantro and dip.

8. Air fried Roasted Sweet and Spicy Carrots

Ingredients
- Cooking oil
- Melted butter - 1 tablespoon
- Grated orange zest - 1 teaspoon
- Carrots - 1/2 pound

- Hot honey - 1 tablespoon
- Cardamom powder - 1/2 teaspoon
- Fresh orange juice - 1 tablespoon
- Black pepper powder - to taste
- Salt - 1 pinch

Method

1. Set the temperature of an air to 200C. Lightly coat its pot with cooking oil.
2. Mix honey, cardamom and orange zest in a clean bowl. Take 1 tablespoon of this sauce in another bowl and place aside. Coat carrots completely by tossing them in remaining sauce. Shift carrots to an air fryer pot.
3. Air fry the carrots and toss them after every 6 minutes. Cook carrots for 15-20 minutes until they are fully cooked and roasted. Combine honey butter sauce with orange juice to make sauce. Coat carrots with this sauce. Season with black pepper and salt and serve this delicious dish.

9. Air fried Chicken Thighs

Ingredients

- Boneless chicken thighs - 4
- Extra virgin olive oil - 2 teaspoons
- Smoked paprika - 1 teaspoon
- Salt - 1/2 teaspoon
- Garlic powder - 3/4 teaspoon
- Black pepper powder - 1/2 teaspoon

Method

1. Set the temperature of an air fryer to 200C.
2. Dry chicken thighs by using tissue paper. Brush olive oil on the skin side of each chicken thigh. Shift the single layer of chicken thighs on a clean tray.
3. Make a mixture of salt, black pepper, paprika and garlic powder in a clean bowl. Use a half of this mixture for the seasoning of 4 chicken thighs on both sides evenly. Then shift single layer of chicken thighs in an air fryer pot by placing skin side up.
4. Preheat the air fryer and maintain its temperature to 75C. Fry chicken for 15-18 minutes until its water become dry and its color changes to brown. Serve immediately.

10. Air fried French Fries

Ingredients
- Peeled Potatoes - 1 pound
- Vegetable oil - 2 tablespoon
- Cayenne pepper - 1 pinch
- Salt - 1/2 teaspoon

Method

1. Lengthwise cut thick slices of potato of 3/8 inches.
2. Soak sliced potatoes for 5 minutes in water. Drain excess starch water from soaked potatoes after 5 minutes. Place these potatoes in boiling water pan for 8-10 minutes.
3. Remove water from the potatoes and dry them completely. Cool them for 10 minutes and shift in a clean bowl. Add some oil and fully coat the potatoes with cayenne by tossing.
4. Set the temperature of an air fryer to 190C. Place two layers of potatoes in air fryer pot and cook them for 10-15 minutes. Toss fries continuously and cook for more 10 minutes until their color changes to golden brown. Season fries with salt and serve this appetizing dish immediately.

11. Air fried Mini Breakfast Burritos

Ingredients

- Mexican style chorizo - 1/4 cup
- Sliced potatoes - 1/2 cup
- Chopped serrano pepper - 1
- 8-inch flour tortillas - 4
- Bacon grease - 1 tablespoon
- Chopped onion - 2 tablespoon
- Eggs - 2
- Cooking avacado oil - to spray
- Salt - to taste
- Black pepper powder - to taste

Method

1. Take chorizo in a large size pan and cook on medium flame for 8 minutes with continuous stirring until its color change into reddish brown. Shift chorizo in a clean plate and place separate.

2. Take bacon grease in same pan and melt it on medium flame. Place sliced potatoes and cook them for 10 minutes with constant stirring. Add serrano pepper and onion meanwhile. Cook for more 2-5 minutes until potatoes are fully cooked, onion and serrano pepper become soften. Then add chorizo and eggs and cook for more 5 minutes until potato mixture is fully incorporated. Use pepper and salt for seasoning.

3. In the meantime, heat tortillas in a large pan until they become soft and flexible. Put 1/3 cup of chorizo mixture at the center of each tortilla. Filling is covered by rolling the upper and lower side of tortilla and give shape of burrito. Spray cooking oil and place them in air fryer pot.

4. Fry these burritos at 200C for 5 minutes. Change the side'scontinuously and spray with cooking oil. Cook in air fryer for 3-4 minutes until color turns into light brown. Shift burritos in a clean dish and serve this delicious dish.

12. Air fried Vegan Tator Tots

Ingredients
- Frozen potato nuggets (Tator Tots) - 2 cups
- Buffalo wing sauce - 1/4 cup
- Vegan ranch salad - 1/4 cup

Method

1. Set the temperature of an air fryer to 175C.
2. Put frozen potato nuggets in air fryer pot and cook for 6-8 minutes with constant shake.
3. Shift potatoes to a large-sized bowl and add wing sauce. Combine evenly by tossing them and place them again in air fryer pot.
4. Cook more for 8-10 minutes without disturbance. Shift to a serving plate. Serve with ranch dressing and enjoy this dish.

13. Air fried Roasted Cauliflower

Ingredients
- Cauliflower florets - 4 cups
- Garlic - 3 cloves
- Smoked paprika - 1/2 teaspoon
- Peanut oil - 1 tablespoon
- Salt - 1/2 teaspoon

Method
1. Set the temperature of an air fryer to 200C.
2. Smash garlic cloves with a knife and mix with salt, oil and paprika. Coat cauliflower in this mixture.
3. Put coated cauliflower in air fryer pot and cook around 10-15 minutes with stirring after every 5 minutes. Cook according to desired color and crispiness and serve immediately.

14. Air fried Cinnamon-Sugar Doughnuts

Ingredients
- White sugar - 1/2 cup
- Brown sugar - 1/4 cup
- Melted butter - 1/4 cup
- Cinnamon powder - 1 teaspoon
- Ground nutmeg - 1/4 TEASPOON
- Packed chilled flaky biscuit dough - 1 (16.3 ounce)

Method

1. Put melted butter in a clean bowl. Add brown sugar, white sugar, nutmeg and cinnamon and mix.
2. Divide and cut biscuit dough into many single biscuits and give them the shape of doughnuts using a biscuit cutter. Shift doughnuts in an air fryer pot.
3. Air fry the doughnuts for 5-6 minutes at 175C until color turns into golden brown. Turn the side of doughnuts and cook for more 1-3 minutes.
4. Shift doughnuts from air fryer to a clean dish and dip them in melted butter. Then completely coat these doughnuts in sugar and cinnamon mixture and serve frequently.

15. Air Fried Broiled Grapefruit

Ingredients

- Chilled red grapefruit - 1
- Melted butter - 1 tablespoon
- Brown sugar - 2 tablespoon
- Ground cinnamon - 1/2 teaspoon
- Aluminium foil

Method
1. Set the temperature of an air fryer to 200C.
2. Cut grapefruit crosswise to half and also cut a thin slice from one end of grapefruit for sitting your fruit flat on a plate.
3. Mix brown sugar in melted butter in a small sized bowl. Coat the cut side of the grapefruit with this mixture. Dust the little brown sugar over it.
4. Take 2 five inch pieces of aluminium foil and put the half grapefruit on each piece. Fold the sides evenly to prevent juice leakage. Place them in air fryer pot.
5. Broil for 5-7 minutes until bubbling of sugar start in an air fryer. Before serving, sprinkle cinnamon on grapefruit.

16. Air Fried Brown Sugar and Pecan Roasted Apples

Ingredients
- Apples - 2 medium
- Chopped pecans - 2 tablespoons
- Plain flour - 1 teaspoon
- Melted butter - 1 tablespoon
- Brown sugar - 1 tablespoon
- Apple pie spice - 1/4 teaspoon

Method
1. Set the temperature of an air fryer to 180C.
2. Mix brown sugar, pecan, apple pie spice and flour in a clean bowl. Cut apples in wedges and put them in another bowl and coat them with melted butter by tossing. Place a single layer in an air fryer pot and add mixture of pecan on the top.
3. Cook apples for 12-15 minutes until they get soft.

17. Air Fried Breaded Sea Scallops

Ingredients
- Crushed butter crackers - 1/2 cup
- Seafood seasoning - 1/2 teaspoon
- Sea scallops - 1 pound
- Garlic powder - 1/2 teaspoon
- Melted butter - 2 tablespoons
- Cooking oil - for spray

Method

1. Set the temperature of an air fryer to 198C.

2. Combine garlic powder, seafood seasoning and cracker crumbs in a clean bowl. Take melted butter in another bowl.

3. Coat each scallop with melted butter. Then roll them in breading until completely enclose. Place them on a clean plate and repeat this step with rest of the scallops.

4. Slightly spray scallops with cooking oil and place them on the air fryer pot at equal distance. You may work in 2-3 batches.

5. Cook them for 2-3 minutes in preheated air fryer. Use a spatula to change the side of each scallop. Cook for more 2 minutes until they become opaque. Dish out in a clean plate and serve immediately.

18. Air Fried Crumbed Fish

Ingredients

- Flounder fillets - 4
- Dry bread crumbs - 1 cup
- Egg - 1
- Sliced lemon - 1
- Vegetable oil - 1/4 cup

Method

1. Set the temperature of an air fryer to 180C.
2. Combine oil and bread crumbs in a clean bowl and mix them well.
3. Coat each fish fillets with beaten egg, then evenly dip them in the crumbs mixture.
4. Place coated fillets in preheated air fryer and cook for 10-12 minutes until fish easily flakes by touching them with fork. Shift prepared fish in a clean plate and serve with lemon slices.

19. Air Fried Cauliflower and Chickpea Tacos

Ingredients

- Cauliflower - 1 small
- Chickpeas - 15 ounce
- Chili powder - 1 teaspoon
- Cumin powder - 1 teaspoon
- Lemon juice - 1 tablespoon
- Sea salt - 1 teaspoon
- Garlic powder - 1/4 teaspoon
- Olive oil - 1 tablespoon

Method

1. Set the temperature of an air fryer to 190C.

2. Mix lime juice, cumin, garlic powder, salt, olive oil and chili powder in a clean bowl. Now coat well the cauliflower and chickpeas in this mixture by constant stirring.

3. Put cauliflower mixture in an air fryer pot. Cook for 8-10 minutes with constant stirring. Cook for more 10 minutes and stir for final time. Cook for more 5 minutes until desired crispy texture is attained.

5. Place cauliflower mixture by using spoon and serve.

20. Air Fried Roasted Salsa

Ingredients

- Roma tomatoes - 4
- Seeded Jalapeno pepper - 1
- Red onion - 1/2
- Garlic - 4 cloves
- Cilantro - 1/2 cup
- Lemon juice - 1
- Cooking oil - to spray

- Salt - to taste

Method

1. Set the temperature of an air fryer to 200C.

2. Put tomatoes, red onion and skin side down of jalapeno in an air fryer pot. Brush lightly these vegetables with cooking oil for roasting them easily.

3. Cook vegetables in an air fryer for 5 minutes. Then add garlic cloves and again spray with cooking oil and fry for more 5 minutes.

4. Shift vegetables to cutting board and allow them to cool for 8-10 minutes.

5. Separate skins of jalapeno and tomatoes and chop them with onion into large pieces. Add them to food processor bowl and add lemon juice, cilantro, garlic and salt. Pulsing for many times until all the vegetables are evenly chopped. Cool them for 10-15 minutes and serve this delicious dish immediately.

21. Air Fried Flour Tortilla Bowls

Ingredients

- Flour tortilla - 1 (8 inch)
- Souffle dish - 1 (4 1/2 inch)

Method

1. Set the temperature of an air fryer to 190C.

2. Take tortilla in a large pan and heat it until it become soft. Put tortilla in the souffle dish by patting down side and fluting up from its sides of dish.

3. Air fry tortilla for 3-5 minutes until its color change into golden brown.

4. Take out tortilla bowl from the dish and put the upper side in the pot. Air fry again for more 2 minutes until its color turns into golden brown. Dish out and serve.

22. Air Fried Cheese and Mini Bean Tacos

Ingredients

- Can Refried beans - 16 ounce
- American cheese - 12 slices
- Flour tortillas - 12 (6 inch)
- Taco seasoning mix - 1 ounce
- Cooking oil - to spray

Method

1. Set the temperature of an air fryer to 200C.

2. Combine refried beans and taco seasoning evenly in a clean bowl and stir.

3. Put 1 slice of cheese in the center of tortilla and place 1 tablespoon of bean mixture over cheese. Again place second piece of cheese over this mixture. Fold tortilla properly from upper side and press to enclose completely. Repeat this step for the rest of beans, cheese and tortillas.

4. Spray cooking oil on the both sides of tacos. Put them in an air fryer at equal distance. Cook the tacos for 3 minutes and turn it side and again cook for more 3 minutes. Repeat this step for the rest of tacos. Transfer to a clean plate and serve immediately.

23. Air Fried Lemon Pepper Shrimp

Ingredients

- Lemon - 1
- Lemon pepper - 1 teaspoon
- Olive oil - 1 tablespoon
- Garlic powder - 1/4 teaspoon
- Paprika - 1/4 teaspoon
- Deveined and peeled shrimps - 12 ounces
- Sliced lemon – 1

Method

1. Set the temperature of an air fryer to 200C.

2. Mix lemon pepper, garlic powder, and olive oil, paprika and lemon juice in a clean bowl. Coat shrimps by this mixture by tossing.

3. Put shrimps in an air fryer and cook for 5-8 minutes until its color turn to pink. Dish out cooked shrimps and serve with lemon slices.

24. Air Fried Shrimp a la Bang Bang

Ingredients

- Deveined raw shrimps - 1 pound
- Sweet chili sauce - 1/4 cup
- Plain flour - 1/4 cup
- Green onions - 2
- Mayonnaise - 1/2 cup
- Sriracha sauce - 1 tablespoon
- Bread crumbs - 1 cup
- Leaf lettuce - 1 head

Method

1. Set the temperature of an air fryer to 200C

2. Make a bang bang sauce by mixing chili sauce, mayonnaise and sriracha sauce in a clean bowl. Separate some sauce for dipping in a separate small bowl.

3. Place bread crumbs and flour in two different plates. Coat shrimps with mayonnaise mixture, then with flour and then bread crumbs. Set coated shrimps on a baking paper.

4. Place them in an air fryer pot and cook for 10-12 minutes. Repeat this step for the rest of shrimps. Transfer shrimps to a clean dish and serve with green onions and lettuce.

25. Air Fried Spicy Bay Scallops

Ingredients

- Bay scallops - 1 pound
- Chili powder - 2 teaspoons
- Smoked paprika- 2 teaspoons
- Garlic powder - 1 teaspoon
- Olive oil - 2 teaspoons
- Black pepper powder - 1/4 teaspoon
- Cayenne red pepper - 1/8 teaspoon

Method

1. Set the temperature of an air fryer to 200C

2. Mix smoked paprika, olive oil, bay scallops, garlic powder, pepper, chili powder and cayenne pepper in a clean bowl and stir properly. Shift this mixture to an air fryer.

3. Air fry for 6-8 minutes with constant shaking until scallops are fully cooked. Transfer this dish in a clean plate and serve immediately.

26. Air Fried Breakfast Fritatta

Ingredients

- Fully cooked breakfast sausages - 1/4 pound
- Cheddar Monterey Jack cheese - 1/2 cup
- Green onion - 1
- Cayenne pepper - 1 pinch
- Red bell pepper - 2 tablespoons
- Eggs - 4
- Cooking oil - to spray

Method

1. Set the temperature of an air fryer to 180C.

2. Mix eggs, sausages, Cheddar Monterey Jack cheese, onion, bell pepper and cayenne in a clean bowl and stir to mix properly.

3. Spray cooking oil on a clean non-stick cake pan. Put egg mixture in the cake pan. Air fry for 15-20 minutes until fritatta is fully cooked and set. Transfer it in a clean plate and serve immediately.

27. Air Fried Roasted Okra

Ingredients

- Trimmed and sliced Okra - 1/2 pound
- Black pepper powder - 1/8 teaspoon
- Olive oil - 1 teaspoon
- Salt - 1/4 teaspoon

Method

1. Set the temperature of an air fryer to 175C.

2. Mix olive oil, black pepper, salt and okra in a clean bowl and stir to mix properly.

3. Make a single layer of this mixture in an air fryer pot. Air fry for 5-8 minutes with constant stirring. Cook for more 5 minutes and again toss. Cook for more 3 minutes and dish out in a clean plate and serve immediately.

28. Air Fried Rib-Eye Steak

Ingredients

- Rib-eye steak - 2 (1 1/2 inch thick)
- Olive oil - 1/4 cup
- Grill seasoning - 4 teaspoons
- Reduced sodium soy sauce - 1/2 cup

Method

1. Mix olive oil, soy sauce, seasoning and steaks in a clean bowl and set aside meat for marination.

2. Take out steaks and waste the remaining mixture. Remove excess oil from steak by patting.

3. Add 1 tablespoon water in an air fryer pot for the prevention from smoking during cooking of steaks.

3. Set the temperature of an air fryer to 200C. Place steaks in an air fryer pot. Air fry for 7-8 minutes and turn its side after every 8 minutes. Cook for more 7 minutes until it is rarely medium. Cook for final 3 minutes for a medium steak and dish out in a clean plate and serve immediately.

29. Air Fried Potato Chips

Ingredients

- Large potatoes - 2
- Olive oil - to spray
- Fresh parsley - optional
- Sea salt - 1/2 teaspoon

Method

1. Set the temperature of an air fryer to 180C.

2. Peel off the potatoes and cut them into thin slices. Shift the slices in a bowl containing ice chilled water and soak for 10 minutes. Drain potatoes, again add chilled water and soak for more 15 minutes.

3. Remove water from potatoes and allow to dry by using paper towel. Spray potatoes with cooking oil and add salt according to taste.

4. Place a single layer of potatoes slices in an oiled air fryer pot and cook for 15-18 minutes until color turns to golden brown and crispy. Stir constantly and turn its sides after every 5 minutes.

5. Dish out these crispy chips and serve with parsley.

30. Air Fried Tofu

Ingredients

- Packed tofu - 14 ounces
- Olive oil - 1/4 cup
- Reduced sodium soy sauce - 3 tablespoons

- Crushed red pepper flakes - 1/4 teaspoon
- Green onions - 2
- Cumin powder - 1/4 teaspoon
- Garlic - 2 cloves

Method

1. Set the temperature of an air fryer to 200C.

2. Mix olive oil, soy sauce, onions, garlic, cumin powder and red pepper flakes in a deep bowl to make marinade mixture.

3. Cut 3/8 inches' thick slices of tofu lengthwise and then diagonally. Coat tofu with marinade mixture. Place them in refrigerate for 4-5 minutes and turn them after every 2 minutes.

4. Place tofu in buttered air fryer pot. Put remaining marinade over each tofu. Cook for 5-8 minutes until color turns to golden brown. Dish out cooked tofu and serve immediately.

31. Air Fried Acorn Squash Slices

Ingredients

- Medium sized acorn squash - 2
- Soft butter - 1/2 cup
- Brown sugar - 2/3 cup

Method

1. Set the temperature of an air fryer to 160C.

2. Cut squash into two halves from length side and remove seeds. Again cut these halves into half inch slices.

3. Place a single layer of squash on buttered air fryer pot. Cook each side of squash for 5 minutes.

4. Mix butter into brown sugar and spread this mixture on the top of every squash. Cook for more 3 minutes. Dish out and serve immediately.

32. Air Fried Red Potatoes

Ingredients

- Baby potatoes - 2 pounds
- Olive oil - 2 tablespoons
- Fresh rosemary - 1 tablespoon
- Garlic - 2 cloves
- Salt - 1/2 teaspoon
- Black pepper - 1/4 teaspoon

Method

1. Set the temperature of an air fryer to 198C.

2. Cut potatoes into wedges. Coat them properly with minced garlic, rosemary, black pepper and salt.

3. Place coated potatoes on buttered air fryer pot. Cook potatoes for 5 minutes until golden brown and soft. Stir them at once. Dish out in a clean plate and serve immediately.

33. Air Fried Butter Cake

Ingredients

- Melted butter - 7 tablespoons
- White sugar - 1/4 cup & 2 tablespoons
- Plain flour - 1 & 2/3 cup
- Egg - 1
- Salt - 1 pinch
- Milk - 6 tablespoons
- Cooking oil - to spray

Method

1. Set the temperature of an air fryer to 180C and spray with cooking oil.

2. Beat white sugar, and butter together in a clean bowl until creamy and light. Then add egg and beautiful fluffy and smooth. Add salt and flour and stir. Then add milk and mix until batter is smooth. Shift batter to an preheated air fryer pot and level its surface by using spatula.

3. Place in an air fryer and set time of 15 minutes. Bake and check cake after 15 minutes by inserting toothpick in the cake. If toothpick comes out clean it means cake has fully baked.

4. Take out cake from air fryer and allow it to cool for 5-10 minutes. Serve immediately and enjoy.

34. Air Fried Jelly and Peanut Butter S'mores

Ingredients

- Chocolate topping peanut butter cup - 1
- Raspberry jam (seedless) - 1 teaspoon
- Marshmallow - 1 large
- Chocolate cracker squares – 2

Method

1. Set the temperature of an air fryer to 200C.

2. Put peanut butter cup on one cracker square and topped with marshmallow and jelly. Carefully transfer it in the preheated air fryer.

3. Cook for 1 minute until marshmallow becomes soft and light brown. Remaining cracker squares is used for topping.

4. Shift this delicious in a clean plate and serve immediately.

35. Air Fried Sun-Dried Tomatoes

Ingredients

- Red grape tomatoes - 5 ounces
- Olive oil - 1/4 teaspoon
- Salt - to taste

Method

1. Set the temperature of an air fryer to 115C.

2. Combine tomatoes halves, salt and olive oil evenly in a clean bowl. Shift tomatoes in an air fryer pot by placing skin side down.

3. Cook in air fryer for 45 minutes. Smash tomatoes by using spatula and cook for more 30 minutes. Repeat this step with the rest of tomatoes.

4. Shift this delicious dish in a clean plate and allow it to stand for 45 minutes to set. Serve this dish and enjoy.

36. Air Fried Sweet Potatoes Tots

Ingredients:

- Peeled Sweet Potatoes - 2 small (14oz.total)
- Garlic Powder - 1/8 tsp
- Potato Starch - 1 tbsp
- Kosher Salt, Divided - 11/4 tsp
- Unsalted Ketchup - 3/4 Cup
- Cooking Oil for spray

Method:

1. Take water in a medium pan and give a single boil over high flame. Then, add the sweet potatoes in the boiled water & cook for 15 minutes till potatoes becomes soft. Move the potatoes to a cooling plate for 15 minutes.

2. Rub potatoes using the wide hole's grater over a dish. Apply the potato starch, salt and garlic powder and toss gently. Make almost 24 shaped cylinders (1-inch) from the mixture.

3. Coat the air fryer pot gently with cooking oil. Put single layer of 1/2 of the tots in the pot and spray with cooking oil. Cook at 400 °F for about 12 to 14 minutes till lightly browned and flip tots midway. Remove from the pot and sprinkle with salt. Repeat with rest of the tots and salt left over. Serve with ketchup immediately.

37. Air Fried Banana Bread

Ingredients:

- White Whole Wheat Flour - 3/4 cup (3 oz.)
- Mashed Ripe Bananas - 2 medium or (about 3/4th cup)
- Cinnamon powder– 4 pinches
- Kosher Salt - 1/2 tsp
- Baking Soda - 1/4 tsp
- Large Eggs, Lightly Beaten - 2
- Regular Sugar - 1/2 cup
- Vanilla Essence - 1 tsp
- Vegetable Oil - 2 tbsp
- Roughly Chopped and toasted Walnuts - 2 table-spoons (3/4 oz.)
- Plain Non-Fat Yogurt - 1/3 cup

- Cooking Oil for Spray - as required

Method:

1. Cover the base of a 6-inches round cake baking pan with baking paper and lightly brush with melted butter. Beat the flour, baking soda, salt, and cinnamon together in a clean bowl and let it reserve.

2. Whisk the mashed bananas, eggs, sugar, cream, oil and vanilla together in a separate bowl. Stir the wet ingredients gently into the flour mixture until everything is blended. Pour the mixture in the prepared pan and sprinkle with the walnuts.

3. Set the temperature of an air fryer to 310 °F and put the pan in the air fryer. Cook until browned, about 30 to 35 minutes. Rotate the pan periodically until a wooden stick put in it and appears clean. Before flipping out & slicing, move the bread to a cooling rack for 15 minutes.

38. Air Fried Avocado Fries

Ingredients:

- Avocados --. 2 - Cut each into the 8 pieces
- All-purpose flour - 1/2 cup (about 21/8 oz.)
- Panko (Japanese Style Breadcrumbs) - 1/2 cup
- Large Eggs - 2
- Kosher Salt - 1/4 tsp
- Apple Cider - 1 tbsp
- Sriracha Chilli Sause - 1 tbsp

- Black pepper - 11/2 tsp
- Water - 1 tbsp
- Unsalted Ketchup - 1/2 cup
- Cooking spray

Method:

1. Mix flour and pepper collectively in a clean bowl. Whip eggs & water gently in another bowl. Take panko in a third bowl. Coat avocado slices in flour and remove extra flour by shaking. Then, dip the slices in the egg and remove any excess. Coat in panko by pushing to stick together. Spray well the avocado slices with cooking oil.

2. In the air fryer's basket, put avocado slices & fry at 400 ° F until it turns into golden for 7-8 minutes. Turn avocado wedges periodically while frying. Take out from an air fryer and use salt for sprinkling.

3. Mix the Sriracha, ketchup, vinegar, and mayonnaise together in a small bowl. Put two tablespoons of sauce on each plate with 4 avocado fries before serving.

39. "Strawberry Pop Tarts" in an Air Fryer

Ingredients:

- Quartered Strawberries - (about 13/4 cups equal to 8 ounces)
- White/Regular Sugar - 1/4 cup
- Refrigerated Piecrusts - 1/2(14.1-oz)
- Powdered Sugar - 1/2 cup (about 2-oz)

- Fresh Lemon Juice - 11/2 tsp
- Rainbow Candy Sprinkles - 1 tbsp(about 1/2 ounce)
- Cooking Spray

Method:

1. Mix strawberries & white sugar and stay for 15 minutes with periodically stirring. Air fryer them for 10 minutes until glossy and reduced with constant stirring. Let it cool for 30 minutes.

2. Use the smooth floured surface to roll the pie crust and make 12-inches round shape. Cut the dough into 12 rectangles of (2 1/2- x 3-inch), re-rolling strips if necessary. Leaving a 1/2-inch boundary, add the spoon around 2 tea-spoons of strawberry mixture into the middle of 6 of dough rectangles. Brush the edges of the rectangles of the filled dough with water. Then, press the edges of rest dough rectangles with a fork to seal. Spray the tarts very well with cooking oil.

3. In an air fryer pot, put 3 tarts in a single layer and cook them at 350 ° F for 10 minutes till golden brown. With the rest of the tarts, repeat the process. Set aside for cooling for 30 minutes.

4. In a small cup, whip the powdered sugar & lemon juice together until it gets smooth. Glaze the spoon over the cooled tarts and sprinkle equally with candy.

40. Lighten up Empanadas in an Air Fryer

Ingredients:

- Lean Green Beef - 3 ounces
- Cremini Mushrooms - Chopped finely - 3 ounces
- White onion - Chopped finely - 1/4th cup
- Garlic – Chopped finely - 2 tsp.
- Pitted Green Olives - 6
- Olive Oil - 1 table-spoon
- Cumin - 1/4th tsp
- Cinnamon - 1/8th tsp
- Chopped tomatoes - 1/2 cup
- Paprika - 1/4 tea-spoon
- Large egg lightly Beaten - 1
- Square gyoza wrappers - 8

Method:

1. In a medium cooking pot, let heat oil on the medium/high temperature. Then, add beef & onion; for 3 minutes, cook them, mixing the crumble, until getting brown. Put the mushrooms; let them cook for 6 mins, till the mushrooms start to brown, stirring frequently. Add the paprika, olives, garlic, cinnamon, and cumin; cook for three minutes until the mushrooms are very tender and most of the liquid has been released. Mix in the tomatoes and cook, turning periodically, for 1 minute. Put the filling in a bowl and let it cool for 5 minutes.

2. Arrange 4 wrappers of gyoza on a worktop. In each wrapper, put around 1 1/2 tablespoons of filling in the middle. Clean the edges of the egg wrappers; fold over the

wrappers and pinch the edges to seal. Repeat with the remaining wrappers and filling process.

3. Place the 4 empanadas in one single layer in an air-fryer basket and cook for 7 minutes at 400 °F until browned well. Repeat with the empanadas that remain.

41. Air Fried Calzones

Ingredients:

- Spinach Leaves --> 3 ounces (about 3 cups)
- Shredded Chicken breast --> 2 ounces (about 1/3 cup)
- Fresh Whole Wheat Pizza Dough --> 6 ounces
- Shredded Mozzarella Cheese --> 11/2 ounces (about 6 tbsp)
- Low Sodium Marinara Sauce --> 1/3 cup

Method:

1. First of all, in a medium pan, let heat oil on medium/high temperature. Include onion & cook, continue mixing then well efficiently, for two min, till get soft. After that, add the spinach; then cover & cook it until softened. After that, take out the pan from the heat; mix the chicken & marinara sauce.

2. Divide the dough in to the four identical sections. Then, roll each section into a 6-inches circle on a gently floured surface. Place over half of each dough circular shape with one-fourth of the spinach mixture. Top with one-fourth of the cheese each. Fold the dough

to make half-moons and over filling, tightening the edges to lock. Coat the calzones well with spray for cooking

3. In the basket of an air fryer, put the calzones and cook them at 325 ° F until the dough becomes nicely golden brown, in 12 mins, changing the sides of the calzones after 8 mins.

42. Air Fried Mexican Style Corns

Ingredients:

- Unsalted Butter - 11/2 tbsp.
- Chopped Garlic -2 tsp
- Shucked Fresh Corns - 11/2 lb
- Fresh Chopped Cilantro - 2 tbsp.
- Lime zest - 1 tbsp.
- Lime Juice - 1 tsp
- Kosher Salt - 1/2 tsp
- Black Pepper - 1/2 tsp

Method:

1. Coat the corn delicately with the cooking spray, and put the corn in the air fryer's basket in one single layer. Let it Cooking for 14 mins at 400 °F till tender then charred gently, changing the corn half the way via cooking.

2. In the meantime, whisk together all the garlic, lime juice, butter, & lime zest in the microwaveable pot. Let an air fryer on Fast, about 30 seconds, until the butter melts and

the garlic is aromatic. Put the corn on the plate and drop the butter mixture on it. Using the salt, cilantro, and pepper to sprinkle. Instantly serve this delicious recipe.

43. Air Fryer Crunchy & Crispy Chocolate Bites

Ingredients:

- Frozen Shortcrust Pastry - Partially thawed -- 4
- Cinnamon for dusting -- as required
- Icing Sugar for dusting -- as required
- Mars Celebration Chocolates -- 24
- Whipped Cream - as required

Method:

1. First of all, cut each pastry sheet into 6 equal rectangles. Brush the egg finely. In the centre of each piece of the pastry, place one chocolate. Fold the pastry over to seal the chocolate. Trim the extra pastry, then press and lock the corners. Put it on a tray lined with baking sheet. Brush the tops with an egg. Use the mixture of cinnamon and sugar to sprinkle liberally.

2. In the air-fryer basket, put a layer of the baking paper, ensuring that the paper is 1 cm smaller than that of the basket to permit air to circulate well. Place the 6 pockets in basket, taking care that these pockets must not to overlap. Then, cook them for 8-9 mins at 190 ° C till they become golden and the pastry are prepared thoroughly. As the pockets cooked, transfer them into a dish. Repeat the process with the pockets that remain.

3. After taking out from the air fryer, dust the Icing sugar and at last with whipped cream. Serve them warm.

44. Doritos-Crumbled Chicken tenders in an Air fryer

Ingredients:

- Buttermilk -- 1 cup (about 250ml)
- Doritos Nacho Cheese Corn Chips -- 170g Packet
- Halved Crossways Chicken Tenderloins -- 500g
- Egg -- 1
- Plain Flour -- 50g
- Mild Salsa -- for serving

Method:

1.Take a ceramic bowl or glass and put the chicken in it. Then, c over the buttermilk with it. Wrap it and put it for 4 hours or may be overnight in the refrigerator to marinate.

2. Let Preheat an air fryer at 180C. Then, cover a Baking tray with grease-proof paper.

3. In a Chopper, add the corn chips then pulse them until the corn chips become coarsely chopped. Then, transfer the chopped chips to a dish. In a deep cup, put the egg and beat it. On another plate, put the flour.

4. Remove the unnecessary water from the chicken, and also discard the buttermilk. Then, dip the chicken in the flour mixture and wipe off the extra flour. After that, dip in the beaten egg and then into the chips of corn, press it firmly to coat well. Transfer it to the tray that made ready to next step.

5. In the air fryer, put half of the chicken and then, fry for 8 to 10 mins until they are golden as well as cooked completely. Repeat the process with the chicken that remain.

Transfer the chicken in the serving dish. Enjoy this delicious recipe with salsa.

45. Air Fryer Ham & Cheese Croquettes

Ingredients:

- Chopped White Potatoes -- 1 kg
- Chopped Ham -- 100g
- Chopped Green Shallots -- 2
- Grated Cheddar Cheese -- 80g (about 1 cup)
- All-purpose flour -- 50g
- eggs -- 2
- Breadcrumbs -- 100g
- Lemon Slices -- for serving
- Tonkatsu Sause -- for serving

Method:

1. In a large-sized saucepan, put the potatoes. Cover with chill water. Carry it over high temperature to a boil. Boil till tender for 10 to 12 minutes. Drain thoroughly. Return over low heat to pan. Mix until it is smooth and has allowed to evaporate the certain water. Withdraw from the sun. Switch to a tub. Fully set aside to chill.

2. Then, add the shallot, Ham and cheese in the mashed potatoes also season with kosher salt. Mix it well. Take the 2 tablespoons of the mixture and make its balls. And repeat process for the rest of mixture.

3. Take the plain flour in a plate. Take another small bowl and beat the eggs. Take the third bowl and add the breadcrumbs in it. Toss the balls in the flour. Shake off the extra flour then in eggs and coat the breadcrumbs well. Make the balls ready for frying. Take all the coated balls in the fridge for about 15 minutes.

4. Preheat an air fryer at 200 ° C. Then, cook the croquettes for 8 to10 mints until they become nicely golden, in two rounds. Sprinkle the tonkatsu sauce and serve the croquettes with lemon slices.

46. Air Fryer Lemonade Scones

Ingredients:

- Self-raising flour -- 525g (about 3 1/2 cups)
- Thickened Cream -- 300ml
- Lemonade -- 185ml (about 3/4 cup)
- Caster Sugar -- 70g (1/3 cup)
- Vanilla Essence -- 1 tsp
- Milk -- for brushing
- Raspberry Jam -- for serving
- Whipped Cream -- for serving

Method:

1. In a large-sized bowl, add the flour and sugar together. Mix it well. Add lemonade, vanilla and cream. In a big bowl, add the flour and sugar. Just make a well. Remove milk, vanilla and lemonade. Mix finely, by using a plain knife, till the dough comes at once.

2. Take out the dough on the flat surface and sprinkle the dry flour on the dough. Knead it gently for about 30 secs until the dough get smooth. On a floured surface, roll out the dough. Politely knead for thirty seconds, until it is just smooth. Form the dough into a round shape about 2.5 cm thick. Toss around 5.5 cm blade into the flour. Cut the scones out. Push the bits of remaining dough at once gently and repeat the process to make Sixteen scones.

3. In the air fryer bucket, put a layer of baking paper, ensuring that the paper is 1 cm shorter than the bucket to allow air to flow uniformly. Put 5 to 6 scones on paper in the bucket, even hitting them. Finely brush the surfaces with milk. Let cook them for about 15 mins at 160 ° C or when they tapped on the top, until become golden and empty-sounding. Move it safely to a wire or cooling rack. Repeat the same process with the rest of scones and milk two more times.

4. Serve the lemonade scones warm with raspberry jam & whipped cream.

47. Air Fryer Baked Potatoes

Ingredients:

- Baby Potatoes -- Halved shape -- 650g
- Fresh rosemary sprigs-- 2 large
- Sour Cream -- for serving

- Sweet Chilli Sauce -- for serving
- Salt -- for seasoning

Method:

1. Firstly, at 180C, pre-heat the air fryer. In an air fryer, put the rosemary sprigs & baby potatoes. Use oil for spray and salt for seasoning. Then, cook them for fifteen min until become crispy and cooked completely, also turning partially.

2. Serve the baked potatoes sweet chilli Sause & sour cream to enhance its flavour.

48. Air Fryer Mozzarella Chips

Ingredients:

- All-purpose flour -- 1 tbsp
- Breadcrumbs -- 2/3 cup
- Garlic Powder -- 3 tbsp
- Lemon Juice -- 1/3 cup
- Avocado -- 1
- Basil Pesto -- 2 tbsp
- Plain Yogurt -- 1/4 cup
- Chopped Green Onion --1
- Cornflakes crumbs -- 1/4 cup
- Mozzarella block -- 550g
- Eggs – 2
- Olive Oil for spray

Method:

1. Start making Creamy and fluffy Avocado Dipped Sauce: In a small-sized food processor, put the yogurt, avocado, lemon juice, onion, and pesto. Also add the pepper & salt, blend properly. Process it well until it get mixed and smooth. Switch the batter to a bowl. Cover it. Place in the fridge, until It required.

2. Take a large-sized tray and place a baking sheet. In a large bowl, add the garlic powder & plain flour together. Also add the salt and season well. Take another medium bowl, whisk the eggs. Mix the breadcrumbs well in bowl.

3. Make the 2 cm thick wedges of mozzarella, then put them into the sticks. For coating, roll the cheese in the flour. Shake off the extra flour. Then, coat the sticks in the egg fusion, then in the breadcrumbs, operating in rounds. Place the prepared plate on it. Freeze till solid, or even for around 1 hour.

4. Spray the oil on the mozzarella lightly. Wrap the air fryer bucket with baking sheet, leaving an edge of 1 cm to enable air to flow. Then, cook at 180C, for 4 to 4 1/2 mins until the sticks become crispy & golden. Serve warm with sauce to dip.

49. Air Fryer Fetta Nuggets

Ingredients:

- All-purpose flour -- 1 tbsp.
- Chilli flakes -- 1 tsp
- Onion powder -- 1 tsp
- Sesame Seeds -- 1/4 cup
- Fetta Cheese Cubes -- Cut in 2 cm 180g
- Fresh Chives -- for serving

- Breadcrumbs -- 1/4 cup

BARBECUE SAUSE:

- apple cider -- 11/2 tsp
- Chilli Flakes -- 1/2 tsp
- Barbecue Sause -- 1//4 cup

Method:

1. Mix the onion powder, flour and chilli flakes in a medium-sized bowl. Use pepper for seasoning. Take another bowl, and beat an egg. Take one more bowl and mix sesame seeds and breadcrumbs. Then, toss the fetta in the chilli flakes, onion powder & flour mixture. Dip the fetta in egg, and toss again in breadcrumbs fusion. Put them on a plate.

2. Pre- heat the air fryer at 180 °C. Put the cubes of fetta in a baking tray, in the basket of the air fryer. cook till fetta cubes become golden, or may be for 6 mins.

3. In the meantime, mix all the wet ingredients and create the Barbecue sauce.

4. Sprinkle the chives on the fetta and serve with Barbecue Sause.

50. Air Fryer Japanese Chicken Tender

Ingredients:

- McCormick Katsu Crumb for seasoning -- 25g
- Pickled Ginger -- 1 tbsp.
- Japanese-Style Mayonnaise -- 1/3 cup
- Chicken Tenderloins -- 500g

- Oil for spray

Method:

1. Put the chicken on tray in the form of single layer. Sprinkle the half seasoning on chicken. Then, turn chicken and sprinkle the seasoning again evenly. Use oil for spray on it.

2. Pre-heat at 180°C, an air fryer. Let the chicken cooking for about 12 - 14 mins until it becomes golden & cooked completely.

3. In the meantime, take a small-sized bowl, mix the mayonnaise and the remaining pickling sauce.

4. Serve the chicken with white sauce and put the ginger on the side, in a platter.

51. Whole-Wheat Pizzas in an Air Fryer

Ingredients:

- Low-sodium Marinara Sauce -- 1/4 cup
- Spinach leaves -- 1 cup
- Pita Breads -- 2
- Shredded Mozzarella Cheese -- 1/4 cup
- Parmigiano- Reggiano Cheese -- 1/4 ounces (about 1 tbsp.)
- Tomato slices -- 8
- Sliced Garlic Clove -- 1

Method:

1. Spread the marinara sauce on 1 side of each pita bread uniformly. Cover the cheese spinach leaves, tomato slices and garlic, with half of each of these.

2. Put one pita bread in an air fryer pot, then cook it at 350°F till the cheese becomes melted and pita becomes crispy, 4 - 5 mins. Repeat the process with the pita leftover.

52. Air Fryer Crispy Veggie Quesadillas

Ingredients:

- 6 inches Whole Grain Flour Tortillas -- 4
- Full fat Cheddar Cheese -- 4 ounces (about 1 cup)
- Sliced Zucchini -- 1 cup
- Lime Zest -- 1 tbsp.
- Lime Juice -- 1 tsp.
- Fresh Cilantro -- 2 tbsp.
- Chopped Red Bell Pepper -- (about 1 cup)
- Cumin -- 1/4 tsp.
- Low-fat Yoghurt -- 2 ounces
- Refrigerated Pico de Gallo -- 1/2 cup
- Oil for spray

Method:

1. Put tortillas on the surface of the work. Sprinkle onto half of each tortilla with 2 tbsp. of grated cheese. Cover each tortilla with 1/4 cup of chopped red bell pepper, zucchini chunks & the black beans on the top of the cheese. Sprinkle finely with 1/2 cup of cheese left. Fold over the tortillas to create quesadillas form like half-moons. Coat the quesadillas slightly with a cooking spray, & lock them with match picks or toothpicks.

2. Lightly brush a bucket of air fryer with cooking oil spray. Place 2 quesadillas carefully in the basket. Cook at 400°F till the tortillas become golden brown & gently crispy. Melt the cheese & gradually tender the vegetables for ten mins, tossing the quesadillas partially throughout the cooking period. Repeat the process with leftover quesadillas.

3. Mix together lime zest, yogurt, cumin, & lime juice, in a small-sized bowl since the quesadillas getting prepare. Break each quesadilla in-to the pieces to serve and then sprinkle the coriander. With one tbsp. of cumin cream and two tablespoons of pico de gallo, and serve each.

53. Air Fried Curry Chickpeas

Ingredients:

- Drained & Rinsed Un-Salted Chickpeas -- 11/2 cups (15-oz.)
- Olive Oil -- 2 tbsp.
- Curry Powder -- 2 tsp.
- Coriander -- 1/4 tsp.
- Cumin -- 1/4 tsp.
- Cinnamon -- 1/4 tsp.
- Turmeric -- 1/2 tsp.
- Aleppo Pepper -- 1/2 tsp.

- Red Wine Vinegar -- 2 tbsp.
- Kosher Salt -- 1/4 tsp.
- Sliced Fresh Cilantro -- as required

Method:

1. Break the chickpeas lightly in a medium-sized bowl with your hands (don't crush them); and then remove the skins of chickpea.

2. Add oil & vinegar to the chickpeas, and stir to coat. Then, add curry powder, turmeric, coriander, cumin, & cinnamon; mix gently to combine them.

3. In the air fryer bucket, put the chickpeas in one single layer & cook at 400°F temperature until becoming crispy, for about 15 min, stirring the chickpeas periodically throughout the cooking process.

4. Place the chickpeas in a dish. Sprinkle the salt, cilantro and Aleppo pepper on chickpeas; and cover it.

54. Air Fried Beet Chips

Ingredients:

- Canola Oil -- 1 tsp.
- Medium-sized Red Beets -- 3
- Black Pepper -- 1/4 tsp.
- Kosher Salt -- 3/4 tsp.

Method:

1. Cut and Peel the red beets. Make sure each beet cutted into 1/8-inch-thick slices. Take a large-sized bowl and toss the beets slices, pepper, salt and oil well.

2. Put half beets in air fryer bucket and then cook at the 320°F temperature about 25 - 30 mins or until they become crispy and dry. Flip the bucket about every 5 mins. Repeat the process for the beets that remain.

55. Double-Glazed Air Fried Cinnamon Biscuits

Ingredients:

- Cinnamon -- 1/4 tsp.
- Plain Flour -- 2/3 cup (about 27/8 oz.)
- Whole-Wheat Flour -- 2/3 cup (about22/3 oz.)
- Baking Powder -- 1 tsp.
- White Sugar -- 2 tbsp.
- Kosher Salt -- 1/4 tsp.
- Chill Salted Butter -- 4 tbsp.
- Powdered Sugar -- 2 cups (about 8-oz.)
- Water -- 3 tbsp.
- Whole Milk -- 1/3 cup
- Oil for spray -- as required

Method:

1. In a medium-sized bowl, stir together salt, plain flour, baking powder, white sugar cinnamon and butter. Use two knives or pastry cutter to cut mixture till butter becomes well mixed with the flour and the mixture seems to as coarse cornmeal. Add the milk, then mix well until the dough becomes a ball. Place the dough on a floury surface and knead for around 30 seconds until the dough becomes smooth. Break the dough into 16 identical parts. Roll each part carefully into a plain ball.

2. Coat the air fryer pot well with oil spray. Put 8 balls in the pot, by leaving the space between each one; spray with cooking oil. Cook them until get browned & puffed, for 10 - 12 mins at 350°F temperature. Take out the doughnut balls from the pot carefully and put them on a cooling rack having foil for five mins. Repeat the process with the doughnut balls that remain.

3. In a medium pot, mix water and powdered sugar together until smooth. Then, spoon half of the glaze carefully over the doughnut balls. Cool for five mins and let it glaze once and enabling to drip off extra glaze.

56. Lemon Drizzle Cake in an Air Fryer

Ingredients:

- Grated Lemon rind -- 2 tsp.
- Cardamom -- 1 tsp.
- Softened Butter -- 150g
- Eggs -- 3
- Honey-flavoured Yoghurt -- 3/4 cup
- Self-raising flour -- 11/2 cups
- Caster Sugar -- 2/3 cup (150g)
- Lemon Zest -- for serving

LEMON ICING:

- Icing Sugar -- 1 cup
- Lemon Juice -- 11/2 tbsps.
- Softened Butter -- 10g

Method:

1. First, grease a 20 cm cake baking pan of round shape having butter paper. Take an electric beater and beat cardamom, sugar, lemon rind, and butter until the mixture becomes smooth & pale. Then, add the eggs one by one and beat well. Put the eggs in the flour and yoghurt. Fold by spatula and make the surface very smooth.

2. Pre-heat the air fryer at 180 C temperature. Put the pan in air fryer's pot. Bake it for about 35 mins. Check it by putting skewer in it that comes out clean without any sticky batter. Reserve it in the pan for 5 minutes to become cool before shifting it to a cooling rack.

3. Make the lemon glaze, add butter and icing sugar in a bowl. By adding lemon juice as required and form a smooth paste.

4. Put the cake on a plate to serve. Sprinkle the lemon zest and lemon icing to serve.

57. Air Fryer dukkah-Crumbed chicken

Ingredients:

- Chicken Thigh Fillets -- 8
- Herb or dukkah -- 45g packet
- Plain Flour -- 1/3 cup (about 50g)
- Kaleslaw kit -- 350g Packet
- Breadcrumbs -- 1 cup (about 80g)
- Eggs -- 2

Method:

1. Put half of the chicken within 2 sheets of cling paper. Gently beat until it remains 2 cm thick by using a meat hammer or rolling pin. Repeat the process with the chicken that remains.

2. In a deep bowl, mix breadcrumbs and dukkah together. Beat an egg in medium bowl., Put the flour and all the seasoning on a tray. Coat chicken pieces one by one in the flour and shake off the extra. Dip chicken pieces into the egg, then in breadcrumbs for coating. Move them to a dish. Cover them with the plastic wrapper & leave it to marinate for 30 mins in the fridge.

3. Pre-heat air fryer at 200°C temperature. Use olive oil to spray the chicken pieces. Put half of the chicken in one single layer in the air fryer pot. Cook them for about 16 mins and turning partially until they become golden & get cooked completely. Move to a plate & wrap them with foil to stay warm. Repeat the process with the chicken pieces that remains.

4. After that, place the kaleslaw kit in a serving bowl by following instructions mentioned in the packets.

5. Divide the prepared chicken & the kaleslaw between serving platters, and season it.

58. Air Fryer Vietnamese-style spring roll salad

Ingredients:

- Rice Noodles -- 340g
- Crushed Garlic -- 1 clove
- Grated Ginger -- 2 tsp.
- Pork Mince -- 250g

- Lemongrass paste -- 1 tsp
- Cutted into matchsticks the Peeled Carrots -- 2
- Sliced Spring onion -- 3
- Fish sauce -- 2 tsp.
- Spring roll pastries -- 10 sheets
- Coriander -- 1/2 cup
- Sliced Red Chilli - 1 long
- Vietnamese-style Salad -- for dressing
- Mint Leaves -- 1/2
- Bean Sprouts -- 1 cup

Method:

1. Take a large-sized saucepan and cook the noodles for about 4 mins until get soft. Take the cold water and discharge thoroughly. Cutting 1 cup of the boiled noodles into the short lengths, with the leftover noodles reserved.

2. Take a large-sized bowl, add the mince, lemongrass, ginger, garlic, half carrot, spring onion, and fish sauce together and mix them well.

3. On a clean surface, put one pastry paper. Add two tablespoons across 1 side of the mince fusion diagonally. With just a little spray, brush its opposite side. Fold and roll on the sides to completely cover the mince filling. Repeat the process with the sheets of pastry and fill the thin layer of mince mixture, that remain.

4. Pre-heat at 200°C, an air fryer. Use olive oil, spray on the spring rolls. Put in the bucket of air fryer and cook the spring rolls for fifteen mins until cooked completely. Change the sides half-way during cooking.

5. After that, equally split reserved noodles in the serving bowls. Place coriander, bean sprouts, mint and the remaining spring onion and carrots at the top of the serving bowl.

6. Then, break the spring rolls in the half and place them over the mixture of noodles. Sprinkle the chili and serve with Vietnamese-style salad dressing according to your taste.

59. Air Fryer Pizza Pockets

Ingredients:

- Olive oil - 2 tsp.
- Sliced Mushrooms - 6 (about 100g)
- Chopped Leg Ham - 50g
- Crumbled Fetta - 80g
- White Wraps - 4
- Basil Leaves - 1/4 cup
- Baby Spinach - 120g
- Tomato Paste - 1/3 cup
- Chopped Red Capsicum - 1/2
- Dried Oregano - 1/2 tsp
- Olive oil - for spray
- Green Salad - for serving

Method:

1. Heat oil on medium temperature in an air fryer. Cook capsicum for about five minutes until it starts to soften. Add mushrooms and cook them for another five mins until

mushrooms become golden and evaporating any water left in the pan. Move mushrooms to another bowl. Leave them to cool for 10 mins.

2. Take a heatproof bowl and put spinach in it. Cover it with boiling water. Wait for 1 min until slightly wilted. Drain water and leave it to cool for about 10 mins.

3. Excessive spinach moisture is squeezed and applied to the capsicum mixture. Add the oregano, basil, ham and fetta. Season it with both salt & pepper. Mix it well to combine properly.

4. Put one wrapper on the smooth surface. Add 1 tbsp of tomato paste to the middle of the wrap. Cover it with a combination of 1-quarter of the capsicum. Roll up the wrap to completely enclose the filling, give it as the shape of parcel and folding the sides. To build four parcels, repeat the procedure with the remaining wraps, mixture of capsicum & tomato paste. Use oil spray on the tops.

5. Pre-heat the air fryer at 180 C temperature. Cook the parcels for 6 - 8 mins until they become golden & crispy, take out them and move to 2 more batches. Serve along with the salad.

60. Air Fryer Popcorn Fetta with Maple Hot Sauce

Ingredients:

- Marinated Fetta cubes - 265g
- Cajun for seasoning - 2 tsp.
- Breadcrumbs - 2/3 cups
- Corn flour - 2 tbsp.
- Egg - 1
- Chopped Fresh Coriander - 1 tbsp.
- Coriander leaves - for serving

Maple hot sauce:

- Maple syrup - 2 tbsp.
- Sriracha - 1 tbsps.

Method:

1. Drain the fetta, then reserve 1 tbsp of oil making sauce.

2. Take a bowl, mix the cornflour and the Cajun seasoning together. Beat the egg in another bowl. Take one more bowl and combine the breadcrumbs & cilantro in it. Season it with salt & pepper. Work in batches, coat the fetta in cornflour mixture, then dip in the egg. After that, toss them in breadcrumb mixture for coating. Place them on the plate and freeze them for one hour.

3. Take a saucepan, add Sriracha, reserved oil and maple syrup together and put on medium low heat. Stir it for 3 - 4 minutes continuously until sauce get start to thicken. Then, remove the maple sauce from heat.

4. Pre-heat the air fryer at 180C. Place the cubes of fetta in a single layer in the air fryer's pot. Cook them for 3 - 4 mins until just staring softened, and fettas become golden. Sprinkled with extra coriander leaves and serve them with the maple hot sauce.

61. Air fryer Steak Fajitas

Ingredients:

- Chopped tomatoes - 2 large
- Minced Jalapeno pepper - 1
- Cumin - 2 tsp.
- Lime juice - 1/4 cup
- Fresh minced Cilantro - 3 tbsp.
- Diced Red Onion - 1/2 cup
- 8-inches long Whole-wheat tortillas - 6

- Large onion - 1 sliced
- Salt - 3/4 tsp divided
- Beef steak - 1

Method:

1. Mix first 5 ingredients in a clean bowl then stir in cumin and salt. Let it stand till before you serve.

2. Pre-heat the air fryer at 400 degrees. Sprinkle the cumin and salt with the steak that remain. Place them on buttered air-fryer pot and cook the steak until the meat reaches the appropriate thickness (a thermometer should read 135 ° for medium-rare; 140 °; moderate, 145 °), for 6 to 8 mins per side. Remove from the air fryer and leave for five min to stand.

3. Then, put the onion in the air-fryer pot. Cook it until get crispy-tender, stirring once for 2 - 3 mins. Thinly slice the steak and serve with onion & salsa in the tortillas. Serve it with avocado & lime slices if needed.

62. Air-Fryer Fajita-Stuffed Chicken

Ingredients:

- Boneless Chicken breast - 4
- Finely Sliced Onion - 1 small
- Finely Sliced Green pepper - 1/2 medium-sized
- Olive oil - 1 tbsp.
- Salt - 1/2 tsp.
- Chilli Powder - 1 tbsp.
- Cheddar Cheese - 4 ounces
- Cumin - 1 tsp.
- Salsa or jalapeno slices - optional

Method:

1. Pre-heat the air fryer at the 375 degrees. In the widest part of every chicken breast, cut a gap horizontally. Fill it with green pepper and onion. Combine olive oil and the seasonings in a clean bowl and apply over the chicken.

2. Place the chicken on a greased dish in the form of batches in an air-fryer pot. Cook it for 6 minutes. Stuff the chicken with cheese slices and secure the chicken pieces with toothpicks. Cook at 165° until for 6 to 8 minutes. Take off the toothpicks. Serve the delicious chicken with toppings of your choosing, if wanted.

63. Nashvilla Hot Chicken in an Air Fryer

Ingredients:

- Chicken Tenderloins - 2 pounds
- Plain flour - 1 cup
- Hot pepper Sauce - 2 tbsp.
- Egg - 1 large

- Salt - 1 tsp.
- Pepper - 1/2 tsp.
- Buttermilk - 1/2 cup
- Cayenne Pepper - 2 tbsp.
- Chilli powder - 1 tsp.
- Pickle Juice - 2 tbsp.
- Garlic Powder - 1/2 tsp.
- Paprika - 1 tsp.
- Brown Sugar - 2 tbsp.
- Olive oil - 1/2 cup
- Cooling oil for spray

Method:

1. Combine pickle juice, hot sauce and salt in a clean bowl and coat the chicken on its both sides. Put it in the fridge, cover it, for a minimum 1 hour. Throwing away some marinade.

2. Pre-heat the air fryer at 375 degrees. Mix the flour, the remaining salt and the pepper in another bowl. Whisk together the buttermilk, eggs, pickle juice and hot sauce well. For coating the both sides, dip the chicken in plain flour; drip off the excess. Dip chicken in egg mixture and then again dip in flour mixture.

3. Arrange the single layer of chicken on a greased air-fryer pot and spray with cooking oil. Cook for 5 to 6 minutes until it becomes golden brown. Turn and spray well. Again, cook it until golden brown, for more 5-6 minutes.

4. Mix oil, brown sugar, cayenne pepper and seasonings together. Then, pour on the hot chicken and toss to cover. Serve the hot chicken with pickles.

64. Southern-style Chicken

Ingredients:

- Crushed Crackers - 2 cups (about 50)
- Fresh minced parsley - 1 tbsp.
- Paprika - 1 tsp.
- Pepper - 1/2 tsp.
- Garlic salt - 1 tsp.
- Fryer Chicken - 1
- Cumin - 1/4 tsp.
- Egg - 1
- Cooking Oil for spray

Method:

1. Set the temperature of an air fryer at 375 degrees. Mix the first 7 ingredients in a deep bowl. Beat an egg in deep bowl. Soak the chicken in egg, then pat in the cracker mixture for proper coat. Place the chicken in a single layer on the greased air-fryer pot and spray with cooking oil.

2. Cook it for 10 minutes. Change the sides of chicken and squirt with cooking oil spray. Cook until the chicken becomes golden brown & juices seem to be clear, for 10 - 20 minutes longer.

65. Chicken Parmesan in an Air Fryer

Ingredients:

- Breadcrumbs - 1/2 cup

- Pepper - 1/4 tsp.
- Pasta Sauce - 1 cup
- Boneless Chicken breast - 4
- Mozzarella Cheese - 1 cup
- Parmesan Cheese - 1/3 cup
- Large Eggs - 2
- Fresh basil - Optional

Method:

1. Set the temperature of an air-fryer at 375 degrees. In a deep bowl, beat the eggs gently. Combine the breadcrumbs, pepper and parmesan cheese in another bowl. Dip the chicken in beaten egg and coat the chicken parmesan with breadcrumbs mixture.

2. In an air-fryer pot, put the chicken in single layer. Cook the chicken for 10 to 12 mins with changing the sides partially. Cover the chicken with cheese and sauce. Cook it for 3 to 4 minutes until cheese has melted. Then, sprinkle with basil leaves and serve.

66. Lemon Chicken Thigh in an Air Fryer

Ingredients:

- Bone-in Chicken thighs- 4
- Pepper - 1/8 tsp.
- Salt - 1/8 tsp.
- Pasta Sauce - 1 cup
- Lemon Juice - 1 tbsp.
- Lemon Zest - 1 tsp.
- Minced Garlic - 3 cloves
- Butter - 1/4 cup

- Dried or Fresh Rosemary - 1 tsp.
- Dried or Fresh Thyme - 1/4 tsp.

Method:

1. Pre-heat the air fryer at 400 degrees. Combine the butter, thyme, rosemary, garlic, lemon juice & zest in a clean bowl. Spread a mixture on each of the thigh's skin. Use salt and pepper to sprinkle.

2. Place the chicken, then side up the skin, in a greased air-fryer pot. Cook for 20 mins and flip once. Switch the chicken again (side up the skin) and cook it for about 5 mins until the thermometer will read 170 degrees to 175 degrees. Then, place in the serving plate and serve it.

67. Salmon with Maple-Dijon Glaze in air fryer

Ingredients:

- Salmon Fillets - 4 (about ounces)
- Salt - 1/4 tsp.
- Pepper - 1/4 tsp.
- Butter - 3 tbsp.
- Mustard - 1 tbsp.
- Lemon Juice - 1 medium-sized
- Garlic clove - 1 minced
- Olive oil

Method:

1. Pre-heat the air fryer at 400 degrees. Melt butter in a medium-sized pan on medium temperature. Put the mustard, minced garlic, maple syrup & lemon juice. Lower the heat and cook for 2 - 3 minutes before the mixture thickens significantly. Take off from the heat and set aside for few mins.

2. Brush the salmon with olive oil and also sprinkle the salt and pepper on it.

3. In an air fryer bucket, put the fish in a single baking sheet. Cook for 5 to 7 mins until fish is browned and easy to flake rapidly with help of fork. Sprinkle before to serve the salmon with sauce.

68. Air Fryer Roasted Beans

Ingredients:

- Fresh Sliced Mushrooms - 1/2 pounds
- Green Beans cut into 2-inch wedges - 1 pound
- Italian Seasoning - 1 tsp.
- Pepper - 1/8 tsp.
- Salt - 1/4 tsp.
- Red onion - 1 small
- Olive oil - 2 tbsp.

Method:

1. Pre-heat the air fryer at 375 degrees. Merge all of the ingredients in the large-sized bowl by tossing.

2. Assemble the vegetables on the greased air-fryer pot. Cook for 8 -10 minutes until become tender. Redistribute by tossing and cook for 8-10 minutes until they get browned.

69. Air Fried Radishes

Ingredients:

- Quartered Radishes - (about 6 cups)
- Fresh Oregano - 1 tbsp.
- Dried Oregano - 1 tbsp.
- Pepper - 1/8 tsp.
- Salt - 1/4 tsp.
- Olive Oil - 3 tbsp.

Method:

1. Set the temperature of an air fryer to 375 degrees. Mix the rest of the ingredients with radishes. In an air-fryer pot, put the radishes on greased dish.

2. Cook them for 12-15 minutes until they become crispy & tender with periodically stirring. Take out from the air fryer and serve the radishes in a clean dish.

70. Air Fried Catfish Nuggets

Ingredients

- Catfish fillets (1 inch) - 1 pound
- Seasoned fish fry coating - 3/4 cup
- Cooking oil - to spray

Method

1. Set the temperature of an air fryer to 200C.

2. Coat catfish pieces with seasoned coating mix by proper mixing from all sides.

3. Place nuggets evenly in an oiled air fryer pot. Spray both sides of nuggets with cooking oil. You can work in batches if the size of your air fryer is small.

4. Air fry nuggets for 5-8 minutes. Change sides of nuggets with the help of tongs and cook for more 5 minutes. Shift these delicious nuggets in a clean plate and serve immediately.

CONCLUSION:

This manual served you the easiest, quick, healthy and delicious foods that are made in an air fryer. It is also very necessary to cook food easily and timely without getting so much tired. We've discussed all the 70 easy, short, quick, delicious and healthy foods and dishes. These recipes can be made within few minutes. This manual provides the handiest or helpful cooking recipes for the busy people who are performing their routine tasks. Instead of ordering the costly or unhealthy food from hotels, you will be able to make the easy, tasty and healthy dishes with minimum cost. By reading this the most informative handbook, you can learn, experience or make lots of recipes in an air with great taste because cooking food traditionally on the stove is quite difficult for the professional persons. With the help of an air fryer, you can make various dishes for a single person as well as the entire family timely and effortlessly. We conclude that this cook book will maintain your health and it would also be the source of enjoying dishes without doing great effort in less and budget.

Air Fryer Cookbook for Two

Cook and Taste Tens of Healthy Fried Recipes with Your Sweetheart. Burn Fat, Kill Hunger, and Improve Your Mood

By

Sean Foster

Table of Contents

Introduction:

You have got the set of important knives, toaster oven, coffee machine, and quick pot along with the cutter you want to good care of. There may be a variety of things inside your kitchen, but maybe you wish to make more space for an air fryer. It's easy to crowd and load with the new cooking equipment even though you've a lot of them. However, an air fryer is something you will want to make space for.

The air fryer is identical to the oven in the way that it roasts and bakes, but the distinction is that elements of hating are placed over the top& are supported by a big, strong fan, producing food that is extremely crispy and, most importantly with little oil in comparison to the counterparts which are deeply fried. Usually, air fryers heat up pretty fast and, because of the centralized heat source & the fan size and placement, they prepare meals quickly & uniformly. The cleanup is another huge component of the air frying. Many baskets & racks for air fryers are dishwasher protected. We recommend a decent dish brush for those who are not dishwasher secure. It will go through all the crannies and nooks that facilitate the movement of air without making you crazy.

We have seen many rave reviews of this new trend, air frying. Since air frying, they argue, calls for fast and nutritious foods. But is the hype worth it? How do the air fryers work? Does it really fry food?

How do air fryers work?

First, let's consider how air fryer really works before we go to which type of air fryer is decent or any simple recipes. Just think of it; cooking stuff without oil is such a miracle. Then, how could this even be possible? Let's try to find out how to pick the best air fryer for your use now when you understand how the air fryer works.

How to pick the best air fryer

It is common to get lost when purchasing gadgets & electrical equipment, given that there're a wide range of choices available on the market. So, before investing in one, it is really ideal to have in mind the specifications and budget.

Before purchasing the air fryer, you can see the things you should consider:

Capacity/size: Air fryers are of various sizes, from one liter to sixteen liters. A three-liter capacity is fine enough for bachelors. Choose an air fryer that has a range of 4–6 liters for a family having two children. There is a restricted size of the basket which is used to put the food. You will have to prepare the meals in batches if you probably wind up using a tiny air fryer.

Timer: Standard air fryers arrive with a range timer of 30 minutes. For house cooking, it is satisfactory. Thought, if you are trying complex recipes which take a longer cooking time, pick the air fryer with a 1-hour timer.

Temperature: The optimum temperature for most common air fryers is 200 degrees C (400 f). You can quickly prepare meat dishes such as fried chicken, tandoori, kebabs etc.

The design, durability, brand value and controls are other considerations you might consider.

Now that you know which air fryer is best for you let's see the advantages of having an air fryer at your place.

What are the benefits of air fryers?

The benefits of air fryers are as follows:

Cooking with lower fat & will promote weight loss

Air fryers work with no oils and contain up to 80 percent lower fat than most fryers relative to a traditional deep fryer. Shifting to an air fryer may encourage loss of weight by decreasing fat & caloric intake for anyone who consumes fried food regularly and also has a problem with leaving the fast foods.

Faster time for cooking

Air frying is easier comparing with other cooking techniques, such as grilling or baking. Few air fryers need a preheat of 60 seconds, but others do not need a preheat any longer than a grill or an oven. So if there is a greater capacity or multiple compartments for the air fryer basket, you may make various dishes in one go.

Quick to clean

It's extremely easy to clean an air fryer. And after each use, air frying usually does not create enough of a mess except you cook fatty food such as steak or chicken wings. Take the air fryer out and clean it with soap & water in order to disinfect the air fryer.

Safer to be used

The air fryer is having no drawbacks, unlike hot plates or deep frying. Air fryers get hot, but splashing or spilling is not a risk.

Minimum use of electricity and environment friendly

Air fryers consume far less electricity than various electric ovens, saving your money & reducing carbon output.

Flexibility

Some of the air fryers are multi-functional. It's possible to heat, roast, steam, broil, fry or grill food.

Less waste and mess

Pan-fries or deep fryer strategies leave one with excess cooking oil, which is difficult to rid of and usually unsustainable. You can cook fully oil-less food with an air fryer. All the pieces have a coating of nonstick, dishwasher safe and nonstick coating.

Cooking without the use of hands

The air fryer includes a timer, & when it is full, it'll stop by itself so that you may feel secure while multitasking.

Feasible to use

It is very much convenient; you can use an air fryer whenever you want to. Few air fryers involve preheating, which is less than 5 minutes; with the air fryer, one may begin cooking immediately.

Reducing the possibility of the development of toxic acrylamide

Compared to making food in oil, air frying will decrease the potential of producing acrylamides. Acrylamide is a compound that, under elevated temperature cooking, appears in certain food and may have health impacts.

Chapter 1: Air fryer breakfast recipes

1. Air fryer breakfast frittata

Cook time: 20 minutes

Servings: 2 people

Difficulty: Easy

Ingredients:

- 1 pinch of cayenne pepper (not necessary)

- 1 chopped green onion

- Cooking spray

- 2 tbsp. diced red bell pepper

- ¼ pound fully cooked and crumbled breakfast sausages

- 4 lightly beaten eggs

- ½ cup shredded cheddar-Monterey jack cheese blend

Instructions:

1. Combine eggs, bell pepper, cheddar Monterey Jack cheese, sausages, cayenne and onion inside a bowl & blend to combine.

2. The air fryer should be preheated to 360 ° f (180° c). Spray a 6 by 2-inch non-stick cake pan along with a spray used in cooking.

3. Place the mixture of egg in the ready-made cake tray.

4. Cook for 18 - 20 minutes in your air fryer before the frittata is ready.

2. Air fryer banana bread

Cook time: 28 minutes

Serving: 8 people

Difficulty: Easy

Ingredients:

- 3/4 cup flour for all purposes

- 1/4 tbsp. salt

- 1 egg

- 2 mashed bananas overripe

- 1/4 cup sour cream

- 1/2 cup sugar

- 1/4 tbsp. baking soda

- 7-inch bundt pan

- 1/4 cup vegetable oil

- 1/2 tbsp. vanilla

Instructions:

1. In one tub, combine the dry ingredients and the wet ones in another. Mix the two slowly till flour is fully integrated, don't over mix.

2. With an anti-stick spray, spray and on a 7-inch bundt pan & then pour in the bowl.

3. Put it inside the air fryer basket & close. Placed it for 28 mins to 310 degrees

4. Remove when completed & permit to rest in the pan for about 5 mins.

5. When completed, detach and allow 5 minutes to sit in the pan. Then flip on a plate gently. Sprinkle melted icing on top, serve after slicing.

3. Easy air fryer omelet

Cook time: 8 minutes

Serving: 2 people

Difficulty: Easy

Ingredients:

- 1/4 cup shredded cheese

- 2 eggs

- Pinch of salt

- 1 teaspoon of McCormick morning breakfast seasoning – garden herb

- Fresh meat & veggies, diced

- 1/4 cup milk

Instructions:

1. In a tiny tub, mix the milk and eggs till all of them are well mixed.

2. Add a little salt in the mixture of an egg.

3. Then, in the mixture of egg, add the veggies.

4. Pour the mixture of egg in a greased pan of 6 by 3 inches.

5. Place your pan inside the air fryer container.

6. Cook for about 8 to 10 mins and at 350 f.

7. While you are cooking, slather the breakfast seasoning over the eggs & slather the cheese on the top.

8. With a thin spoon, loose the omelet from the pan and pass it to a tray.

9. Loosen the omelet from the sides of the pan with a thin spatula and pass it to a tray.

10. Its options to garnish it with additional green onions.

4. Air-fried breakfast bombs

Cook time: 20 mins

Serving: 2

Difficulty: easy

Ingredients:

• Cooking spray

• 1 tbsp. fresh chives chopped

• 3 lightly beaten, large eggs

• 4 ounces whole-wheat pizza dough freshly prepared

• 3 bacon slices center-cut

• 1 ounce 1/3-less-fat softened cream cheese

Instructions:

1. Cook the bacon in a standard size skillet for around 10 minutes, medium to very crisp. Take the bacon out of the pan; scatter. Add the eggs to the bacon drippings inside the pan; then cook, stirring constantly, around 1 minute, until almost firm and yet loose. Place the eggs in a bowl; add the cream cheese, the chives, and the crumbled bacon.

2. Divide the dough into four identical sections. Roll each bit into a five-inch circle on a thinly floured surface. Place a quarter of the egg mixture in the middle of each circle of dough. Clean the underside of the dough with the help of water; wrap the dough all around the mixture of an egg to form a purse and pinch the dough.

3. Put dough purses inside the air fryer basket in one layer; coat really well with the help of cooking spray. Cook for 5 to 6 minutes at 350 degrees f till it turns to a golden brown; check after 4 mins.

5. Air fryer French toast

Cook time: 15 mins

Serving: 2 people

Difficulty: easy

Ingredients:

- 4 beaten eggs

- 4 slices of bread

- Cooking spray (non-stick)

Instructions:

1. Put the eggs inside a container or a bowl which is sufficient and big, so the pieces of bread will fit inside.

2. With a fork, mix the eggs and after that, place each bread slice over the mixture of an egg.

3. Turn the bread for one time so that every side is filled with a mixture of an egg.

4. After that, fold a big sheet of aluminum foil; this will keep the bread together. Switch the foil's side; this will ensure that the mixture of an egg may not get dry. Now put the foil basket in the air fryer basket. Make sure to allow space around the edges; this will let the circulation of hot air.

5. With the help of cooking spray, spray the surface of the foil basket and then put the bread over it. On top, you may add the excess mixture of an egg.

6. For 5 mins, place the time to 365 degrees f.

7. Turn the bread & cook it again for about 3 to 5 mins, until it's golden brown over the top of the French toast & the egg isn't runny.

8. Serve it hot, with toppings of your choice.

6. Breakfast potatoes in the air fryer

Cook time: 15 mins

Servings: 2

Difficulty: easy

Ingredients:

- 1/2 tbsp. kosher salt

- 1/2 tbsp. garlic powder

- Breakfast potato seasoning

- 1/2 tbsp. smoked paprika

- 1 tbsp. oil

- 5 potatoes medium-sized. Peeled & cut to one-inch cubes (Yukon gold works best)

- 1/4 tbsp. black ground pepper

Instructions:

1. At 400 degrees f, preheat the air fryer for around 2 to 3 minutes. Doing this will provide you the potatoes that are crispiest.

2. Besides that, brush your potatoes with oil and breakfast potato seasoning till it is fully coated.

3. Using a spray that's non-stick, spray on the air fryer. Add potatoes & cook for about 15 mins, shaking and stopping the basket for 2 to 3 times so that you can have better cooking.

4. Place it on a plate & serve it immediately.

7. Air fryer breakfast pockets

Cook time: 15 mins

Serving: 5 people

Difficulty: easy

Ingredients:

- 2-gallon zip lock bags

- Salt & pepper to taste

- 1/3 + 1/4 cup of whole milk

- 1 whole egg for egg wash

- Cooking spray

- 1-2 ounces of Velveeta cheese

- Parchment paper

- 1 lb. of ground pork

- 2 packages of Pillsbury pie crust

  - 2 crusts to a package

- 4 whole eggs

Instructions:

1. Let the pie crusts out of the freezer.

2. Brown the pig and rinse it.

3. In a tiny pot, heat 1/4 cup of cheese and milk until it is melted.

4. Whisk four eggs, season with pepper and salt & add the rest of the milk.

5. Fumble the eggs in the pan until they are nearly fully cooked.

6. Mix the eggs, cheese and meat together.

7. Roll out the pie crust & cut it into a circle of about 3 to 4 inches (cereal bowl size).

8. Whisk 1 egg for making an egg wash.

9. Put around 2 tbsp. of the blend in the center of every circle.

10. Now, eggs wash the sides of the circle.

FRY THE PARTY! BY SEAN FOSTER

11. Create a moon shape by folding the circle.

12. With the help of a fork, folded edges must be crimped

13. Place the pockets inside parchment paper & put it inside a ziplock plastic bag overnight.

14. Preheat the air fryer for 360 degrees until it is ready to serve.

15. With a cooking spray, each pocket side must be sprayed.

16. Put pockets inside the preheated air fryer for around 15 mins or till they are golden brown.

17. Take it out from the air fryer & make sure it's cool before you serve it.

8. Air fryer sausage breakfast casserole

Cook time: 20 mins

Serving: 6 people

Difficulty: easy

Ingredients:

- 1 diced red bell pepper

- 1 lb. ground breakfast sausage

- 4 eggs

- 1 diced green bell pepper

- 1/4 cup diced sweet onion

- 1 diced yellow bell pepper

- 1 lb. hash browns

Instructions:

1. Foil line your air fryer's basket.

2. At the bottom, put some hash browns.

3. Cover it with the raw sausage.

4. Place the onions & peppers uniformly on top.

5. Cook for 10 mins at 355 degrees.

6. Open your air fryer & blend the casserole a little if necessary.

7. Break every egg inside the bowl and spill it directly over the casserole.

8. Cook for the next 10 minutes for 355 degrees.

9. Serve with pepper and salt for taste.

9. Breakfast egg rolls

Cook time: 15 mins

Servings: 6 people

Difficulty: easy

Ingredients:

- Black pepper, to taste

- 6 large eggs

- Olive oil spray

- 2 tbsp. chopped green onions

- 1 tablespoon water

- 1/4 teaspoon kosher salt

- 2 tablespoons diced red bell pepper

- 1/2 pound turkey or chicken sausage

- 12 egg roll wrappers

- The salsa that is optional for dipping

Instructions:

1. Combine the water, salt and black pepper with the eggs.

2. Cook sausage in a non-stick skillet of medium size, make sure to let it cook in medium heat till there's no pink color left for 4 minutes, splitting into crumbles, then drain.

3. Stir in peppers and scallions & cook it for 2 minutes. Put it on a plate.

4. Over moderate flame, heat your skillet & spray it with oil.

5. Pour the egg mixture & cook stirring till the eggs are cooked and fluffy. Mix the sausage mixture.

6. Put one wrapped egg roll on a dry, clean work surface having corners aligned like it's a diamond.

7. Include an egg mixture of 1/4 cup on the lower third of your wrapper.

8. Gently raise the lower point closest to you & tie it around your filling.

9. Fold the right & left corners towards the middle & continue rolling into the compact cylinder.

10. Do this again with the leftover wrappers and fillings.

11. Spray oil on every side of your egg roll & rub it with hands to cover them evenly.

12. The air fryer must be preheated to 370 degrees f.

13. Cook the egg rolls for about 10 minutes in batches till it's crispy and golden brown.

14. Serve instantly with salsa, if required.

10. Air fryer breakfast casserole

Cook time: 45 mins

Servings: 6 people

Difficulty: medium

Ingredients:

- 1 tbsp. extra virgin olive oil

- Salt and pepper

- 4 bacon rashers

- 1 tbsp. oregano

- 1 tbsp. garlic powder

- 2 bread rolls stale

- 1 tbsp. parsley

- 320 grams grated cheese

- 4 sweet potatoes of medium size

- 3 spring onions

- 8 pork sausages of medium size

- 11 large eggs

- 1 bell pepper

Instructions:

1. Dice and peel the sweet potato in cubes. Mix the garlic, salt, oregano and pepper in a bowl with olive oil of extra virgin.

2. In an air fryer, put your sweet potatoes. Dice the mixed peppers, cut the sausages in quarters & dice the bacon.

3. Add the peppers, bacon and sausages over the sweet potatoes. Air fry it at 160c or 320 f for 15 mins.

4. Cube and slice the bread when your air fryer is heating & pound your eggs in a blending jug with the eggs, including some extra parsley along with pepper and salt. Dice the spring onion.

5. Check the potatoes when you hear a beep from the air fryer. A fork is needed to check on the potatoes. If you are unable to, then cook for a further 2 to 3 minutes. Mix the basket of the air fryer, include the spring onions & then cook it for an additional five minutes with the same temperature and cooking time.

6. Using the projected baking pans, place the components of your air fryer on 2 of them. Mix it while adding bread and cheese. Add your mixture of egg on them & they are primed for the actual air fry.

7. Put the baking pan inside your air fryer & cook for 25 minutes for 160 c or 320 f. If you planned to cook 2, cook 1 first and then the other one. Place a cocktail stick into the middle & then it's done if it comes out clear and clean.

11. Air fryer breakfast sausage ingredients

Cook time: 10 mins

Serving: 2 people

Difficulty: easy

Ingredients:

- 1 pound breakfast sausage

- Air fryer breakfast sausage ingredients

Instructions:

1. Insert your sausage links in the basket of an air fryer.

2. Cook your sausages or the sausage links for around 8 to 10 minutes at 360°.

12. Wake up air fryer avocado boats

Cook time: 5 mins

Servings: 2

Difficulty: easy

Ingredients:

- 1/2 teaspoon salt

- 2 plum tomatoes, seeded & diced

- 1/4 teaspoon black pepper

- 1 tablespoon finely diced jalapeno (optional)

- 4 eggs (medium or large recommended)

- 1/4 cup diced red onion

- 2 avocados, halved & pitted

- 1 tablespoon lime juice

- 2 tablespoons chopped fresh cilantro

Instructions:

1. Squeeze the avocado fruit out from the skin with a spoon, leaving the shell preserved. Dice the avocado and put it in a bowl of medium-sized. Combine it with onion, jalapeno (if there is a need), tomato, pepper and cilantro. Refrigerate and cover the mixture of avocado until ready for usage.

2. Preheat the air-fryer for 350° f

3. Place the avocado shells on a ring made up of failing to make sure they don't rock when cooking. Just roll 2 three-inch-wide strips of aluminum foil into rope shapes to create them, and turn each one into a three-inch circle. In an air fryer basket, put every avocado shell over a foil frame. Break an egg in every avocado shell & air fry for 5 - 7 minutes or when needed.

4. Take it out from the basket; fill including avocado salsa & serve.

12. Air fryer cinnamon rolls

Cook time: 15 mins

Serving: 2 people

Difficulty: easy

Ingredients:

- 1 spray must non-stick cooking spray

- 1 can cinnamon rolls we used Pillsbury

Instructions:

1. put your cinnamon rolls inside your air fryer's basket, with the help of the rounds of 2. Parchment paper or by the cooking spray that is non-stick.

2. Cook at around 340 degrees f, 171 degrees for about 12 to 15 minutes, for one time.

3. Drizzle it with icing, place it on a plate and then serve.

13. Air-fryer all-American breakfast dumplings

Cook: 10 minutes

Servings: 1 person

Difficulty: easy

Ingredients:

- Dash salt

- 1/2 cup (about four large) egg whites or liquid egg fat-free substitute

- 1 tbsp. Pre-cooked real crumbled bacon

- 1 wedge the laughing cow light creamy Swiss cheese (or 1 tbsp. reduced-fat cream cheese)

- 8 wonton wrappers or gyoza

Instructions:

1. By using a non-stick spray, spray your microwave-safe bowl or mug. Include egg whites or any substitute, salt and cheese wedge. Microwave it for around 1.5 minutes, mixing in between until cheese gets well mixed and melted and the egg is set.

2. Mix the bacon in. Let it cool completely for about 5 minutes.

3. Cover a wrapper of gyoza with the mixture of an egg (1 tablespoon). Moist the corners with water & fold it in half, having the filling. Tightly push the corners to seal. Repeat this step to make seven more dumplings. Make sure to use a non-stick spray for spraying.

4. Insert the dumplings inside your air fryer in one single layer. (Save the leftover for another round if they all can't fit). Adjust the temperature to 375 or the closest degree. Cook it for around 5 mins or till it's crispy and golden brown.

Chapter 2: Air fryer seafood recipe

1. Air fryer 'shrimp boil'

Cook time: 15 mins

Servings: 2 people

Difficulty: easy

Ingredients:

- 2 tbsp. vegetable oil

- 1 lb. easy-peel defrosted shrimp

- 3 small red potatoes cut 1/2 inch rounds

- 1 tbsp. old bay seasoning

- 2 ears of corn cut into thirds

- 14 oz. smoked sausage, cut into three-inch pieces

Instructions:

1. Mix all the items altogether inside a huge tub & drizzle it with old bay seasoning, peppers, oil and salt. Switch to the air fryer basket attachment & place the basket over the pot.

2. Put inside your air fryer & adjust the setting of fish; make sure to flip after seven minutes.

3. Cautiously remove & then serve.

2. Air fryer fish & chips

Cook time: 10 mins

Serving: 6 people

Difficulty: easy

Ingredients:

- Tartar sauce for serving

- ½ tbsp. garlic powder

- 1 pound cod fillet cut into strips

- Black pepper

- 2 cups panko breadcrumbs

- ½ cup all-purpose flour

- ¼ tbsp. salt

- Large egg beaten

- Lemon wedges for serving

- 2 teaspoons paprika

Instructions:

1. In a tiny tub, combine the flour, adding salt, paprika and garlic powder. Put your beaten egg in one bowl & your panko breadcrumbs in another bowl.

2. Wipe your fish dry with a towel. Dredge your fish with the mixture of flour, now the egg & gradually your panko breadcrumbs, pushing down gently till your crumbs stick. Spray both ends with oil.

3. Fry at 400 degrees f. Now turn halfway for around 10 to 12 mins until it's lightly brown and crispy.

4. Open your basket & search for preferred crispiness with the help of a fork to know if it easily flakes off. You may hold fish for an extra 1 to 2 mins as required.

5. Serve instantly with tartar sauce and fries, if required.

3. Air-fryer scallops

Cook time: 20 mins

Servings: 2 people

Difficulty: easy

Ingredients:

- ¼ cup extra-virgin olive oil

- ½ tbsp. garlic finely chopped

- Cooking spray

- ½ teaspoons finely chopped garlic

- 8 large (1-oz.) Sea scallops, cleaned & patted very dry

- 1 tbsp. finely grated lemon zest

- ⅛ tbsp. salt

- 2 tbsps. Very finely chopped flat-leaf parsley

- 2 tbsp. capers, very finely chopped

- ¼ tbsp. ground pepper

Instructions:

1. Sprinkle the scallops with salt and pepper. Cover the air fryer basket by the cooking spray. Put your scallops inside the basket & cover them by the cooking spray. Put your basket inside the air fryer. Cook your scallops at a degree of 400 f till they attain the temperature of about 120 degrees f, which is an international temperature for 6 mins.

2. Mix capers, oil, garlic, lemon zest and parsley inside a tiny tub. Sprinkle over your scallops.

4. Air fryer tilapia

Cook time: 6 mins

Servings: 4 people

Difficulty: easy

Ingredients:

- 1/2 tbsp. paprika

- 1 tbsp. salt

- 2 eggs

- 4 fillets of tilapia

- 1 tbsp. garlic powder

- 1/2 teaspoon black pepper

- 1/2 cup flour

- 2 tbsp. lemon zest

- 1 tbsp. garlic powder

- 4 ounces parmesan cheese, grated

Instructions:

1. Cover your tilapia fillets:

Arrange three deep dishes. Out of these, put flour in one. Blend egg in second and make sure that the eggs are whisked in the last dish mix lemon zest, cheese, pepper, paprika and salt. Ensure that the tilapia fillets are dry, and after that dip, every fillet inside the flour & covers every side. Dip into your egg wash & pass them for coating every side of the fillet to your cheese mixture.

2. Cook your tilapia:

Put a tiny sheet of parchment paper in your bask of air fryer and put 1 - 2 fillets inside the baskets. Cook at 400°f for around 4 - 5 minutes till the crust seems golden brown, and the cheese completely melts.

5. Air fryer salmon

Cook time: 7 mins

Serving: 2 people

Difficulty: easy

Ingredients:

- 1/2 tbsp. salt

- 2 tbsp. olive oil

- 1/4 teaspoon ground black pepper

- 2 salmon fillets (about 1 1/2-inches thick)

- 1/2 teaspoon ginger powder

- 2 teaspoons smoked paprika

- 1 teaspoon onion powder

- 1/4 teaspoon red pepper flakes

- 1 tbsp. garlic powder

- 1 tablespoon brown sugar (optional)

Instructions:

1. Take the fish out of the refrigerator, check if there are any bones, & let it rest for 1 hour on the table.

2. Combine all the ingredients in a tub.

3. Apply olive oil in every fillet & then the dry rub solution.

4. Put the fillets in the Air Fryer basket.

5. set the air fryer for 7 minutes at the degree of 390 if your fillets have a thickness of 1-1/2-inches.

6. As soon as the timer stops, test fillets with a fork's help to ensure that they are ready to the perfect density. If you see that there is any need, then you cook it for a further few minutes. Your cooking time may vary with the temperature & size of the fish. It is best to set your air fryer for a minimum time, and then you may increase the time if there is a need. This will prevent the fish from being overcooked.

6. Blackened fish tacos in the air fryer

Cook time: 9 mins

Serving: 4 people

Difficulty: easy

Ingredients:

- 1 lb. Mahi mahi fillets (can use cod, catfish, tilapia or salmon)

- Cajun spices blend (or use 2-2.5 tbsp. store-bought Cajun spice blend)

- ¾ teaspoon salt

- 1 tbsp. paprika (regular, not smoked)

- 1 teaspoon oregano

- ½-¾ teaspoon cayenne (reduces or skips to preference)

- ½ teaspoon garlic powder

- ½ teaspoon onion powder

- ½ teaspoon black pepper

- 1 teaspoon brown sugar (skip for low-carb)

Additional ingredients for tacos:

- Mango salsa

- Shredded cabbage (optional)

- 8 corn tortillas

Instructions:

1. Get the fish ready

2. Mix cayenne, onion powder, brown sugar, salt, oregano, garlic powder, paprika and black pepper in a deep mixing tub.

3. Make sure to get the fish dry by using paper towels. Drizzle or brush the fish with a little amount of any cooking oil or olive oil. This allows the spices to stick to the fish.

4. Sprinkle your spice mix graciously on a single edge of your fish fillets. Rub the fish softly, so the ingredients stay on the fish.

5. Flip and brush the fish with oil on the other side & sprinkle with the leftover spices. Press the ingredients inside the fish softly.

6. Turn the air fryer on. Inside the basket put your fish fillets. Do not overlap the pan or overfill it. Close your basket.

7. Air fry the fish

8. Set your air fryer for 9 mins at 360°f. If you are using fillets which are thicker than an inch, then you must increase the cooking time to ten minutes. When the air fryer timer stops, with the help of a fish spatula or long tongs, remove your fish fillets.

9. Assembling the tacos

10. Heat the corn tortillas according to your preference. Conversely, roll them inside the towel made up of wet paper & heat them in the microwave for around 20 to 30 seconds.

11. Stack 2 small fillets or insert your fish fillet. Add a few tablespoons of your favorite mango salsa or condiment & cherish the scorched fish tacos.

12. Alternatively, one can include a few cabbages shredded inside the tacos & now add fish fillets on the top.

7. Air fryer cod

Cook time: 16 mins

Servings: 2 people

Difficulty: easy

Ingredients:

- 2 teaspoon of light oil for spraying

- 1 cup of plantain flour

- 0.25 teaspoon of salt

- 12 pieces of cod about 1 ½ pound

- 1 teaspoon of garlic powder

- 0.5 cup gluten-free flour blend

- 2 teaspoon of smoked paprika

- 4 teaspoons of Cajun seasoning or old bay

- Pepper to taste

Instructions:

1. Spray some oil on your air fryer basket & heat it up to 360° f.

2. Combine the ingredients in a tub & whisk them to blend. From your package, take the cod out and, with the help of a paper towel, pat dry.

3. Dunk every fish piece in the mixture of flour spice and flip it over & push down so that your fish can be coated.

4. Get the fish inside the basket of your air fryer. Ensure that there is room around every fish piece so that the air can flow round the fish.

5. Cook for around 8 minutes & open your air fryer so that you can flip your fish. Now cook another end for around 8 mins.

6. Now cherish the hot serving with lemon.

8. Air fryer miso-glazed Chilean sea bass

Cook time: 20 mins

Serving: 2 people

Difficulty: easy

Ingredients:

- 1/2 teaspoon ginger paste

- Fresh cracked pepper

- 1 tbsp. unsalted butter

- Olive oil for cooking

- 1 tbsp. rice wine vinegar

- 2 tbsp. miring

- 1/4 cup white miso paste

- 2 6 ounce Chilean sea bass fillets

- 4 tbsp. Maple syrup, honey works too.

Instructions:

1. Heat your air fryer to 375 degrees f. Apply olive oil onto every fish fillet and complete it with fresh pepper. Sprat olive oil on the pan of the air fryer and put the skin of the fish. Cook for about 12 to 15 minutes till you see the upper part change into golden brown color & the inner temperature now reached 135-degree f.

2. When the fish is getting cooked, you must have the butter melted inside a tiny saucepan in medium heat. When you notice that the butter melts, add maple syrup, ginger paste, miso paste, miring and rice wine vinegar, mix all of them till they are completely combined, boil them in a light flame and take the pan out instantly from the heat.

3. When your fish is completely done, brush the glaze and fish sides with the help of silicone pastry. Put it back inside your air fryer for around 1 to 2 extra minutes at 375 degrees f, till the glaze is caramelized. Complete it with green onion (sliced) & sesame seeds.

Instructions for oven

1. Heat the oven around 425 degrees f and put your baking sheet and foil sprayed with light olive oil. Bake it for about 20 to 25 minutes; this depends on how thick the fish is. The inner temperature must be around 130 degrees f when your fish is completely cooked.

2. Take out your fish, placed it in the oven & heat the broiler on a high flame. Now the fish must be brushed with miso glaze from the sides and the top & then put the fish inside the oven in the above rack. If the rack is very much near with your broiler, then place it a bit down, you might not want the fish to touch the broiler. Cook your fish for around 1 to 2

minutes above the broiler till you see it's getting caramelize. Make sure to keep a check on it as it happens very quickly. Complete it with the help of green onions (sliced) and sesame seeds.

9. Air fryer fish tacos

Cook time: 35 mins

Serving: 6 people

Difficulty: Medium

Ingredients:

- ¼ teaspoon salt

- ¼ cup thinly sliced red onion

- 1 tbsp. water

- 2 tbsp. sour cream

- Sliced avocado, thinly sliced radishes, chopped fresh cilantro leaves and lime wedges

- 1 teaspoon lime juice

- ½ lb. skinless white fish fillets (such as halibut or mahi-mahi), cut into 1-inch strips

- 1 tbsp. mayonnaise

- 1 egg

- 1 package (12 bowls) old el Paso mini flour tortilla taco bowls, heated as directed on package

- 1 clove garlic, finely chopped

- ½ cup Progresso plain panko crispy bread crumbs

- 1 ½ cups shredded green cabbage

- 2 tbsp. old el Paso original taco seasoning mix (from 1-oz package)

Instructions:

1. Combine the sour cream, garlic, salt, mayonnaise and lime juice together in a medium pot. Add red onion and cabbage; flip to coat. Refrigerate and cover the mixture of cabbage until fit for serving.

2. Cut an 8-inch circle of parchment paper for frying. Place the basket at the bottom of the air fryer.

3. Place the taco-seasoning mix in a deep bowl. Beat the egg & water in another small bowl. Place the bread crumbs in another shallow dish. Coat the fish with your taco seasoning mix; dip inside the beaten egg, then cover with the mixture of bread crumbs, pressing to hold to it.

10. Air fryer southern fried catfish

Cook time: 13 mins

Servings: 4 people

Difficulty: easy

Ingredients:

- 1 lemon

- 1/4 teaspoon cayenne pepper

- Cornmeal seasoning mix

- 1/4 teaspoon granulated onion powder

- 1/2 cup cornmeal

- 1/2 teaspoon kosher salt

- 1/4 teaspoon chili powder

- 2 pounds catfish fillets

- 1/4 teaspoon garlic powder

- 1 cup milk

- 1/4 cup all-purpose flour

- 1/4 teaspoon freshly ground black pepper

- 2 tbsp. dried parsley flakes

- 1/2 cup yellow mustard

Instructions:

1. Add milk and put the catfish in a flat dish.

2. Slice the lemon in two & squeeze around two tbsp. of juice added into milk so that the buttermilk can be made.

3. Place the dish in the refrigerator & leave it for 15 minutes to soak the fillets.

4. Combine the cornmeal-seasoning mixture in a small bowl.

5. Take the fillets out from the buttermilk & pat them dry with the help of paper towels.

6. Spread the mustard evenly on both sides of the fillets.

7. Dip every fillet into a mixture of cornmeal & coat well to create a dense coating.

8. Place the fillets in the greased basket of the air fryer. Spray gently with olive oil.

9. Cook for around 10 minutes at 390 to 400 degrees. Turn over the fillets & spray them with oil & cook for another 3 to 5 mins.

11. Air fryer lobster tails with lemon butter

Cook time: 8 mins

Serving: 2 people

Difficulty: easy

Ingredients:

- 1 tbsp. fresh lemon juice

- 2 till 6 oz. Lobster tails, thawed

- Fresh chopped parsley for garnish (optional)

- 4 tbsp. melted salted butter

Instructions:

1. Make lemon butter combining lemon and melted butter. Mix properly & set aside.

2. Wash lobster tails & absorb the water with a paper towel. Butter your lobster tails by breaking the shell, take out the meat & place it over the shell.

3. Preheat the air fryer for around 5 minutes to 380 degrees. Place the ready lobster tails inside the basket of air fryer, drizzle with single tbsp. melted lemon butter on the meat of lobster. Cover the basket of the air fryer and cook for around 8 minutes at 380 degrees f, or when the lobster meat is not translucent. Open the air fryer halfway into the baking time, and then drizzle with extra lemon butter. Continue to bake until finished.

4. Remove the lobster tails carefully, garnish with crushed parsley if you want to, & plate. For dipping, serve with additional lemon butter.

12. Air fryer crab cakes with spicy aioli + lemon vinaigrette

Cook time: 20 mins

Servings: 2 people

Difficulty: easy

Ingredients:

For the crab cakes:

- 1. Avocado oil spray

- 16-ounce lump crab meat

- 1 egg, lightly beaten

- 2 tbsp. finely chopped red or orange pepper

- 1 tbsp. Dijon mustard

- 2 tbsp. finely chopped green onion

- 1/4 teaspoon ground pepper

- 1/4 cup panko breadcrumbs

- 2 tbsp. olive oil mayonnaise

For the aioli:

- 1/4 teaspoon cayenne pepper

- 1/4 cup olive oil mayonnaise

- 1 teaspoon white wine vinegar

- 1 teaspoon minced shallots

- 1 teaspoon Dijon mustard

For the vinaigrette:

- 2 tbsp. extra virgin olive oil

- 1 tbsp. white wine vinegar

- 4 tbsp. fresh lemon juice, about 1 ½ lemon

- 1 teaspoon honey

- 1 teaspoon lemon zest

To serve:

- Balsamic glaze, to taste

- 2 cups of baby arugula

Instructions:

1. Make your crab cake. Mix red pepper, mayonnaise, ground pepper, crab meat, onion, panko and Dijon in a huge bowl. Make sure to mix the ingredients well. Then add eggs & mix the mixture again till it's mixed well. Take around 1/4 cup of the mixture of crab into cakes which are around 1 inch thick. Spray with avocado oil gently.

2. Cook your crab cakes. Organize crab cakes in one layer in the air fryer. It depends on the air fryer how many batches will be required to cook them. Cook for 10 minutes at 375 degrees f. Take it out from your air fryer & keep it warm. Do this again if required.

3. Make aioli. Combine shallots, Dijon, vinegar, cayenne pepper and mayo. Put aside for serving until ready.

4. Make the vinaigrette. Combine honey, white vinegar, and lemon zest and lemon juice in a ting jar. Include olive oil & mix it well until mixed together.

5. Now serve. Split your arugula into 2 plates. Garnish with crab cakes. Drizzle it with vinaigrette & aioli. Include few drizzles of balsamic glaze if desired.

Chapter 3: Air Fryer Meat and Beef recipe

1. Air fryer steak

Cook time: 35 mins

Servings: 2

Difficulty: Medium

Ingredients:

- Freshly ground black pepper

- 1 tsp. freshly chopped chives

- 2 cloves garlic, minced

- 1(2 lb.) Bone-in rib eye

- 4 tbsp. Butter softened

- 1 tsp. Rosemary freshly chopped

- 2 tsp. Parsley freshly chopped

- 1 tsp. Thyme freshly chopped

- Kosher salt

Instructions:

1. In a tiny bowl, mix herbs and butter. Put a small layer of the wrap made up of plastic & roll in a log. Twist the ends altogether to make it refrigerate and tight till it gets hardened for around 20 minutes.

2. Season the steak with pepper and salt on every side.

3. Put the steak in the air-fryer basket & cook it around 400 degrees for 12 - 14 minutes, in medium temperature, depending on the thickness of the steak, tossing half-way through.

4. Cover your steak with the herb butter slice to serve.

2. Air-fryer ground beef wellington

Cook time: 20 mins

Serving: 2 people

Difficulty: easy

Ingredients:

- 1 large egg yolk

- 1 tsp. dried parsley flakes

- 2 tsp. flour for all-purpose

- 1/2 cup fresh mushrooms chopped

- 1 tbsp. butter

- 1/2 pound of ground beef

- 1 lightly beaten, large egg, it's optional

- 1/4 tsp. of pepper, divided

- 1/4 tsp. of salt

- 1 tube (having 4 ounces) crescent rolls refrigerated

- 2 tbsp. onion finely chopped

- 1/2 cup of half & half cream

Instructions:

1. Preheat the fryer to 300 degrees. Heat the butter over a moderate flame in a saucepan. Include mushrooms; stir, and cook for 5-6 minutes, until tender. Add flour & 1/8 of a tsp.

of pepper when mixed. Add cream steadily. Boil it; stir and cook until thickened, for about 2 minutes. Take it out from heat & make it aside.

2. Combine 2 tbsp. of mushroom sauce, 1/8 tsp. of the remaining pepper, onion and egg yolk in a tub. Crumble over the mixture of beef and blend properly. Shape it into two loaves. Unroll and divide the crescent dough into two rectangles; push the perforations to close. Put meatloaf over every rectangle. Bring together the sides and press to seal. Brush it with one beaten egg if necessary.

3. Place the wellingtons on the greased tray inside the basket of the air fryer in a single sheet. Cook till see the thermometer placed into the meatloaf measures 160 degrees, 18 to 22 minutes and until you see golden brown color.

Meanwhile, under low pressure, warm the leftover sauce; mix in the parsley. Serve your sauce, adding wellington.

3. Air-fried burgers

Cook time: 10 mins

Serving: 4 people

Difficulty: easy

Ingredients:

- 500 g of raw ground beef (1 lb.)

- 1 tsp. of Maggi seasoning sauce

- 1/2 tsp. of ground black pepper

- 1 tsp. parsley (dried)

- Liquid smoke (some drops)

- 1/2 tsp. of salt (salt sub)

- 1 tbsp. of Worcestershire sauce

- 1/2 tsp. of onion powder

- 1/2 tsp. of garlic powder

Instructions:

1. Spray the above tray, and set it aside. You don't have to spray your basket if you are having an air fryer of basket-type. The cooking temperature for basket types will be around 180 c or 350 f.

2. Mix all the spice things together in a little tub, such as the sauce of Worcestershire and dried parsley.

2. In a huge bowl, add it inside the beef.

3. Mix properly, and make sure to overburden the meat as this contributes to hard burgers.

4. Divide the mixture of beef into four, & the patties are to be shape off. Place your indent in the middle with the thumb to keep the patties from scrunching up on the center.

5. Place tray in the air fry; gently spray the surfaces of patties.

6. Cook for around 10 minutes over medium heat (or more than that to see that your food is complete). You don't have to turn your patties.

7. Serve it hot on a pan with your array of side dishes.

4. Air fryer meatloaf

Cook time: 25 mins

Serving: 4 people

Difficulty: easy

Ingredients:

- 1/2 tsp. of Salt

- 1 tsp. of Worcestershire sauce

- 1/2 finely chopped, small onion

- 1 tbsp. of Yellow mustard

- 2 tbsp. of ketchup, divided

- 1 lb. Lean ground beef

- 1/2 tsp. Garlic powder

- 1/4 cup of dry breadcrumbs

- 1 egg, lightly beaten

- 1/4 tsp. Pepper

- 1 tsp. Italian seasoning

Instructions:

1. Put the onion,1 tbsp. Ketchup, garlic powder, pepper, ground beef, egg, salt, breadcrumbs, Italian seasoning and Worcestershire sauce in a huge bowl.

2. Use hands to blend your spices with the meat equally, be careful you don't over-mix as it would make it difficult to over mix.

3. Shape meat having two inches height of 4 by 6, loaf. Switch your air fryer to a degree of 370 f & Put that loaf inside your air fryer.

4. Cook for fifteen min at a degree of 370 f.

5. In the meantime, mix the leftover 1 tbsp. of ketchup & the mustard in a tiny bowl.

6. Take the meatloaf out of the oven & spread the mixture of mustard over it.

7. Return the meatloaf to your air fryer & begin to bake at a degree of 370 degrees f till the thermometer placed inside the loaf measures 160 degrees f, around 8 to 10 further minutes.

8. Remove the basket from your air fryer when the meatloaf has touched 160 degrees f & then make the loaf stay inside the air fryer basket for around 5 to 10 minutes, after that slice your meatloaf.

5. Air fryer hamburgers

Cook time: 16 mins

Serving: 4 people

Difficulty: easy

Ingredients:

- 1 tsp. of onion powder

- 1 pound of ground beef (we are using 85/15)

- 4 pieces burger buns

- 1 tsp. salt

- 1/4 tsp. of black pepper

- 1 tsp. of garlic powder

- 1 tsp. of Worcestershire sauce

Instructions:

1. Method for standard ground beef:

2. Your air fryer must be preheated to 360 °.

3. In a bowl, put the unprocessed ground beef & add the seasonings.

4. To incorporate everything, make the of use your hands (or you can use a fork) & then shape the mixture in a ball shape (still inside the bowl).

5. Score the mixture of ground beef into 4 equal portions by having a + mark to split it.

Scoop out and turn each segment into a patty.

6. Place it in the air fryer, ensuring each patty has plenty of room to cook (make sure not to touch). If required, one can perform this in groups. We've got a bigger (5.8 quart) air fryer, and we did all of ours in a single batch.

7. Cook, turning half-way back, for 16 minutes. (Note: for bigger patties, you may have a need to cook longer.)

Process for Patties (pre-made):

1. In a tiny bowl, mix onion powder, pepper, garlic powder and salt, then stir till well mixed.

2. In a tiny bowl, pour in a few quantities of Worcestershire sauce. You may require A little more than one teaspoon (such as 1.5 tsp.), as some of it will adhere in your pastry brush.

3. Put patties on a tray & spoon or brush on a thin layer of your Worcestershire sauce.

4. Sprinkle with seasoning on every patty, saving 1/2 for another side.

5. With your hand, rub the seasoning to allow it to stick better.

6. Your air fryer should be preheated to 360 ° f.

7. Take out the basket when it's preheated & gently place your patties, seasoned one down, inside the basket.

8. Side 2 of the season, which is facing up the exact way as per above.

9. In an air fryer, put the basket back and cook for around 16 minutes, tossing midway through.

6. Air Fryer Meatloaf

Cook time: 25 mins

Serving: 4 people

Difficulty: Easy

Ingredients:

• Ground black pepper for taste

• 1 tbsp. of olive oil, or as required

• 1 egg, lightly beaten

• 1 tsp. of salt

• 1 pound of lean ground beef

• 1 tbsp. fresh thyme chopped

• 3 tbsp. of dry bread crumbs

• 1 finely chopped, small onion

• 2 thickly sliced mushrooms

Instructions:

1. Preheat your air fryer to a degree of 392 f (200°C).

2. Mix together egg, onion, salt, ground beef, pepper, bread crumbs and thyme in a tub. 3. Thoroughly knead & mix.

4. Transfer the mixture of beef in your baking pan & smooth out the surface. The mushrooms are to be pressed from the top & coated with the olive oil. Put the pan inside the basket of the air fryer & slide it inside your air fryer.

5. Set the timer of the air fryer for around 25 minutes & roast the meatloaf till it is nicely browned.

6. Make sure that the meatloaf stays for a minimum of 10 minutes, and after that, you can slice and serve.

7. Air Fryer Beef Kabobs

Cook time: 8 mins

Serving: 4 people

Difficulty: Easy

Ingredients:

• 1 big onion in red color or onion which you want

• 1.5 pounds of sirloin steak sliced into one-inch chunks

- 1 large bell pepper of your choice

For the marinade:

- 1 tbsp. of lemon juice

- Pinch of Salt & pepper

- 4 tbsp. of olive oil

- 1/2 tsp. of cumin

- 1/2 tsp. of chili powder

- 2 cloves garlic minced

Ingredients:

1. In a huge bowl, mix the beef & ingredients to marinade till fully mixed. Cover & marinate for around 30 minutes or up to 24 hours inside the fridge.

2. Preheat your air fryer to a degree of 400 f until prepared to cook. Thread the onion, pepper and beef onto skewers.

3. Put skewers inside the air fryer, which is already heated and the air fryer for about 8 to 10 minutes, rotating half-way until the outside is crispy and the inside is tender.

8. Air-Fried Beef and Vegetable Skewers

Cook time: 8 mins

Serving: 2

Difficulty: easy

Ingredients:

- 2 tbs. of olive oil

- 2 tsp. of fresh cilantro chopped

- Kosher salt & freshly black pepper ground

- 1 tiny yellow summer squash, sliced into one inch (of 2.5-cm) pieces

- 1/4 tsp. of ground coriander

- Lemon wedges to serve (optional)

- 1/8 tsp. of red pepper flakes

- 1 garlic clove, minced

- 1/2 tsp. of ground cumin

- 1/2 yellow bell pepper, sliced into one inch (that's 2.5-cm) pieces

- 1/2 red bell pepper, sliced into one inch (that's 2.5-cm) pieces

- 1/2 lb. (that's 250 g) boneless sirloin, sliced into one inch (of 2.5-cm) cubes

- 1 tiny zucchini, sliced into one inch (that's 2.5-cm) pieces

- 1/2 red onion, sliced into one inch (that's 2.5-cm) pieces

Ingredients:

1. Preheat your air fryer at 390 degrees f (199-degree c).

2. In a tiny bowl, mix together one tablespoon of cumin, red pepper flakes and coriander. Sprinkle the mixture of spices generously over the meat.

3. In a tub, mix together zucchini, oil, cilantro, bell peppers, summer squash, cilantro, onion and garlic. Season with black pepper and salt to taste.

4. Tightly thread the vegetables and meat onto the four skewers adding two layers rack of air fryer, rotating the bits and equally splitting them. Put the skewers over the rack & carefully set your rack inside the cooking basket. Put the basket inside the air fryer. Cook, without covering it for around 7 - 8 minutes, till the vegetables are crispy and tender & your meat is having a medium-rare.

5. Move your skewers to a tray, and if you want, you can serve them with delicious lemon wedges.

9. Air fryer taco calzones

Cook time: 10 mins

Serving: 2 people

Difficulty: easy

Ingredients:

- 1 cup of taco meat

- 1 tube of Pillsbury pizza dough thinly crust

- 1 cup of shredded cheddar

Instructions:

1. Spread out the layer of your pizza dough over a clean table. Slice the dough into four squares with the help of a pizza cutter.

2. By the use of a pizza cutter, cut every square into a big circle. Place the dough pieces aside to create chunks of sugary cinnamon.

3. Cover 1/2 of every dough circle with around 1/4 cup of taco meat & 1/4 cup of shredded cheese.

4. To seal it firmly, fold the remaining over the cheese and meat and push the sides of your dough along with the help of a fork so that it can be tightly sealed. Repeat for all 4 calzones.

5. Each calzone much is gently picked up & spray with olive oil or pan spray. Organize them inside the basket of Air Fryer.

Cook your calzones at a degree of 325 for almost 8 to 10 minutes. Monitor them carefully when it reaches to 8 min mark. This is done so that there is no chance of overcooking.

6. Using salsa & sour cream to serve.

7. For the making of cinnamon sugary chunks, split the dough pieces into pieces having equal sides of around 2 inches long. Put them inside the basket of the air fryer & cook it at a degree of 325 for around 5 minutes. Instantly mix with the one ratio four sugary cinnamon mixtures.

10. Air Fryer Pot Roast

Cook time: 30 mins

Serving: 2 people

Difficulty: Medium

Ingredients:

- 1 tsp. of salt

- 3 tbsp. of brown sugar

- 1/2 cup of orange juice

- 1 tsp. of Worcestershire sauce

- 1/2 tsp. of pepper

- 3–4 pound thawed roast beef chuck roast

- 3 tbsp. of soy sauce

Instructions:

1. Combine brown sugar, Worcestershire sauce, soy sauce and orange juice.

2. Mix till the sugar is completely dissolved.

3. Spillover the roast & marinade for around 8 to 24 hours.

4. Put the roast in the basket of an air fryer.

5. Sprinkle the top with pepper and salt.

6. Air fry it at a degree of 400 f for around 30 minutes, turning it half-way through.

7. Allow it to pause for a period of 3 minutes.

8. Slice and serve into thick cuts.

Chapter 4: midnight snacks

1. Air fryer onion rings

Cook time: 7 mins

Serving: 2 people

Difficulty: easy

Ingredients:

- 2 beaten, large eggs

- Marinara sauce for serving

- 1 ½ tsp. of kosher salt

- ½ tsp. of garlic powder

- 1 medium yellow onion, cut into half in about (1 1/4 cm)

- 1 cup of flour for all-purpose (125 g)

- 1 ½ cups of panko breadcrumbs (172 g)

- 1 tsp. of paprika

- ⅛ tsp. of cayenne

- ½ tsp. of onion powder

- ½ tsp. black pepper freshly ground

Instructions:

1. Preheat your air fryer to 190°c (375°f).

2. Use a medium-size bowl to mix together onion powder, salt, paprika, cayenne, pepper, flour and garlic powder.

3. In 2 separate small cups, add your panko & eggs.

4. Cover onion rings with flour, then with the eggs, and afterward with the panko.

Working in lots, put your onion rings in one layer inside your air fryer & "fry" for 5 to 7 minutes or till you see golden brown color.

5. Using warm marinara sauce to serve.

2. Air fryer sweet potato chips

Cook time: 15 mins

Serving: 2

Difficulty: easy

Ingredients:

- 1 ½ tsp. of kosher salt

- 1 tsp. of dried thyme

- 1 large yam or sweet potato

- ½ tsp. of pepper

- 1 tbsp. of olive oil

Instructions:

1. Preheat your air fryer to a degree of 350 f (180 c).

2. Slice your sweet potato have a length of 3- to 6-mm (1/8-1/4-inch). In a medium tub, mix your olive oil with slices of sweet potato until well-seasoned. Add some pepper, thyme and salt to cover.

3. Working in groups, add your chips in one sheet & fry for around 14 minutes till you see a golden brown color and slightly crisp.

Fun.

3. Air fryer tortilla chips

Cook time: 5 mins

Serving: 2 people

Difficulty: easy

Ingredients:

- 1 tbsp. of olive oil

- Guacamole for serving

- 2 tsp. of kosher salt

- 12 corn of tortillas

- 1 tbsp. of McCormick delicious jazzy spice blend

Instructions:

1. Preheat your air fryer at a degree of 350 f (180 c).

2. Gently rub your tortillas with olive oil on every side.

3. Sprinkle your tortillas with delicious jazzy spice and salt mix on every side.

Slice every tortilla into six wedges.

4. Functioning in groups, add your tortilla wedges inside your air fryer in one layer & fry it for around 5 minutes or until you see golden brown color and crispy texture.

Serve adding guacamole

4. Air fryer zesty chicken wings

Cook time: 20 mins

Serving: 2 people

Difficulty: easy

Ingredients:

- 1 ½ tsp. of kosher salt

- 1 ½ lb. of patted dry chicken wings (of 680 g)

- 1 tbsp. of the delicious, zesty spice blend

Instructions:

1. Preheat your air fryer at 190°c (375°f).

2. In a tub, get your chicken wings mixed in salt & delicious zesty spice, which must be blend till well-seasoned.

3. Working in lots, add your chicken wings inside the air fryer in one layer & fry it for almost 20 minutes, turning it halfway through.

4. Serve it warm

5. Air fryer sweet potato fries

Cook time: 15 mins

Serving: 2 people

Difficulty: easy

Ingredients:

- 1/4 tsp. of sea salt

- 1 tbsp. of olive oil

- 2 (having 6-oz.) sweet potatoes, cut & peeled into sticks of 1/4-inch

- Cooking spray

- 1/4 tsp. of garlic powder

- 1 tsp. fresh thyme chopped

Instructions:

1. Mix together thyme, garlic powder, olive oil and salt in a bowl. Put sweet potato inside the mixture and mix well to cover.

2. Coat the basket of the air fryer gently with the help of cooking spray. Place your sweet potatoes in one layer inside the basket & cook in groups at a degree of 400 f until soft inside & finely browned from outside for around 14 minutes, rotating the fries halfway through the cooking process.

6. Air fryer churros with chocolate sauce

Cook time: 30 mins

Serving: 12

Difficulty: easy

Ingredients:

- 1/4 cup, adding 2 tbsp. Unsalted butter that's divided into half-cup (around 2 1/8 oz.)

- 3 tbsp. of heavy cream

- Half cup water

- 4 ounces of bitter and sweet finely chopped baking chocolate

- Flour for All-purpose

- 2 tsp. of ground cinnamon

- 2 large eggs

- 1/4 tsp. of kosher salt

- 2 tbsp. of vanilla kefir

- 1/3 cup of granulated sugar

Instruction:

1. Bring salt, water & 1/4 cup butter and boil it in a tiny saucepan with a medium-high flame. Decrease the heat to around medium-low flame; add flour & mix actively with a spoon made up of wood for around 30 seconds.

2. Stir and cook continuously till the dough is smooth. Do this till you see your dough continues to fall away from the sides of the pan & a film appears on the bottom of the pan after 2 to 3 minutes. Move the dough in a medium-sized bowl. Stir continuously for around 1 minute until slightly cooled. Add one egg from time to time while stirring continuously till you see it gets smoother after every addition. Move the mixture in the piping bag, which is fitted with having star tip of medium size. Chill it for around 30 minutes.

3. Pipe 6 (3" long) bits in one-layer inside a basket of the air fryer. Cook at a degree of 380 f for around 10 minutes. Repeat this step for the leftover dough.

4. Stir the sugar & cinnamon together inside a medium-size bowl. Use 2 tablespoons of melted butter to brush the cooked churros. Cover them with the sugar mixture.

5. Put the cream and chocolate in a tiny, microwaveable tub. Microwave with a high temperature for roughly 30 seconds until molten and flat, stirring every 15 seconds. Mix in kefir.

6. Serve the churros, including chocolate sauce.

7. Whole-wheat pizzas in an air fryer

Cook time: 10 mins

Serving: 2 people

Difficulty: easy

Ingredients:

- 1 small thinly sliced garlic clove

- 1/4 ounce of Parmigiano-Reggiano shaved cheese (1 tbsp.)

- 1 cup of small spinach leaves (around 1 oz.)

- 1/4 cup marinara sauce (lower-sodium)

- 1-ounce part-skim pre-shredded mozzarella cheese (1/4 cup)

- 1 tiny plum tomato, sliced into 8 pieces

- 2 pita rounds of whole-wheat

Instructions:

1. Disperse marinara sauce equally on one side of every pita bread. Cover it each with half of the tomato slices, cheese, spinach leaves and garlic.

2. Put 1 pita in the basket of air-fryer & cook it at a degree of 350 f until the cheese is melted and the pita is crispy. Repeat with the leftover pita.

8. Air-fried corn dog bites

Cook time: 15 mins

Serving: 4 people

Difficulty: easy

Ingredients:

- 2 lightly beaten large eggs

- 2 uncured hot dogs of all-beef

- Cooking spray

- 12 bamboo skewers or craft sticks

- 8 tsp. of yellow mustard

- 1 1/2 cups cornflakes cereal finely crushed

- 1/2 cup (2 1/8 oz.) Flour for All-purpose

Instructions:

1. Split lengthwise every hot dog. Cut every half in three same pieces. Add a bamboo skewer or the craft stick inside the end of every hot dog piece.

2. Put flour in a bowl. Put slightly beaten eggs in another shallow bowl. Put crushed cornflakes inside another shallow bowl. Mix the hot dogs with flour; make sure to shake the surplus. Soak in the egg, helping you in dripping off every excess. Dredge inside the cornflakes crumbs, pushing to stick.

3. Gently coat the basket of the air fryer with your cooking spray. Put around six bites of corn dog inside the basket; spray the surface lightly with the help of cooking spray. Now cook at a degree of 375 f till the coating shows a golden brown color and is crunchy for about 10 minutes, flipping the bites of corn dog halfway in cooking. Do this step with other bites of the corn dog.

4. Put three bites of corn dog with 2 tsp. of mustard on each plate to, and then serve immediately.

9. Crispy veggie quesadillas in an air fryer

Cook time: 20 mins

Serving: 4 people

Difficulty: easy

Instructions:

- Cooking spray

- 1/2 cup refrigerated and drained pico de gallo

- 4 ounces far educing cheddar sharp cheese, shredded (1 cup)

- 1 tbsp. of fresh juice (with 1 lime)

- 4(6-in.) whole-grain Sprouted flour tortillas

- 1/4 tsp. ground cumin

- 2 tbsp. fresh cilantro chopped

- 1 cup red bell pepper sliced

- 1 cup of drained & rinsed black beans canned, no-salt-added

- 1 tsp. of lime zest plus

- 1 cup of sliced zucchini

- 2 ounces of plain 2 percent fat reduced Greek yogurt

Instructions:

1. Put tortillas on the surface of your work. Sprinkle two tbsp. Shredded cheese on the half of every tortilla. Each tortilla must be top with cheese, having a cup of 1/4 each black beans, slices of red pepper equally and zucchini slices. Sprinkle equally with the leftover 1/2 cup

of cheese. Fold the tortillas making a shape of a half-moon. Coat quesadillas lightly with the help of cooking spray & protect them with toothpicks.

2. Gently spray the cooking spray on the basket of the air fryer. Cautiously put two quesadillas inside the basket & cook it at a degree of 400 f till the tortillas are of golden brown color & slightly crispy, vegetables get softened, and the cheese if finally melted for around 10 minutes, rotating the quesadillas halfway while cooking. Do this step again with the leftover quesadillas.

3. As the quesadillas are cooking, mix lime zest, cumin, yogurt and lime juice altogether in a small tub. For serving, cut the quesadilla in slices & sprinkle it with cilantro. Serve it with a tablespoon of cumin cream and around 2 tablespoons of pico de gallo.

10. Air-fried curry chickpeas

Cook time: 10 mins

Serving: 4 people

Difficulty: easy

Ingredients:

- 2 tbsp. of curry powder

- Fresh cilantro thinly sliced

- 1(15-oz.) Can chickpeas (like garbanzo beans), rinsed & drained (1 1/2 cups)

- 1/4 tsp. of kosher salt

- 1/2 tbsp. of ground turmeric

- 1/2 tsp. of Aleppo pepper

- 1/4 tsp. of ground coriander

- 2 tbsp. of olive oil

- 1/4 tsp. and 1/8 tsp. of Ground cinnamon

- 2 tbsp. of vinegar (red wine)

- 1/4 tsp. of ground cumin

Instructions:

1. Smash chickpeas softly inside a tub with your hands (don't crush); remove chickpea skins.

2. Apply oil and vinegar to chickpeas, & toss for coating. Add turmeric, cinnamon, cumin, curry powder and coriander; whisk gently so that they can be mixed together.

3. Put chickpeas in one layer inside the bask of air fryer & cook at a degree of 400 f till it's crispy for around 15 mins; shake the chickpeas timely while cooking.

4. Place the chickpeas in a tub. Sprinkle it with cilantro, Aleppo pepper and salt; blend to coat.

11. Air fry shrimp spring rolls with sweet chili sauce.

Cook time: 20 mins

Serving: 4

Difficulty: easy

Ingredients:

- 1 cup of matchstick carrots

- 8 (8" square) wrappers of spring roll

- 2 1/2 tbsp. of divided sesame oil

- 4 ounces of peeled, deveined and chopped raw shrimp

- 1/2 cup of chili sauce (sweet)

- 1 cup of (red) bell pepper julienne-cut

- 2 tsp. of fish sauce

- 3/4 cup snow peas julienne-cut

- 2 cups of cabbage, pre-shredded

- 1/4 tsp. of red pepper, crushed

- 1 tbsp. of lime juice (fresh)

- 1/4 cup of fresh cilantro (chopped)

Instructions:

1. In a large pan, heat around 1 1/2 tsp. of oil until softly smoked. Add carrots, bell pepper and cabbage; Cook, stirring constantly, for 1 to 1 1/2 minutes, until finely wilted. Place it on a baking tray; cool for 5 minutes.

2. In a wide tub, place the mixture of cabbage, snow peas, cilantro, fish sauce, red pepper, shrimp and lime juice; toss to blend.

3. Put the wrappers of spring roll on the surface with a corner that is facing you. Add a filling of 1/4 cup in the middle of every wrapper of spring roll, extending from left-hand side to right in a three-inch wide strip.

4. Fold each wrapper's bottom corner over the filling, stuffing the corner tip under the filling. Fold the corners left & right over the filling. Brush the remaining corner softly with water; roll closely against the remaining corner; press gently to cover. Use 2 teaspoons of the remaining oil to rub the spring rolls.

5. Inside the basket of air fryer, put four spring rolls & cook at a degree of 390 f till it's golden, for 6 - 7 minutes, rotating the spring rolls every 5 minutes. Repeat with the leftover spring rolls. Use chili sauce to serve.

Chapter 5: Dessert recipes

1. Air fryer mores

Cook time: 2 mins

Serving: 2 people

Difficulty: easy

Ingredients:

- 1 big marshmallow

- 2 graham crackers split in half

- 2 square, fine quality chocolate

Instructions:

1. Preheat the air fryer at a degree of 330 f.

2. When preheating, break 2 graham crackers into two to form four squares. Cut 1 big marshmallow into half evenly so that one side can be sticky.

3. Add every half of your marshmallow in a square of one graham cracker & push downwards to stick the marshmallow with graham cracker. You must now have two marshmallows coated with graham crackers & two regular graham crackers.

4. In one layer, put two graham crackers and marshmallows inside your air fryer & cook for about 2 minutes till you can see the marshmallow becoming toasted slightly.

5. Remove immediately and completely and add 1 chocolate square to the toasted marshmallow. Add the rest of the squares of the graham cracker and press down. Enjoy instantly.

2. Easy air fryer brownies

Cook time: 15 mins

Serving: 4 people

Difficulty: easy

Ingredients:

- 2 large eggs

- ½ cup flour for all-purpose

- ¼ cup melted unsalted butter

- 6 tbsp. of cocoa powder, unsweetened

- ¼ tsp. of baking powder

- ¾ cup of sugar

- ½ tsp. of vanilla extract

- 1 tbsp. of vegetable oil

- ¼ tsp. of salt

Instructions:

1. Get the 7-inch baking tray ready by gently greasing it with butter on all the sides and even the bottom. Put it aside

2. Preheat the air fryer by adjusting its temperature to a degree of 330 f & leaving it for around 5 minutes as you cook the brownie batter.

3. Add baking powder, cocoa powder, vanilla extract, flour for all-purpose, butter, vegetable oil, salt, eggs and sugar in a big tub & mix it unless well combined.

4. Add up all these for the preparation of the baking pan & clean the top.

5. Put it inside the air fryer & bake it for about 15 minutes or as long as a toothpick can be entered and comes out easily from the center.

6. Take it out and make it cool in the tray until you remove and cut.

3. Easy air fryer churros

Cook time: 5 mins

Serving: 4 people

Difficulty: easy

Ingredients:

- 1 tbsp. of sugar

- Sifted powdered sugar & cinnamon or cinnamon sugar

- 1 cup (about 250ml) water

- 4 eggs

- ½ cup (113g) butter

- ¼ tsp. salt

• 1 cup (120g) all-purpose flour

Instructions:

1. Mix the ingredients bringing them to boil while stirring continuously.

2. Add flour & start mixing properly. Take it out from the heat & mix it till it gets smooth & the dough can be taken out from the pan easily.

3. Add one egg at one time and stir it until it gets smooth. Set it to cool.

4. Preheat your air fryer degree of 400 for 200 c.

5. Cover your bag of cake decorations with dough & add a star tip of 1/2 inch.

6. Make sticks which are having a length of 3 to 4 inches by moving your dough out from the bag in paper (parchment). You can now switch it inside your air fryer if you are ready to do so. If it is hard to handle the dough, put it inside the refrigerator for around 30 minutes.

7. Use cooking spray or coconut oil to spray the tray or the basket of your air fryer.

8. Add around 8 to 10 churros in a tray or inside the basket of the air fryer. Spray with oil.

9. Cook for 5 minutes at a degree of 400 for 200 c.

10. Until finished and when still hot, rill in regular sugar, cinnamon or sugar mixture.

11. Roll in the cinnamon-sugar blend, cinnamon or normal sugar until finished and when still high.

4. Air fryer sweet apples

Cook time: 8 mins

Serving: 4 people

Difficulty: easy

Ingredients:

- ¼ cup of white sugar

- ⅓ Cup of water

- ¼ cup of brown sugar

- ½ tsp. of ground cinnamon

- 6 apples diced and cored

- ¼ tsp. of pumpkin pie spice

- ¼ tsp. of ground cloves

Instructions:

1. Put all the ingredients in a bowl that is oven safe & combine it with water and seasonings. Put the bowl inside the basket, oven tray or even in the toaster of an air fryer.

2. Air fry the mixture of apples at a degree of 350 f for around 6 minutes. Mix the apples & cook them for an extra 2 minutes. Serve it hot and enjoy.

5. Air fryer pear crisp for two

Cook time: 20 mins

Serving: 2

Difficulty: easy

Ingredients:

- ¾ tsp. of divided ground cinnamon

- 1 tbsp. of softened salted butter

- 1 tsp. of lemon juice

- 2 pears. Peeled, diced and cored

- 1 tbsp. of flour for all-purpose

- 2 tbsp. of quick-cooking oats

- 1 tbsp. of brown sugar

Instructions:

1. Your air fryer should be preheated at a degree of 360 f (180 c).

2. Mix lemon juice, 1/4 tsp. Cinnamon and pears in a bowl. Turn for coating and then split the mixture into 2 ramekins.

3. Combine brown sugar, oats, leftover cinnamon and flour in the tub. Using your fork to blend in the melted butter until the mixture is mushy. Sprinkle the pears.

4. Put your ramekins inside the basket of an air fryer & cook till the pears become bubbling and soft for around 18 - 20 minutes.

6. Keto chocolate cake – air fryer recipe

Cook time: 10 mins

Serving: 6 people

Difficulty: easy

Ingredients:

- 1 tsp. of vanilla extract

- 1/2 cup of powdered Swerve

- 1/3 cup of cocoa powder unsweetened

- 1/4 tsp. of salt

- 1 & 1/2 cups of almond flour

- 2 large eggs

- 1/3 cups of almond milk, unsweetened

- 1 tsp. of baking powder

Instructions:

1. In a big mixing tub, mix every ingredient until they all are well mixed.

2. Butter or spray your desired baking dish. We used bunt tins in mini size, but you can even get a 6-inch cake pan in the baskets of the air fryer.

3. Scoop batter equally inside your baking dish or dishes.

4. Set the temperature of the air fryer to a degree of 350 f & set a 10-minute timer. Your cake will be ready when the toothpick you entered comes out clear and clean.

Conclusion:

The air fryer seems to be a wonderful appliance that will assist you with maintaining your diet. You will also enjoy the flavor despite eating high amounts of oil if you prefer deep-fried food.

Using a limited quantity of oil, you will enjoy crunchy & crispy food without the additional adverse risk, which tastes exactly like fried food. Besides, the system is safe & easy to use. All you must do is choose the ingredients needed, and there will be nutritious food available for your family.

An air fryer could be something which must be considered if a person is attempting to eat a diet having a lower-fat diet, access to using the system to prepare a range of foods, & want trouble cooking experience.

Bariatric Air Fryer Cookbook

70+ Healthy, Tasty Recipes for After-Surgery Recovery and Lifelong Weight Management

By

Sean Foster

Table of Contents

Introduction

Weight loss surgery has proved to be an invaluable tool in the process of losing weight and becoming healthier. However, this tool must be used correctly in order to achieve positive results. The most important step is to follow your doctor's Directions and accordingly try to ease back into eating and taking care of your healing body. In the long-term, you must be careful of not only your portion sizes and also of what foods are good for you and which ones you should avoid.

Bariatric surgery, on its own, is not enough to enable you to lose weight and keep it off. After the bariatric surgery, your diet will have to change drastically. You will need to follow a healthy diet of bariatric recipes to ensure your long-term weight loss.

Eat healthy

The most important step in following a bariatric diet is to eat healthily.

. In general, your bariatric diet should consist only of 'FOG' foods, which are as follows:

Farm- The food that is raised on farms i.e. chicken, eggs, dairy products.

Ocean- The food that comes from the ocean i.e. fish.

Ground- The food that is grown in the ground i.e. fruits, vegetables, nuts, whole grains.

Proteins-the essential part of diet

Proteins are one of the most important nutrients required by your body. You need up to 80 grams/day of proteins, in order to stay healthy. However, now that your stomach is down to the size of a golf ball, 80 grams is a big percentage of the available space.

If you are not eating enough proteins, your body will begin to break down muscle, in order to get the number of proteins required by the body.

This can cause nausea, irritability, weakness, and tiredness.

Proteins can be found in a number of foods including, meat, fish, dairy products, legumes, and nuts.

Stages of a bariatric diet

The stages of a bariatric diet in the first few months may vary, depending on the type of weight loss surgery you had. This is a general, four-stage plan for successful healing and weight loss process. However, it is important to follow your surgeon and dietitian's Directions, before you follow any diet.

Stage 1: clear liquids

Basically, clear liquids, as the name implies, are liquids you can see through. Apart from water, there are several other liquids, which are included in this category as well:

- Pulp-free juices that have been diluted 50/50 with water (however, orange juice and tomato juice are not considered clear liquids)

- Clear beef, chicken, or vegetable broth (high-protein broths)

- Clear, sugar-free gelatin

- Sugar-free ice pops

- Decaf coffee

- tea

- Sugar-free, noncarbonated fruit drinks

- Flavored sugar-free, noncarbonated water

- Clear liquid supplements

Stage 2: full liquids

Full liquids are liquids or semi-liquids, which are pourable at room temperature. You also cannot see through them. You can start to have these liquids as early as the second day after surgery, provided you can tolerate clear liquids.

Full liquids include all those liquids which are in their clear liquid phase as well as the following foods:

- Low-fat soups that have been strained or puréed.

- Cooked wheat or rice cereals that have been thinned and are of a soupy consistency

- All juices (diluted fruit juice, 50/50 with water)

- Skimmed or 1 percent milk; plain, low-fat soy milk; or buttermilk (or lactose-free milk if you're lactose intolerant)

- Sugar-free custards or puddings

- Sugar-free hot chocolate

- Protein shakes with at least 10 grams of protein per 100 calories

- No-sugar-added or light yogurt

Stage 3: smooth foods

Smooth foods, also known as puréed foods, are those foods which have been put through the food processor in order to turn them into a puree with a smooth texture. You may follow the stage three for up to four weeks, depending on your surgeon's recommendations.

Smooth foods include the following:

- Blended low-fat cottage cheese

- Blended scrambled eggs

- Mashed potatoes made with skim milk

- Sugar-free applesauce

- Blended meats

- Part-skim ricotta cheese

Stage 4: soft foods

The stage 4 diet is the easiest to follow, as you can easily fulfill your protein requirements without using supplements. Your diet can include the following soft foods:

- Finely ground tuna

- Soft, tender, moist proteins like chicken salad (no onions or celery), turkey, veal, pork, beef, shrimp, scallops, and white fish that have been minced or ground in the food processor

- Soft, cooked vegetables

- Canned fruit packed in its own juice or water

- Eggs

- Low-fat soft cheese

- Low-fat cottage cheese

- Beans

- Crackers

Bariatric recipes

A good bariatric recipe is one which is high in protein and low in fat. Fish and lean meat are the excellent sources of proteins. Fried foods and recipes with lots of oil and butter must be avoided at all costs. Therefore, baking and grilling is a better option than frying. Spices and lemon juice can also be used, as they provide healthier flavors as compared to the oil and   butter.

You should also try to avoid foods that are heavy in carbohydrates like pasta or white bread. Whole wheat bread and brown rice are better alternatives.

Best ways to prepare bariatric recipes

The preparation of bariatric food is the most important step in determining whether the food is healthy and meets all the requirements of a bariatric diet. Therefore, the following things must be kept in mind, when preparing your food:

- The food must be baked, grilled, poached or broiled. Frying is not an option.
- Use skimmed milk instead of whole milk.
- Use chicken or vegetable broth instead of oil.
- Oil must be replaced with applesauce or yogurt.
- Add spices or lemon juice to add flavors instead of olive oil or butter.

Chapter 1: Tips for Weight Loss

This is by no means an exhaustive list but just something to let you kick start the weight loss journey if you haven't already. The tips are all quickly actionable and easy to follow, though some may require a little more effort than the other, these are all ideas which have been known to work for people in pursuit of weight loss.

Record what you eat – Get a notebook if you are of the more pen and paper variety, or simply just use the note function on your smartphone to record down the food that you are consuming throughout the day. This gives you a sense of accountability when you sit down at the end of the day and review what you have eaten. You might be surprised at the amount of food you have taken in, and this will serve as a timely reminder to do better the next day. Get an accountability partner – Many people do better in tasks that require discipline when they are required to report to somebody else.

Getting an accountability partner will give that added sense of responsibility as well as the desire not to disappoint the partner when you report on your weight loss daily activities. Having someone to cajole and encourage you during this period can also be immensely gratifying, and that could be the added push to keep you on track for the weight loss journey.

Get enough sleep – It is by no means a measure of surprise to know that lack of sleep hampers your weight loss efforts by the simple increase of the hormone cortisol in our body system. Cortisol increases our appetite and hunger sensations, which is why getting sufficient sleep can do simple wonders in letting you shed the excess pounds. You will feel less cranky and more energized too!

Be mindful when eating – We get the feeling of fullness and satiation when we concentrate on the food that we are chewing and not get distracted by the ever-present mobile devices or the other assorted distractions available in this modern world while we have our meals. When eating, just eat! I know, it is easier said than done, but you can try counting the number of chews for that mouthful of food, get to seven or ten chews before swallowing. It helps to focus your mind back onto the food that you consume, and as a bonus, you are helping your stomach with better digestion as well!

Avoid processed foods – Yeap, that means the ice-creams, donuts and creamy cakes have got to take a backseat when it comes to your food selection. Pile on the whole and natural foods because those are nutrient dense items that will ensure you do not take in empty calories. Most of the processed food found today contain quite a bit of sugar and are pretty much deficient in the nutrients department, hence the term empty calories! The sugar eats into your daily calorie limit while not providing you with the essential nutrients your body needs. Go for chicken meat instead of chicken nuggets, whole potatoes instead of fries. You get the idea. Putting whole foods on your platter gives you more bang for the buck regarding your daily calorie limit, where you ensure that the calories you take in supplies your body with the nutrients that it needs to function well.

How can Hypnosis change the way you think?

Human information on the genuine substance of daze and entrancing is gotten from the Assumption Satisfaction Hypothesis of Dreams by Joe Griffin. For, obviously, dreaming is the most profound daze of all. At the point when the baby initially starts to show REM (quick eye development) rest, it is the most crucial type of daze that creates in the belly. Dreams deactivate the enthusiastic excitement, permitting the mind to react newly to each new day, thus safeguarding our senses' uprightness.

Because of the reasonable physiological similitudes with the territory of REM rest, we allude to daze as the REM state in the human giving methodology.

Profound daze reflects numerous parts of REM rest when instigated by spellbinding, for example, impenetrability to outside tangible data, less agony affectability, muscle loss of motion, and so forth Moreover, parts of how the REM state functions when we dream equal techniques utilized for daze enlistment. To help create daze, numerous hypnotists may utilize cadenced movement (for instance, making dull hand developments or getting people to gaze at turning optical figments), which connections back to the crude cerebrum of fish that we have advanced from. Obviously, on account of their consistent need to move, steer and equilibrium themselves in water, which they do by 'turning' their balances, fish respond incredibly capably to cadence. Centering consideration mirrors retention in a fantasy. Another closeness is in the focal point of consideration: creating a noisy clamor or unexpected development can place an individual in a daze, as that quickly catches their consideration and includes electrical cerebrum action known as the direction reaction, a similar PGO waves as found in REM rest. The direction reaction fires angrily when we initially begin to dream.

The fantasy hypothesis of assumption satisfaction clarifies that this is the instrument for making the mind aware of the presence of unexpressed passionate feelings of excitement that should be released in a fantasy. Considerably more likenesses exist. As we nod off, the profound unwinding that psychotherapists use as enlistment into daze matches what occurs. Also, whenever clients are loose, the guided symbolism we use to permit them to see and beat their issues from an alternate point of view equal dream material emerging, the distinction being that the advisor manages the interaction in a misleadingly incited daze, while the 'fantasy script symbolism' in our rest gives the 'unused enthusiastic feelings of excitement from the earlier day.' As we probably are aware, allegory, when given to an individual in a daze, is profoundly incredible in treatment; and dreams are illustrations. Clear daze encounters may include mental trips. For instance, clients may report the glow of the sun they envisioned on their appearances, and dreams are additionally illusory. Exploration has shown that in the two conditions, a similar cerebrum pathways are dynamic. Likewise, visionaries additionally immediately experience wonders that can be actuated in a daze, like an amnesia (for the fantasy), sedation and absense of pain, body hallucinations, catalepsy, separation, and twisting of time.

Be that as it may, similarly as spellbinding isn't a daze, so the REM state isn't a fantasy. In actuality, it is the venue wherein the fantasy happens. The fantasy script isn't like the REM theater, our inward 'reality generator' as Joe Griffin appeared, and inside, it is carried on or made genuine.

In a wide range of daze, the REM state at that point is dynamic. It's not simply a condition of 'loose' or 'latent.' It's dynamic. All types of learning, scholarly or something else (counting molding, treatment, and teaching), are engaged with programming inborn and learned information, and furthermore when we wander off in fantasy land and take care of issues. At the point when we are damaged, the REM state is the medium through which the mind catches the horrible mishap and turns into a learned part of the models of endurance. Along these lines, the REM state, especially on the off chance that we are associated with conveying treatment, is fundamentally critical to comprehend.

Chapter 2: Breakfast

Italian Poached Eggs

Serves: 6

Time: 30 minutes

Ingredients

16 oz. marinara sauce

4 shredded basil leaves

3-4 roasted red pepper, sliced

Pepper

4 eggs

Salt

Directions

Grab a skillet and let it heat up. Add the marinara sauce and the peppers then mix them together and allow them to heat up.

Once they are hot, use a spoon to make four wells into the marinara sauce. Now, crack one egg into each of the wells you have made.

Sprinkle pepper and salt over each of the eggs.

Allow this to cook for about 12 minutes. You can cook the eggs as long as you want until it reaches your desired doneness. You can also place a lid on your skillet so that the eggs cook a bit faster.

Remove the skillet from the stove and sprinkle the torn basil over the top. Scoop the eggs out along with a bit of sauce and enjoy.

Egg Burrito

Serves: 4

Time: 30 minutes

Ingredients

Pepper

1 tbsp. shredded Mexican cheese blend

Salt

2 tbsp. salsa

1 egg + 1 egg white

1 oz. protein of choices such as ground beef, chicken, or tofu

2 tbsp. plain fat-free Greek yogurt

Directions

Place the egg white and egg into a small bowl. Whisk until well combined. Spray cooking spray on a skillet. When warmed, pour eggs into the hot pan. Tilt pan to spread the eggs evenly on the bottom. Let it sit until edges are set. Sprinkle with pepper and salt then gently flip over.

Allow the other side to cook until the eggs are done. Place on a plate. Put your protein of choice and cheese onto the center of the egg. Roll up the egg in the form of a burrito. Add salsa and Greek yogurt, if desired.

Bunless Breakfast Sandwich

Serves: 4

Time: 35 minutes

Ingredients

¼ c shredded cheddar cheese

2 eggs

2 tbsp. water

½ avocado, mashed

2 sliced cooked bacon

Directions

Place two canning jar lids into a skillet and spray with cooking spray. Let everything warm up. Crack one egg in each lid and whisk the egg gently with a fork to break the yolks.

Pour a small amount of water into the pan and put the lid on the skillet. Allow to cook and steam the eggs. Cook for three minutes. Take off the lid and put cheese on just one of the eggs. Allow cheese to melt for about one minute.

Put the egg without the cheese on a plate. Add avocado and then the bacon on top. Put the other egg on top with the cheesy side down. Enjoy.

Chocolate Porridge

Serves: 4

Time: 5 minutes

Ingredients

Chopped nuts, fruits, or seeds of choice

4 tbsp. porridge oats

1 c skim milk

Sugar-free syrup

1 square dark unsweetened chocolate

1 tbsp. cocoa powder

Directions

Place the chocolate, cocoa powder, oats, and milk in a microwavable bowl.

Cook for two minutes. Give everything a good stir and cook for an additional 15 to 20 seconds.

Put in a serving bowl and add desired toppings. Enjoy.

Cheesy Spiced Pancakes

Serves: 4

Time: 55 minutes

Ingredients

Pancakes:

1 tbsp. artificial sweetener

1 tsp. mixed spice, ground

Low-fat cooking spray

8 oz. spreadable goat cheese

Pinch salt

3 eggs, separated

½ c all-purpose flour

Optional Adult Toppings:

Sweetener

1 measure Brandy

4 tangerines, peeled

2 oz. cranberries

Directions

To make the pancakes: Combine the egg yolks, cheese, and mixed spice. Add the salt and flour and mix well.

Beat the egg whites until they are stiff peaks and whisk in sweetener. Fold this into the cheese mixture.

If using the optional topping, place sweetener and tangerines into a pot. Stir occasionally until tangerines begin to release some juices and begin to look a bit syrupy. Add the Brandy and cranberries. Let this cook for few minutes. Keep warm until ready to use.

Spray the skillet with cooking spray. Allow to warm up. Add three large spoonful of batter into the pan. Cook for about two minutes until bubbles form on top. Flip and cook until the other side is browned. Remove from the pan and keep warm. Continue until all batter has been used. You should get 12 pancakes from this batter.

Divide among four plates and spoon the topping. Enjoy.

Pumpkin Pie Oatmeal

Serves: 6

Time: 10 minutes

Ingredients

½ c canned pumpkin

1 tsp. Truvia

Dash ground cloves

1/3 c old fashioned oats

Dash ground ginger

½ c no salt 1% cottage cheese

1/8 tsp. cinnamon

Directions

Place the sweetener, spices, pumpkin, and oats into a microwavable bowl. Mix to combine. Microwave on high for 90 seconds. Add the cottage cheese and stir well. Microwave for another 60 seconds. Wait for few minutes before eating then enjoy.

Egg Muffin

Serves: 4

Time: 45 minutes

Ingredients

¼ tsp. salt

12 slices turkey bacon

¼ tsp. Italian seasoning

6 large eggs

¼ tsp. pepper

¾ c shredded low-fat shredded cheese of choice

½ c 1% milk

Directions

Spray cooking spray into muffin pan. Your oven needs to be warmed to 350.

Place three slices of bacon on the bottom of each muffin cup.

Mix all remaining ingredients together until well combined. Reserve ¼ cup of shredded cheese. Put a fourth cup of this mixture into every muffin cup. Add a bit more cheese on top.

Bake for about 25 minutes. The eggs should be set.

Flour-Less Pancakes

Serves: 8

Time: 70 minutes

Ingredients

Milk to mix

1 egg

Low-fat cooking spray

1 c rolled oats

1 banana

Directions

Place the banana, egg, and oats into a food processor. Process until smooth. Add a small amount of milk and blend again. Add the milk until the mixture has reached a runny consistency. Three tablespoons should be the maximum amount you use.

Allow to sit for about 15 minutes. This lets the mixture thicken slightly.

Spray a small amount of cooking spray into a skillet. Allow to get warm. Add a spoonful of the batter to form a small pancake. Put as many as your pan will allow. Just make sure you have room to flip each. Allow the first side to cook for about a minute until bubbles begin to form on the surface. Flip and cook until browned. Remove from the skillet onto a plate and keep warm while you continue to cook the remaining batter.

Serve warm with fruit, yogurt, sugar-free syrup, a dusting of powdered sugar, or a drizzle of lemon. You might prefer them plain. Either way, enjoy.

Broccoli Quiche

Serves: 4

Time: 60 minutes

Ingredients

½ c fat-free half and half

3 oz. low-fat Swiss cheese

¼ c skim milk

½ c canned mushrooms

1 c egg substitute

1 large head broccoli

Directions

Your oven should be set to 400. Coat a pie plate with nonstick spray.

Put the broccoli in a steamer basket. In a pot that the basket will fit into, add about an inch of water. Place a steamer basket into the pot then steam for about five minutes. Allow to cool slightly then give the broccoli a rough chop.

Put the mushrooms and broccoli into the pie plate.

Whisk together the half and half, skim milk, and egg substitute. Whisk until well combined.

Pour the egg mixture over the mushrooms and broccoli. Add some cheese on top.

Cook for about 40 minutes until the eggs are set.

Cut into four equal servings and enjoy.

Oatmeal Cookie Shake

Serves: 8

Time: 20 minutes

Ingredients

Low-fat cream, cinnamon, and nuts – garnish

1 c low-fat nut milk

Ice

½ tsp. cinnamon

¼ tsp. vanilla

1 scoop vanilla whey protein powder

1 tbsp. oatmeal

Directions

Place the protein powder, mice, milk, vanilla, cinnamon, and oatmeal into a strong blender, and pulse couple of times until all of the ingredients come together.

Pour the shake into a glass and top with some cinnamon, cream, and nuts.

Soft Eggs with Chives and Ricotta

Serves: 4

Time: 40 minutes

Ingredients

2 eggs

Olive oil

½ c milk

1 tbsp. chopped chives

½ c ricotta

Directions

Add the eggs and milk to a jar. Place the lid on tightly and shake it until everything is mixed together well.

Grab yourself a skillet and place it on the stove. Once it is warm, pour the eggs into the skillet and scramble them. Allow them to cook until they are soft-set. Once soft-set, let it cook and gently stir them once in a while.

After the eggs are done, stir the ricotta and the chives. Add the eggs to a plate and drizzle some oil over the top if you would like.

Ham and Egg Roll-Ups

Serves: 6

Time: 35 minutes

Ingredients

2 tsp. garlic powder

1 c baby spinach

1 c chopped tomatoes

10 eggs

Pepper

2 tbsp. butter

Salt

1 ½ c shredded cheddar cheese

20 ham slices

Directions

Turn oven to broil. Crack all the eggs into a bowl and beat together. Add the garlic powder, pepper, and salt. Mix well.

Warm a skillet on stove top. Add the butter and allow it to melt. Add the eggs and scramble until they are done. Mix the cheese, stirring until it melts. Fold in the spinach and tomatoes.

Put two pieces of ham on a cutting board. Add a spoonful of eggs then roll up. Repeat this process until all ham and eggs are used.

Place the roll-ups on a baking sheet and broil about five minutes.

Cottage Cheese Pancakes

Serves: 7

Time: 45 minutes

Ingredients

1/3 c all-purpose flour

½ tbsp. canola oil

½ tsp. baking soda

3 eggs, lightly beaten

1 c low-fat cottage cheese

Directions

Sift the baking soda and flour in a small bowl.

Mix the remaining ingredients together.

Mix the flour into the wet ingredients and stir to incorporate.

Spray cooking spray into a skillet and warm. When warmed, place one-third cup of the batter into the pan and cook until you see bubbles. Flip and cook until the other side is browned.

Serve warm with sugar-free syrup. Enjoy.

Mocha Frappuccino

Serves: 4

Time: 15 minutes

Ingredients

¼ c brewed coffee

Low-sugar chocolate syrup

¼ c unsweetened almond milk

Low-fat whipped cream

½ c 0% fat Greek yogurt

1 c ice

3-4 drops liquid sweetener

1 tbsp. cocoa powder

Directions

Place the coffee, ice, milk, cocoa, yogurt, and sweetener in a blender and pulse until all of the ingredients come together and it's all smooth.

Pour the Frappuccino into a glass and swirl some whipped cream and chocolate syrup over the top.

PB&J Pancakes

Serves: 8

Time: 50 minutes

Ingredients

½ c instant oatmeal

1 c frozen mixed berries

½ c low-fat cottage cheese

4 large egg whites

2 tbsp. powdered peanuts

Directions

The ingredients have to be put in the blender in a specific order. You will add the cottage cheese first. Next, will be the oatmeal. Followed by the powdered peanuts. Last, will be the egg whites. Blend until smooth and the consistency is of a pancake batter. Pour into a bowl and add the mixed fruit. Spray a skillet with cooking spray. Put ¼ cup batter into the heated skillet and cook until the top forms bubbles. Flip and cook until browned on the other side. Should make between four and seven pancakes. Serve warm with sugar-free syrup.

Breakfast Popsicles

Serves: 4

Time: 50 minutes

Ingredients

½ c oats

1 c Greek yogurt

1 c mixed berries

½ c 1% milk

Directions

Mix together the yogurt and milk. Divide the mixture equally into popsicle molds. Place some berries into each one. Divide the oatmeal mixture equally into each popsicle mold. Place a popsicle stick into each and place in the freezer. Freeze at least four hours. If popsicles are reluctant to come out of their molds, dip into warm water for a few seconds. Enjoy.

Chapter 3: Protein Shakes & Smoothies

Blueberry Cacao Blast V 20

Serves: 1

Time: 5 minutes

Ingredients:

1 cup blueberries

1 tablespoon raw cacao nibs

1 tablespoon Chia seeds

1 dash cinnamon

½ Spinach (chopped)

½ Cup Bananas (chopped)

1½ Cup Almond milk

2 scoops Whey protein powder

Directions:

Place raspberries, cacao nibs, Chia seeds and cinnamon in a blender.

Add enough almond milk to reach the max line.

Process for 30 seconds or until you get a smooth mixture.

Serve immediately in the chilled tall glass.

Cucumber and Avocado Dill Smoothie V 20

Serves: 2

Time: 5 minutes

Ingredients:

1 cucumber, peeled, sliced

2 tablespoons dill, chopped

2 tablespoons lemon juice

1 avocado, pitted

1 cup coconut milk

1 teaspoon coconut, shredded

2 kiwis, peeled, sliced

Directions

In a blender add all ingredients and blend well.

Drain the extract and discard residue.

Serve and enjoy.

Coco - Banana Milkshake V 20

Serves: 1

Time: 5 minutes

Ingredients

1 cup coconut milk

2 ripe bananas

2 tablespoons cinnamon

¼ teaspoon cardamom powder

2 scoops protein powder

7 ice cubes

Directions

In a blender add coconut milk with cardamom powder, cinnamon, bananas and blend well.

Pour into glass and add ice chunks.

Serve and enjoy.

Stuffed Southwest Style Sweet Potatoes

Serves: 4

Time: 60 minutes

Ingredients:

Pepper

Salt

Chopped cilantro, 2 tbs

Frozen corn kernels, ½ cup

Ground cumin, 1 tsp

Cooked black beans, ½ cup

Chopped tomatoes with juices, 1 cup

Chili powder, ½ tsp

Diced red onion, 1 small

Olive oil, 1 tsp

Small sweet potatoes, 4

Minced garlic, 1 clove

Directions:

Set your oven to 400 degrees.

Sit the sweet potatoes on a cookie sheet and allow them to bake in your heated oven for 30 minutes.

Take the potatoes out of the oven and prick them a few times and then place them back in for another 30 minutes, or until they have become tender.

As the sweet potatoes are baking, place a pan on medium heat and allow it to heat up.

Add in the olive oil and the onions and allow them to cook for two minutes. The onions should be soft, but they should not be translucent.

Add in the garlic and allow it to cook for 30 seconds or until you can start to smell the garlic.

Mix in the salt, chili powder, and cumin. Mix everything together until well combined. Mix in the cilantro and season the mixture with a bit more pepper and salt.

Taste and adjust the flavorings as you need.

To serve the potatoes:

Take the sweet potatoes out of the oven and slice them down the middle.

Fluff the meat inside of the potato up a little and season it with a bit of salt.

Divide the filling you just made between the different potatoes.

Enjoy.

Chocolate Coconut Chia Smoothie V 20

Serves: 1

Time: 5 minutes

Ingredients:

1 tablespoon raw cacao nibs

1 tablespoon Chia seeds

1 dash cinnamon

½ Spinach (chopped)

½ Cup Coconut (shredded)

1½ Cup Almond milk

Directions:

Place coconut, cacao nibs, Chia seeds and cinnamon in Vitamix.

Add enough almond milk to reach the max line.

Process for 30 seconds or until you get a smooth mixture.

Serve immediately in the tall chilled glass.

Banana-Cherry Smoothie V 20

Serves: 1

Time: 5 minutes

Ingredients:

1 banana

1 cup cherries, pitted

¼ teaspoon nutmeg

1scoop protein powder

1 cup almond milk

Directions:

Place all ingredients in a blender

Process ingredients until smooth, for 20 seconds.

Serve immediately.

Avocado Smoothie V 20

Serves: 1

Time: 5 minutes

Ingredients:

1 medium ripe avocado

¼ cup crushed peanuts

1 tablespoon flax seed

1 ½ cups vanilla Greek yogurt

1 cup Liquid (milk, water, coconut milk, etc.)

Directions:

Place all ingredients in Vitamix.

Process ingredients until smooth, for 20 seconds

Serve immediately.

Sweet Pepper Poppers

Serves: 6

Time: 20 minutes

Ingredients:

Salsa, for serving

2% shredded cheese, ½ cup

Chopped cilantro, 2 tbs

Taco seasoning packet

93% lean ground turkey, 1 pound

A bag of mini sweet bell peppers

Directions:

Start by halving the peppers and removing their seeds.

Set your oven to 350 degrees.

While the oven is heating up, brown the ground turkey.

Once the turkey is thoroughly cooked, drain off any fat that may have accumulated, and then sprinkle in the taco seasoning packet. Follow the directions on the packet for seasoning.

Place the halved bell peppers onto a baking sheet.

Ease the ground, seasoned turkey into the bell peppers.

Make sure you try to get an even amount of turkey into each bell pepper half.

Sprinkle the tops of each of the peppers with some cheese.

Place the baking tray in the oven and allow it to cook for five minutes.

Allow the peppers to cool slightly and then place over onto a serving plate. Sprinkle them with cilantro and serve them with some salsa for dipping.

Mango Smoothie V 20

Serves: 2

Time: 5 minutes

Ingredients:

2 Mangos (seeded, diced, frozen)

Milk (1 cup)

½ cup crushed ice

1 cup plain yogurt

2 scoops protein powder

Directions:

Combine all ingredients in Vitamix.

Process for 30 seconds or until smooth

Serve immediately in a tall glass.

Pink Lady Cornmeal Cake

Serves: 12

Time: 1 hour 25 minutes

Ingredients:

Juice and zest of one lemon

Baking powder, 1 tsp

Ground almonds, 2 cups

Salt

Cornmeal, 1 cup

Vanilla, 1 tsp

Eggs, 3 large beaten

Splenda, ¾ cup

Butter, ⅔ cup

Pink lady apple, cored, peeled, and chopped, 1

Topping:

Pink lady apple, cored and sliced thin, 1

Confectioner's sugar, ¼ heaped cup

Zest and juice of one lemon

Crème fraîche to top

Directions:

Preheat your oven to 350 degrees. Grease and line an eight-inch round cake pan.

Place the chopped apple in a little bit of water for about six minutes until fork tender. Take off heat and drain. Let this cool.

Beat the sugar and butter together until creamy and light. Slowly mix in the eggs and beat until smooth. Mix in the baking powder, ground almonds, salt, cornmeal, and vanilla. Fold until well combined. Add in the cooled apple, lemon juice, and zest. Stir until well combined.

Carefully spoon the batter into your pan and smooth out the top. Slide into the oven for 45 minutes until golden brown and firm.

Carefully remove from oven and let it cool for around 20 minutes. Carefully turn the cake out onto a wire rack so that it can cool entirely.

While cake is cooling, make the topping. Add confectioner's sugar, four tablespoons of water, and lemon zest into a pot. Allow it to boil. Place in the sliced apples and allow it to simmer for five minutes. Spoon over the cake and let cool.

Slice into 12 even portions and serve with crème fraiche.

Bean and Spinach Burrito

Serves: 6

Time: 30 minutes

Ingredients:

Whole grain tortillas, 6

Salt, to taste

Fat-free Greek yogurt, 6 tbs

Salsa, ½ cup

Reduced-fat grated cheddar cheese, ½ cup

Chopped romaine lettuce, ½ cup

Cooked Mexican rice, 1 ½ cups

Drained and rinsed black beans, 15 ounces

Baby spinach, 6 cups

Directions:

Set your oven to 300 degrees.

Stack all of the tortillas on top of each other and wrap them in a large piece of aluminum foil.

Sit the stack of tortillas on a baking sheet and bake them for 15 minutes until heated through.

Allow them to warm as you prepare the rest of the ingredients.

Add the spinach to the food processor and pulse it until they are finely chopped. If you don't have a food processor, you can also use a knife to slice up the leaves.

Place a large pan on medium heat and allow it to heat up.

Add in the spinach and black beans. Cook the mixture until the spinach has wilted. This should take around three minutes.

Evenly distribute this mixture between the six tortillas. Make sure that you leave about two inches on the end of the wrap to aid in folding it up.

Add about a quarter cup of the mixture to each tortilla and top with the lettuce, salsa, cheese, and the yogurt. Make sure you distribute the toppings evenly among them. Fold the tortilla over and under on the ends.

Cilantro Lime Cauliflower Rice

Serves: 4

Time: 6 minutes

Ingredients:

Chopped cilantro, 1 ½ tbs

Sea salt, ¼ tsp

Fresh lime juice, 1 tbs

Frozen riced cauliflower, 10 oz

Directions:

Follow the directions on the package of riced cauliflower to cook it.

As the cauliflower is cooking, chop up your cilantro.

Take the cauliflower out of the microwave and open the bag to allow all of the steam to release. Make sure that you don't get burned.

Pour the cooked cauliflower into a bowl and add in the salt, cilantro, and lime juice. Stir everything together to combine all of the flavors.

Chicken Curry

Serves: 4

Time: 60 minutes

Ingredients:

Cornmeal, 2 tbs

Cilantro, chopped, 2 tbs

Chicken stock, ¾ cup

Light coconut milk, 14 ounces

Sweet potato, 7 ounces peeled and chopped

Granny Smith apple that has been peeled, cored, and chopped, 1

Chicken breast, skinless, boneless, 1 pound, cut into cubes

Cinnamon stick

Cardamom pods, 6, crushed

Ground cumin, 1 tsp

Turmeric, 1 tsp

Red chili that has been seeded and chopped, 1

Garlic cloves, 2 crushed

One large onion that has been chopped

Low-fat cooking spray

Directions:

Coat a skillet with nonstick spray. Warm up the skillet on the burner and then add the onion and garlic, cooking until soft. This should take about five minutes. Place in the cinnamon stick, cardamom pods, cumin, turmeric, and chili and cook for an additional two minutes.

Place chicken into skillet and cook for three minutes. Stir to combine everything. Add cilantro, chicken stock, coconut milk, sweet potato, and apple. Stir well again. Partially cover the skillet and turn the heat down to a simmer. Let this cook for 35 minutes. Add water as needed.

Mix the cornmeal with a small amount of water. Mix together. Add to chicken mixture. Stir well until mixture is slightly thickened.

Serve hot over rice if desired.

Corn and Black Bean Salad

Serves: 30

Time: 6 minutes

Ingredients

Pepper, ¼ tsp

Olive oil, 2 tbs

Dash of salt

Brown sugar or honey, 1 tsp

Minced garlic, 1 tsp

Balsamic vinegar, ¼ cup

Minced red onion, 2 tbs

Chopped parsley, ¼ cup

Drained and rinsed black beans, 2, 16-ounce cans

Whole kernel corn, 1 cup

Directions:

 Place the parsley, red onion, black beans, and corn in a large bowl and mix everything together.

 Whisk the pepper, salt, honey, garlic, lemon juice, olive oil, and balsamic vinegar together. Make sure that all of the seasonings are mixed together well.

 Pour the dressing you just made over the corn and bean mixture.

Toss everything together and allow the vegetables to marinate for at least 30 minutes before you serve them.

This will allow all of the flavors to mix together, and the flavor will be a lot more intense.

Enjoy.

Chicken Nuggets

Serves: 4

Time: 50 minutes

Ingredients

2 tbsp. parmesan

3 tsp. canola oil

Nonstick spray

1 lb. chicken breasts, diced

3 tbsp. panko breadcrumbs

½ tsp. salt

¼ tsp. oregano

½ tsp. Italian herbs

¼ tsp. pepper

½ tsp. garlic salt

Directions

Heat your oven to 450.

Coat the chicken with oil. Sprinkle with pepper, garlic salt, oregano, salt, and Italian herbs. Massage into each piece of chicken.

Put the breadcrumbs and parmesan cheese into a gallon zippered bag and add the chicken. Seal the bag and shake and squeeze the chicken to coat it well.

Spray cooking spray on a cookie sheet.

Put chicken nugget in a single layer on the cookie sheet.

Spritz the chicken with some cooking spray.

Place in the oven and cook for eight minutes until no longer pink.

Chia Blueberry Banana Oatmeal Smoothie V 20

Serves: 1

Time: 10m

Ingredients:

Soy milk (1 cups)

Frozen banana (1, sliced)

Frozen blueberries (1/4 cup)

Oats (1/4 cup)

Vanilla extract (1 tsp.)

Cinnamon (1 tsp., to taste)

Chia seed (1 tbs.)

Directions:

Add all ingredients into a blender and blend until the ingredients are combined and smooth.

Serve and enjoy!

Strawberry and Cherry Shake V 20

Serves: 2

Time: 5 minutes

Ingredients:

1 cup strawberries

1 cup cherries

1 cup almond milk

½ cup coconut milk

2 scoops protein powder

Few ice chunks

Directions

In a blender add all ingredients and blend well.

Serve and enjoy.

Pineapple Shake V 20

Serves: 6

Time: 20 minutes

Ingredients:

Frozen pineapple (3 cups)

Whey Protein Powder (2 scoops)

Greek yogurt (1 cup, pineapple/vanilla flavored)

Unsweetened vanilla almond milk (1 cup)

Vanilla extract (1 tbs.)

Directions:

Add the ingredients in the blender and blend until smooth.

Serve and enjoy!

Spicy Peanut Vegetarian Chili

Serves: 12

Time: 50 minutes

Ingredients:

Vegetable broth, 2 cups

Tomato sauce, 15 ounces

Diced tomato, 28 ounces

Powdered peanuts, ⅔ cup

Rinsed and drained white beans, 16 ounces

Rinsed and drained, black beans, 16 ounces

Dried oregano, ¼ tsp

Chipotle chili pepper, 1 tsp (optional)

Chili powder, 2 tbs

Minced garlic, 2 cloves

Chopped onion, 1 cup

Peanut oil, 1 tbs

Directions:

In a Dutch oven, pour the oil in and let it heat up over medium-high heat.

Place in the onion and garlic and sauté them together for three to four minutes. The onions should become tender, but make sure that you don't let your garlic burn.

Mix in the salt, oregano, pepper, and chili powder. Allow this mixture to sauté for another two minutes, or until it becomes fragrant.

Mix in the broth, tomato sauce, tomatoes, powdered peanuts, corn, and cleaned beans.

Stir everything together and let it all come to a boil.

Lower the heat down to a simmer and allow the mixture to cook for 30 minutes.

If you want, this can also be fixed in a slow cooker.

Add everything to the slow cooker and mix everything together.

Cover the slow cooker and set it to high for two to three hours.

Halloumi Wraps

Serves: 6

Time: 30 minutes

Ingredients

Dressing:

1 olive oil

2 tbsp. sweet chili sauce

Filling and Salad:

6 radishes, sliced

9 oz. Halloumi cheese

4 spring onions, sliced

4 wraps, low-carb

1 head lettuce, leaves separated

1 lime, juiced

2 celery stalks, sliced

Directions

Combine the dressing ingredients and stir well to combine.

Slice the Halloumi into eight equal slices and coat with the dressing.

Put them on the grill or in a pan and brown on both sides about three minutes. They need to be crispy and browned on the outside.

While these are cooking, combine the radishes, lettuce, spring onions, and celery together. Add the rest of the dressing on the salad and toss.

Divide this between the wraps and place two of the grilled cheese slices on each. Serve immediately.

Enjoy.

Sichuan Roasted Eggplant

Serves: 4

Time: 80 minutes

Ingredients

1 tbsp. dark soy sauce

4 cloves crushed garlic

3 eggplants

2 tbsp. tomato paste

Pepper

3 tsp. chopped ginger

2 tbsp. olive oil

1 red chili, chopped finely

Salt

2 tbsp. sweet chili sauce

2 tsp. honey

Optional Toppings

Sesame oil

6 spring onions, chopped

Directions

Set your oven to 400. Put foil or silicone pad on a baking sheet. To make cleanup easier.

Mix pepper, ginger, honey, chili, salt, sweet chili sauce, tomato paste, oil, and soy sauce.

Slice eggplants in half lengthwise and make deep crisscross scores into the eggplants. Don't cut through the skins. Mark the flesh only. Put eggplants on the baking sheet and spoon the paste you made earlier on the flesh. Cover the eggplants loosely with foil and cook for about 30 minutes.

Remove the foil and allow to cook for another 30 minutes. They need to be brown and tender. Drizzle with some sesame oil and let stand for five minutes.

Top with chopped onions.

Enjoy.

Crustless Pizza Bites

Serves: 5

Time: 45 minutes

Ingredients

Shredded mozzarella cheese

Pizza toppings of choice

Thick cut Canadian bacon

Pizza sauce

Directions

Spray cooking spray in a regular muffin tin. Put three slices of Canadian bacon in the bottom of each cup. Let the overlap to look like a three-leaf clover. Press down to form them to the cups. They don't like to stay well, but it's okay. When you put the toppings in, they will stay.

Get your cheese, sauce, and toppings together.

Put one tablespoon pizza sauce in each cup.

Add whatever toppings you would like that the cups will hold.

Sprinkle with a good amount of mozzarella cheese.

Heat your oven to 350. Put the pizzas in the oven for 27 minutes or until browned and bubbly. Watch them closely, so they don't burn.

Remove the pizzas from the pan with a fork. There will be some liquid in the bottom of the muffin cups, just throw away and enjoy your pizza bites.

Thai Sea Bass

Serves: 5

Time: 20 minutes

Ingredients

2 tbsp. chopped cilantro

8 oz. bok choy, quartered

1 tbsp. soy sauce

4 oz. asparagus, trimmed

2 sea bass fillets

2 spring onions, chopped

Zest and juice of one lemon

1 mild red chili, sliced and seeded

2 cloves crushed garlic

4 tsp. grated ginger

1 tbsp. fish sauce

3 tbsp. oil

Directions

Heat your oven to 400.

Place the onions, bok choy, and asparagus in a roasting pan.

Mix lemon juice, fish sauce, garlic, lemon zest, chili, oil, soy sauce, and ginger together. Pour half over the vegetables and toss to coat. Slide this into the oven and cook for five minutes.

Take the veggies out and put the sea bass on top. Put back into the oven for another eight minutes until fish is cooked through. It should flake when you poke it with a fork.

Pour remaining dressing on top of fish, top with cilantro and enjoy.

Pacific Cod with Fajita Vegetables (Dairy-Free)

Serves: 4

Time: 20 minutes

Ingredients:

Pepper

Salt

Large julienned carrot, 1

Sliced yellow bell pepper, 2

Sliced red bell pepper, 2

Low-fat nonstick spray

Scallions, 6

Juice and zest of a lime

Wild Alaskan Pacific cod, 4, 6-ounce fillets

Directions:

Heat up your grill or broiler.

Place some aluminum foil over the grill rack and place the cod fillets on top.

Top the fillets with the lime juice, zest, and some slices of the scallions.

Allow them to grill or broil for six to eight minutes, or until it is cooked all the way through. The fish will turn opaque and will easily flake once it is cooked through.

As the fish cooks, spray a large skillet with some low-fat nonstick spray and allow it to heat up for a few moments on high.

Add in the bell peppers, the rest of the scallions, and carrot.

Allow them to cook, stirring often, for three to five minutes.

Divide your cooked veggies between four different plates and top each of them with a cod fillet.

Season the top of the fish with some pepper and salt to taste.

Mini Meatloaves

Serves: 4

Time: 50 minutes

Ingredients

¼ c whole wheat panko breadcrumbs

¾ c reduced fat shredded cheese

½ c chopped green bell pepper

¼ c egg whites

1 tsp. garlic powder

¼ tsp. pepper

3 tbsp. ketchup

½ tsp. salt

1 c chopped onion

1 tsp. onion powder

1 lb. ground beef

1 tsp. mustard

Optional Toppings:

Ketchup

Mustard

Dill pickles

Directions

Heat your oven to 375. Spray cooking spray in a regular muffin tin.

Stir together all of the ingredients, except for the cheese and toppings. Everything needs to be combined well. Divide the meat evenly among the cups and smooth out the tops.

Bake for 35 minutes until edges are browned and the meatloaf is firm.

Sprinkle with the cheese and cook for another three minutes until the cheese is melted and browned.

Take the dish from the oven and take out of the muffin pan with a knife or fork. Serve with toppings of choice and enjoy.

Salmon with Summer Salsa (Dairy-Free)

Serves: 4

Time: 55 minutes

Ingredients:

Lime wedges

Chopped cilantro, ¼ cup

Pepper

Balsamic vinegar, 1 tbs

Salt

Minced red onion, ¼ cup

Cooked corn kernels, ½ cup

Olive oil, 1 tsp

Crushed garlic clove

Chopped avocado, ½ an avocado

Chopped tomato, 1 cup

Skinless salmon, 4, 4-ounce fillets

Directions:

Set your oven to 325 degrees.

Stir all of the ingredients together, except for the lime and salmon.

Allow the mixture to refrigerate for around 30 minutes so that all of the flavors can meld together.

Place the salmon in your preheated oven and let it cook for 15 to 20 minutes, or until it has cooked all the way through. The salmon should flake easily and should be opaque when it is fully cooked.

Serve the cooked salmon topped with the salsa and lime wedge. A great summer option is to allow the salmon to cool off completely after it has cooked. Serving cool salmon with the chilled salsa is delicious.

Roasted Corn Guacamole

Serves: 6

Time: 15 minutes

Ingredients:

Pepper

Salt

Chili pepper, 1 tsp

Garlic powder, 1 ½ tsp

Chopped cilantro, ¼ cup

Diced onion, ¼ cup

Diced small tomato

Lime juice, 2 tsp

Large avocados, 2-3

Cumin, 2 tsp, divided

Butter, 1 tbs

An ear of corn

Directions:

Heat up a grill. Brush the corn with some butter and sprinkle it with a teaspoon of the cumin.

Lay the corn on the grill and cook it for five minutes. Make sure you turn it often during the cooking process to make sure it browns evenly.

The corn should char slightly during the cooking process.

Take it off the grill, and with a sharp knife, slice off the kernels. Set the kernels aside and discard the cob.

Pit the avocados and scoop out the meat of the avocados and place it in a bowl.

Mash up the avocados using a fork until they are creamy, but they still have a little bit of texture.

Mix in the garlic powder, chili powder, cilantro, and lime juice. Mix all of the ingredients together to make sure everything is evenly distributed.

Add in some pepper and salt to taste. Carefully stir in the corn, tomatoes, and onion.

Serve the guacamole immediately.

This is a great topper for any of the recipes in the beef and poultry sections of this book.

Spinach Green Smoothie V 20

Serves: 2

Time: 5 min

Ingredients:

1 cup baby spinach leaves

2-3 mint leave

1 cup 100% grapes juice

1 cup 100% pineapple juice

2 tablespoons lime juice

2 scoops protein powder

Directions

In a blender add ingredients and blend well till puree.

Transfer to serving glasses.

Serve and enjoy.

Vegetable Chili

Serves: 12

Time: 8 hours 15 minutes

Ingredients:

Cilantro, ½ cup

Corn kernels, 1 cup

Vegetable broth, 2 ½ cups

Tomato paste, 6 ounces

Diced green chilis, 4 ounces

Cumin, 1 tsp

Drained black beans, 2 cans

Diced tomatoes, 2, 15-ounce cans

Salt, 1 tsp

Pepper, ½ tsp

Diced sweet potato

Diced celery, 1 cup

Diced sweet onion, 1 cup

Chili powder, 3 tbs

Sliced carrots, 2 cups

Dark red kidney beans, 1 can

Directions:

Place all of the chili ingredients, except for the cilantro, into a slow cooker.

Stir everything together and place the lid on the cooker and then set it to cook for six to eight hours on low.

Once it has finished cooking, sprinkle in the cilantro. You can also top the chili with some diced avocado, sour cream, and shredded cheese.

Black Bean, Rice, and Zucchini Skillet

Serves: 4

Time: 25 minutes

Ingredients:

Monterey Jack and Cheddar cheese blend, shredded, ½ cup

Uncooked instant white rice, 1 cup

Dried oregano, ¼ tsp

Water, ¾ cup

Undrained fire roasted diced tomatoes with garlic, 14.5 ounces

Rinsed and drained black beans, 15 ounces

Diced green bell pepper, ½ cup

Chopped onion, ½ cup

Small sliced zucchini

Canola oil, 1 tbs

Directions:

Start out by heating the oil in a large pan over medium heat.

Once it is well heated, add in the bell pepper, zucchini, and onion. Allow the veggies to cook for five minutes, or until softened.

Make sure that you stir them occasionally.

Add in the oregano, water, undrained tomatoes, and beans.

Bring the heat up a bit and allow it to come to a boil.

Mix in the rice, stirring well to distribute all of the flavors.

Place the lid on the pan and then set it off the heat.

Allow the mixture to sit for seven minutes, or until the rice has absorbed all of the water.

Sprinkle everything with cheese and enjoy.

Mini Chicken Parmesan

Serves: 4

Time: 35 minutes

Ingredients

1 egg

¾ c pasta sauce

1 ½ lb. ground chicken breast

¾ c mozzarella cheese, reduced fat

1 egg white

2 cloves minced garlic

6 tbsp. breadcrumbs

¾ c parmesan cheese

¾ tsp. dried basil

1/3 tsp. pepper

¾ tsp. oregano

¾ tsp. dried thyme

½ small chopped onion

¾ tsp. salt

Directions

Heat the oven to 350. Spray cooking spray into a muffin tin.

Mix the parmesan, pepper, egg, onion, salt, egg whites, garlic, oregano, breadcrumbs, thyme, basil, and chicken. Don't overmix. Make sure all the ingredients are distributed throughout the chicken.

Divide the mixture evenly into the muffin cups. Put pasta sauce over the meat mixture. Slide this in the oven for 20 minutes. Remove from the oven and add one tablespoon shredded cheese. Put back in the oven to let the cheese melt.

Take out of the muffin pan with a knife and enjoy.

Stuffed Chicken

Serves: 4

Time: 40 minutes

Ingredients

Pepper

4 chicken cutlets, pounded thin

Salt

½ c breadcrumbs

Tomato sauce

¼ c parmesan, divided

Mozzarella cheese

1 egg

½ c ricotta cheese

½ pack frozen spinach, thawed and well drained

Directions

Heat your oven to 425.

Add half the breadcrumbs and parmesan cheese to a bowl, mix to combine. Set to the side.

Squeeze the spinach to get rid of all the liquid in it. Mix the rest of the parmesan with the ricotta and spinach in a bowl.

Put the cutlet on a cutting board and spread two tablespoons of the spinach on the top.

Roll up and secure with toothpicks.

In a shallow dish, whisk the eggs.

Coat each cutlet with egg and then the breadcrumbs.

Place them seam side down in a baking dish that you prepared with nonstick spray. Slide this in the oven for 25 minutes.

Take this out and top with some tomato sauce and mozzarella cheese.

Slide this back into the oven for five more minutes.

Remove from the oven and enjoy.

Fajita Chicken

Serves: 4

Time: 8 hours 10 minutes

Ingredients

1 bag frozen pepper and onion blend

1 packet taco seasoning

Garlic powder

3 lb. frozen boneless chicken breast

3 c chunky salsa

Directions

Place the frozen chicken into a Crock-Pot. Sprinkle with taco seasoning and spoon salsa on each one. Sprinkle with garlic powder then add frozen onions and pepper on top.

Place the lid on and set on low for eight hours.

Serve as it is or shred for tacos, nachos, taco salad, fajitas, burritos or add to a baked potato. Leftovers can be stored in the refrigerator for a week or frozen.

Lamb Koftas

Serves: 4

Time: 40 minutes

Ingredients

2 tbsp. mint, chopped

8 oz. lean ground lamb

2 tbsp. fat-free dressing

2 tbsp. chopped parsley

2 oz. bulgur wheat

4 oz. light feta cheese

½ small chopped onion

8 oz. cherry tomatoes, halved

1 clove crushed garlic

½ cucumber, sliced and halved

½ tsp. cumin

½ tsp. ground coriander

1 ½ oz. craisins

Directions

Put the wheat into a skillet then cover with water and allow to boil. Cook for five minutes. The wheat needs to be tender then drain completely.

Combine garlic, lamb, onion, and wheat together. Mix the parsley, cumin, craisins, and coriander. Stir until all is incorporated. Divide the meat into 12 even portions.

Set your oven to broil or warm up a grill. Take one portion of the meat and press it around a skewer to form an oval. Continue with the remaining portions. Put them on a broiler pan or grill. Cook for about ten minutes. Turn about halfway through to brown both sides.

While the meat is cooking, combine parsley, cucumbers, mint, tomatoes, and feta. Toss in the dressing. Serve with the koftas.

Vegetable Chili

Serves: 3

Time: 20 minutes

Ingredients

1 tsp. chopped rosemary

7 oz. Romano peppers, seeded and sliced

1 red onion, sliced

Cilantro - garnish

14 oz. black beans, drained and rinsed

½ c strong low-fat grated cheese

12 oz. cherry tomato and basil sauce

2 tsp. chipotle paste

Cooking spray

Directions

Coat a pan generously with nonstick spray. Allow it to heat up and add the rosemary, peppers, and red onion. Cook for five minutes.

Add the chipotle paste, beans, and cherry tomato and basil sauce. Allow to simmer for about ten minutes. The peppers need to be tender.

Serve with some grated cheese and cilantro.

Enjoy.

Beef and Broccoli Stir-Fry

Serves: 4

Time: 50 minutes

Ingredients

1 tsp. rice vinegar

1 tsp. ginger, grated

4 scallions, shredded

4 tbsp. oyster sauce

12 oz. beef steak, cut into 1/2 -inch strips

2 red chilies, thinly sliced

Cooking spray

5 oz. shiitake mushrooms, sliced

1 tbsp. light soy sauce

1 red thickly sliced onion

8 oz. broccoli, cut in half

Directions

Combine the soy sauce and ginger and add the steak and coat well. Allow to sit for 15 minutes.

Use cooking spray to coat a wok then allow to heat up. When hot, place the steak mixture. Stir-fry the steak for five minutes until browned. Put the steak in a bowl for later use.

Put chili, broccoli, mushrooms, and onion in the wok and cook for about five minutes until veggies are tender. Add water or more cooking spray, so food doesn't burn.

Put the steak along with its juices back into the wok and add the rice vinegar and oyster sauce. Stir to combine. Cook a few minutes more until everything is heated through.

Garnish with scallions. Enjoy.

Spicy Peanut Vegetarian Chili

Serves: 4

Time: 50 minutes

Ingredients

2 c vegetable broth

¼ tsp. dried oregano

1 16 oz. can white beans, drained and rinsed

1 c chopped onion

1 15 oz. can tomato sauce

1 can black beans, drained and rinsed

2 tbsp. chili powder

1 28 oz. can diced tomatoes

2/3 c powdered peanuts

1 tsp. chipotle chili powder

1 tbsp. peanut oil

2 cloves minced garlic

Directions

Add oil to a Dutch oven and allow to heat up. Add the onion and garlic then sauté until tender and fragrant. Add the salt, chili powder, oregano, and pepper. Cook for another two minutes. Add the broth, beans, tomato sauce, corn, tomatoes, and powdered peanuts. Allow to boil then reduce the heat and simmer for 30 minutes.

Spoon into serving bowls and enjoy.

Chicken and Vegetables

Serves: 6

Time: 50 minutes

Ingredients

4 yellow or red sliced bell peppers

3 to 4 cloves minced garlic

2 small diced Vidalia onions

1 8 oz. can tomato sauce

3 small zucchini, sliced

3 16 oz. cans diced tomatoes

8 oz. sliced mushrooms

3 lb. bag boneless skinless chicken breast

Directions

Cut the chicken into cubes. Put into a large pan along with the garlic and onion. Cook until almost done.

Add the tomato sauce, bell peppers, canned tomatoes, zucchini, and mushrooms. Cover and allow to cook for about 20 minutes. The vegetables need to be tender then taste to see if you need more pepper and salt

Serve over rice or as it is. Store leftovers in the refrigerator for one week or can be frozen to be eaten later.

Taco Chicken

Serves: 2

Time: 40 minutes

Ingredients

1 c salsa

1 packet taco seasoning

¼ c nonfat sour cream

4 4 oz. chicken breast

Directions

Heat your oven to 375.

Put the taco seasoning in a reseal-able bag. Place the chicken and shake to coat. Place the chicken in a baking dish that is greased with nonstick spray. Bake for 30 minutes but take out of the oven at 25 minutes and top with salsa. Place back in the oven and bake for five more minutes. Remove from the oven and top with sour cream. Serve as it is or shred for tacos. Enjoy.

Vegetable Stir-Fry

Serves: 5

Time: 25 minutes

Ingredients

1 chili, finely chopped

4 tbsp. soy sauce

2 red peppers, sliced and cored

1 onion, sliced

11 oz. baby corn, halved

1 lb. oriental mushrooms

2 tsp. sesame oil

2 cloves crushed garlic

1 lb. Chinese leaf lettuce, shredded

Cilantro for Garnish

Directions

Put oil in a wok and heat it.

Place the garlic and chili and let cook for 30 seconds.

Add the peppers, mushrooms, Chinese lettuce, and corn. Stir-fry for four minutes until they are tender-crisp.

Pour soy sauce over everything and toss to coat.

Serve garnished with cilantro.

Black Bean and Turkey Sloppy Joes

Serves: 4

Time: 70 minutes

Ingredients

1 14 oz. can diced tomatoes with green chilies

1 tsp. minced garlic

1 tsp. Mrs. Dash onion and herb blend

1 lb. ground turkey

1 6 oz. can tomato paste

1 14 oz. can black beans, drained and rinsed

1 ½ c low sodium tomato juice

1 tsp. paprika

1 tbsp. olive oil

1 medium chopped onion

2 tsp. chili powder

Directions

Put the turkey into a skillet and brown then drain any fat. Put all of the ingredients into the skillet and cook until the desired thickness.

Serve on buns or over toast.

Lemon Chicken Kebabs

Serves: 4

Time: 55 minutes

Ingredients

2 tbsp. olive oil

Vegetables such as tomatoes and zucchini

2 lemons, juiced

1 tbsp. lemon zest

4 chicken breasts, cubed

Dipping Sauce:

2 cloves crushed garlic

Zest and juice of ½ lemon

3 tbsp. chopped basil

8 oz. plain goat cheese yogurt

Garnish:

2 tsp. basil

Directions

Put lemon juice, oil, pepper, salt, and lemon zest in a bowl and mix together well. Place the chicken and coat well. Cover the bowl and allow to marinate about 30 minutes.

While this marinates, combine the yogurt, pepper, garlic, lemon juice, salt, lemon zest, and basil in a bowl to make the dipping sauce. Put in the refrigerator until needed.

Thread the vegetables and the chicken onto eight to 12 skewers. Make sure you alternate them. Grill kebabs about five minutes per side. Turn them often, so they don't burn. As they cook, baste them with leftover marinade.

When chicken is done, serve with dipping sauce. Garnish with basil.

Enjoy.

Chapter 4: Veggies and Fruits

Black Bean and Rice Casserole

Serves: 8

Time: 90 minutes

Ingredients

1 cup vegetable broth

1/3 cup each:

Diced onion

Brown rice

1 tablespoon olive oil

1 lb. chopped chicken breast (no skin or bones)

1 medium thinly sliced zucchini

½ cup sliced mushrooms

¼ teaspoon cayenne pepper

½ teaspoon cumin

1/3 cup shredded carrots

1 can (4 ounces) diced green chilies

1 can (15 ounces) drained black beans

2 cups shredded Swiss cheese

Directions

Prepare a pot with the vegetable broth and rice, bringing it to a boil. Lower the heat setting and cook covered on low for 45 minutes.

Program the oven temperature to 350°F.

Spray a baking dish with some cooking spray.

Pour the oil in a pan over medium heat. Toss in the onion and cook until tender, and blend in the chicken, zucchini, mushrooms, and seasonings. Continue cooking until the chicken is heated and the zucchini is lightly browned.

In a large mixing dish, combine the onion, cooked rice, chicken, zucchini, beans, chilies, mushrooms, one cup of Swiss cheese, and the carrots.

Empty the ingredients into the casserole dish along with the remainder of the Swiss cheese as a topping. Cover and bake 30 minutes. Uncover, and continue cooking ten more minutes.

Broccoli Casserole

Serves: 12

Time: 50 minutes

Ingredients

4 cups cut up broccoli

1 sleeve Ritz crackers

2 cups cheddar cheese

Directions

Add the casserole ingredients into a Pyrex dish with the crumbled crackers on top.

Bake long enough to melt the cheese at 375°F.

Veggies with Grilled Pineapple

Serves: 6

Time: 40 minutes

Ingredients

1 cup of each:

Diced potatoes

Bell peppers

Raw mushrooms

1 cup cherry tomatoes

1 medium chopped onion

1 can of pineapple chunks – natural juices

2 teaspoons each:

Dill weed

Chopped garlic

1 teaspoon celery seed/salt

3 tablespoons olive oil

1 ½ teaspoons each: **Optional**:

Onion powder

Cayenne pepper

Garlic powder

Pepper and salt to taste

Directions

Chop the veggies

Option 1: Add the veggies on a piece of oil sprayed foil. Arrange the package on the grill using medium heat for 20-25 minutes (turning every five minutes).

Option 2: Place the veggies on wooden skewers that have been soaked in water. Cook on a med-high grill, turning every five minutes or so.

Oven: Bake at 400°F, checking every 10 minutes.

Vegetarian Frittata

Serves: 6

Time: 60 minutes

Ingredients

6 ounces button mushrooms

1 pound asparagus

1 shallot

1 garlic clove

1 tablespoon olive oil

1 small zucchini

6 large eggs

1/3 cup 1% milk

¼ teaspoon of freshly ground black pepper

1 teaspoon salt

1 tablespoon chopped chives

Dash of nutmeg

2 medium/1 large tomato

¼ cup freshly grated parmesan cheese

Directions

Set the oven temperature to 350°F.

Prepare the Asparagus: Wash and trim cutting it into one-inch pieces. Blanche the cut asparagus for one to two minutes. Shock it by adding it to ice water. Drain and set to the side.

Wash and slice the mushrooms. Saute them in the oil for ten minutes using medium heat. Mince the shallots and garlic and add – cooking two more minutes. Transfer the mushrooms to a plate and set aside.

Slice the zucchini lengthwise and into half-moon shapes.

Whisk the eggs, milk, chives, pepper, salt, and nutmeg in a large mixing dish. Add the mushroom mixture, asparagus, and zucchini.

Spray a two-quart baking dish with cooking spray and add the egg/veggie mixture.

Arrange the thinly sliced tomatoes on top and sprinkle with the parmesan cheese.

Bake 30-35 minutes. You can place the frittata under the broiler for two to three minutes to brown the top.

Cool and serve at room temperature or straight from the fridge.

Chickpea and Feta Salad

Serves: 1

Time: 55 minutes

Ingredients

¾ cup chopped raw vegetables

¼ cup each:

Can/fresh chickpeas

Crumbled feta cheese

1 tablespoon lemon juice

2 tablespoons olive oil

1 teaspoon dried oregano

Dash each of:

Pepper

Salt

Directions

Use your imagination for the chopped veggies. Include peppers, avocado, tomatoes, onions, and celery or your favorites.

Rinse and drain the chickpeas.

Combine all of the ingredients and chill in the fridge until ready to serve.

Cucumber and Onion Salad with Vinegar

Serves: 6

Time: 70 minutes

Ingredients

Pinch of salt and pepper

1 red onion

3-5 cucumbers (peeled)

½ cup each:

White vinegar

Water

1/3 cup sugar

Directions

Slice the cucumbers and onions very thin and add to a salad dish.

Combine the water, vinegar, salt, pepper, and sugar and pour over the veggies.

Add a cover and marinate for a minimum of one hour.

Coleslaw

Serves: 6

Time: 35 minutes

Ingredients

1 small shredded carrot

3 cups green cabbage – shredded

¼ cup minced onion

1 tablespoon vinegar

1/3 cup mayonnaise

2 teaspoons sugar

½ teaspoon each:

Celery seed

Salt

Directions

Prepare the onion, carrots, and cabbage into a bowl.

Mix the dressing and pour over the slaw.

Lentil Vegetarian Loaf

Serves: 10

Time: 2 hours 20 minutes

Ingredients

1 ½ cups rinsed – dried lentils

2 yellow onions

3 cups cooked brown rice

2 tablespoons canola/olive oil

½ cup ketchup

1 can tomato paste (6 ounces)

1 teaspoon each of:

Marjoram

Garlic powder

Sage

½ cup - quartered cherry tomatoes

¾ cup tomato/pasta sauce

To Taste:

Salt

More ketchup

Directions

Preheat the oven to 350°F.

Rinse and cook the lentils in 3 to 4 cups of water for approximately 30 minutes.

Drain and slightly mash the lentils.

Peel and chop the onions. Cook in the oil until golden.

Combine the onions, lentils, tomato paste, rice, tomatoes, sauce and spices into a large pot. Mix well.

Press the mixture into a well-greased baking dish with ½ cup of ketchup over the top.

Bake for one hour.

Baked Tomatoes

Serves: 6

Time: 60 minutes

Ingredients

Olive oil spray

5-6 large tomatoes

Greek seasoning

¼ cup low-fat parmesan cheese

Optional: ¼ cup pine nuts

Directions

Set the oven temperature in advance to 350°F. Spray a baking pan with the olive oil.

Slice the tomatoes lengthwise into halves and arrange them on the baking pan.

Sprinkle them with the cheese, nuts, and a bit of Greek seasoning as you desire.

Bake on the middle oven rack for 50 minutes.

Acorn Squash- Stuffed with Cheese

Serves: 4

Time: 60 minutes

Ingredients

1 pound ground turkey breast (extra-lean)

2 acorn squash

1 can (8 ounces) tomato sauce

1 cup each:

Sliced fresh mushrooms

Chopped onion

Diced celery

1 teaspoon each:

Garlic powder

Basil

Oregano

1 pinch black pepper

1/8 teaspoon salt

1 cup shredded cheddar cheese (reduced-fat)

Directions

Program the oven temperature to 350°F.

Slice the squash in half and remove the seeds. Arrange the squash, cut side down, in a dish and microwave on high for 20 minutes.

Brown the turkey in a skillet and add the onion and celery. Saute two to three minutes. Blend in the mushrooms, and add the sauce and seasonings. Divide into quarters and spoon into the squash.

Cover and bake for 15 minutes.

Garnish with the cheese and bake until the cheese has melted.

Spicy Sweet Potato Fries

Serves: 4

Time: 40 minutes

Ingredients

1 ½ tablespoons olive oil

2 medium sweet potatoes

¼ teaspoon salt

1 teaspoon ground cumin

½ teaspoon each:

Onion powder

Chili powder

Directions

Program the oven setting to 450°F.

Wash and cut the potatoes lengthwise into fry strips. Combine all ingredients together in a dish and shake

Arrange them on a baking sheet on some parchment paper or foil.

Bake and turn every 5 to 6 minutes - for a total of 20 minutes cooking time.

Spinach Lasagna

Serves: 8

Time: 2 hours

Ingredients

1 large egg

2 cups cottage cheese (1% milkfat)

2 cups part-skim mozzarella cheese

10 ounces baby spinach

1 jar spaghetti/marinara tomato sauce

1 cup water

9 lasagna noodles

1/8 teaspoon black pepper

Directions

Program the oven temperature to 350°F.

Combine the thawed, drained spinach, one cup of mozzarella, cottage cheese, egg, and the seasonings in a large mixing bowl.

Spray a 9x13x2-inch casserole dish with some cooking spray.

Layer ½ cup of the sauce, 3 noodles, and ½ of the cheese mixture. Repeat, and top with the noodles one cup of mozzarella. Pour water around the edges and toothpicks on top to place a piece of foil over the noodles.

Bake covered for one hour to 1 ½ hours. Let it rest 15 minutes.

Squash and Apple Bake

Serves: 6

Time: 70 minutes

Ingredients

2 medium apples

1 medium butternut squash

1 tablespoon each:

Splenda

All-purpose flour

½ teaspoon salt

¼ cup melted butter

2 teaspoons ground cinnamon

Directions

Program the oven temperature to 350°F.

Peel and core the apples and cut them into thin wedges. Peel and cut the squash into ¾-inch cubes.

Combine the squash and apples together in a baking dish.

Add the remainder of ingredients together and add to the top of the mixed apples and squash.

Bake for 50 to 60 minutes in a covered dish. For the last ten minutes, you can remove the top if you prefer the topping crispier.

Eggplant Pesto Mini Pizza

Serves: 4

Time: 55 minutes

Ingredients

1 each chopped:

Bell pepper

Tomato

Eggplant

1 medium sliced red onion

1/8 teaspoon salt

3 cloves of garlic

Pinch of oregano

¼ cup each:

Extra-virgin olive oil

Pesto sauce

Hummus

Vegan Parmesan cheese

Sandwich thins – Arnold Orowheat used

Optional: Pepper flakes

Directions

Set the oven to 400°F.

Chop the vegetables and combine the oil, pepper, salt, oregano, and pepper flakes if desired. Arrange on a baking tin and toast for approximately 30 to 45 minutes or until they are done the way you like them.

Toast the buns and spread the hummus on them, add the veggies, and a bit of pesto sauce. Sprinkle with the vegan cheese and enjoy.

Vegetarian Chili

Serves: 8

Time: 15 minutes

Ingredients

1 can (15 ounces) each:

Dark red kidney beans

Pinto beans

Light red kidney beans

Black beans

2 cans (28 ounces) crushed tomatoes

1 can (28 ounces) diced tomatoes

3 cups celery

1 small diced each of bell peppers:

Yellow

Red

1 medium red onion

4 tablespoons chili powder

3 tablespoons garlic powder

2 tablespoons ground cumin

Directions

Drain and rinse all of the beans. Dice the veggies.

Lightly spray a large pan on the stovetop using medium heat and cook the veggies about six to seven minutes or until they are softened.

Combine the spices, beans, and tomatoes in a slow cooker or a Dutch oven.

Chapter 5: Fruit Salads

California Roll in a Bowl

Serves: 4

Time: 15 minutes

Ingredients

1 head chopped lettuce

1 cup cooked brown rice

1 English cucumber – seedless – thinly sliced

1 (8 ounces) package cooked shrimp/crabmeat – chopped

1 grated carrot

1 ripe diced avocado

3 tablespoons pickled ginger

Ingredients for the Dressing

1 tablespoon light soy sauce

½ teaspoon wasabi powder – to taste

3 tablespoons rice wine vinegar

Garnishes:

1 large sheet seaweed/nori (toasted and in small bits)

1 tablespoon sesame seeds

Directions

Combine each of the fixings for the dressing in a mixing dish and whisk well.

Divide it into four sections and enjoy.

Note: You can locate the ginger in the Asian section of the supermarket.

Israeli Salad

Serves: 8

Time: 5 minutes

Ingredients

1 medium peeled cucumber

3 medium tomatoes

1 yellow/green bell pepper

2 tbsp. lemon juice

3 tbsp. extra-virgin olive oil

1 tsp. of salt and fresh ground pepper

Directions

Chop all of the veggies into small bits.

Combine the rest of the ingredients and enjoy.

Grape Salad

Serves: 16

Time: 65 minutes

Ingredients

2-4 pounds of grapes (green, red, or both)

1 package of fat-free– 8 ounces each:

Sour cream

Softened cream cheese

½ cup each:

Splenda/your choice

Walnuts/Pecans

¼ cup brown sugar

4 tablespoons vanilla extract

Directions

Wash and drain the grapes.

Combine the sour cream, cream cheese, vanilla, and sugar — blending well for about three to four minutes on high with a mixer.

Toss in the grapes and toss until covered.

Pour into a 9x13 cake pan. Sprinkle lightly with the brown sugar. Add the nuts.

Chill about one hour before serving.

Caramel Apple Salad

Serves: 16

Time: 30 minutes

Ingredients

1 tub (8 ounces) Cool Whip Free

1 box Instant Butter Scotch Pudding mix (sugar-free)

1 can (14 ounces) pineapple tidbits with the juice

4 large each:

Fuji apples/Red Delicious

Granny Smith apples

Directions

Mix the pineapple with its juice and the pudding mix in a large mixing container.

Dice the apples into small portions and fold in the Cool Whip.

Mix well, and chill in the refrigerator until ready to eat.

Caprese Salad

Serves: 2

Time: 10 minutes

Ingredients

6 ounces strawberries

1 ripe avocado

1 (7 ounces) sliced mozzarella ball

Small handful salad leaves

2-3 tablespoons balsamic dressing – your choice

Pepper and salt

Directions

Toss in the salad leaves, avocado, strawberries, and cheese into a serving dish.

Add the tasty dressing and sprinkle with the pepper and salt. Gently toss and enjoy.

Sunshine Fruit Salad

Serves: 10

Time: 65 minutes

Ingredients

2 cans (15 ounces each) mandarin oranges in light syrup

3 cans (20 ounces each) pineapple chunks in 100% juice

2 large bananas

3 medium kiwi fruits – bite-sized

Directions

Drain the oranges and pineapple. Reserve the pineapple juice.

Combine all of the fruit (omit the bananas).

Submerge the fruit with the juice and chill for a minimum of one hour.

Slice and stir in the bananas before serving.

Chapter 6: Snacks and Desserts

Mini Cheesecakes

Serves: 20

Time: 2 hours 15 minutes

Ingredients

3 ounces cream cheese

12 ounces fat-free cream cheese

12 low-fat vanilla wafers

½ teaspoon vanilla

½ cup sugar

2 eggs

Cherry pie filling

Directions

Set the oven temperature to 350°F.

Let the cream cheese sit out at room temperature.

Line 12 muffin tins with foil cake liners and add a wafer to each one.

Combine the regular and fat-free cheese until smooth. Blend in the sugar, vanilla, and eggs – beating until smooth.

Pour the batter into the tins and bake for 20 minutes.

Refrigerate for a minimum of two hours – preferably overnight.

Add the cherry filling to each one and serve.

Black Bean Brownies

Serves: 16

Time: 40 minutes

Ingredients

4 large eggs

1 can (15 ounces) black beans

3 tablespoons cocoa powder

½ cup granulated Splenda

1 tablespoon instant coffee*

2 tablespoons olive/canola oil

1 teaspoon each:

Baking powder

Vanilla

Directions

Set the oven temperature to 350°F. Spray an 8x8 pan with some non-stick cooking spray.

*Dissolve the coffee in one tablespoon of hot water and mix with the rest of the ingredients. Drain and rinse the black beans, adding them last.

Bake 30 minutes, and perform the toothpick test for doneness.

Let cool before slicing into 2x2-inch brownies.

Coconut Meringue Cookies

Serves: 20

Time: 30 minutes

Ingredients

2 egg whites

Dash of salt

1 ½ cups coconut sweetened shredded

2/3 cup granulated sugar

¼ teaspoon vanilla extract

Directions

Whip the eggs with a dash of salt to form stiff peaks. Stir in the sugar and fold in the coconut.

Bake 18 to20 minutes at 325ºF.

Healthy Breakfast Cookie

Serves: 30

Time: 20 minutes

Ingredients

2 large eggs

¼ cup butter

½ cup each:

Honey

Chopped - dried apricots

Raisins

1 cup each:

Grated carrots

Chopped walnuts

All-purpose flour

Rolled oats

1 ½ cups Cheerios

1 teaspoon each:

Cinnamon

Nutmeg

Directions

Mix the butter, honey, and egg in a mixing bowl. Combine the mixture with the apricots, walnuts, and raisins.

In a separate container, mix the cinnamon, nutmeg, flour, and oats.

Combine all components and mix well. Fold in the Cheerios.

Drop the dough onto a baking sheet about one inch apart.

Bake 15 minutes or until the cookie is firm.

Blueberry Muffin

Serves: 12

Time: 35 minutes

Ingredients

1 cup of each:

Flour

Old-fashioned oats

1 tsp. each:

Cinnamon

Baking soda

½ tsp. of salt

½ cup each:

Unsweetened applesauce

Water

Sugar

2 egg whites

1 cup frozen blueberries

Directions

Prepare 12 muffin tins and program the oven to 350°F.

Combine the salt, soda, cinnamon, oats, and flour.

Add the egg whites, sugar, water, and applesauce.

Blend in the blueberries

Bake 20 to 25 minutes until lightly browned.

Pumpkin Muffins

Serves: 18

Time: 40 minutes

Ingredients

1 can/1 pound pumpkin

½ cup flaxseed meal

1 box spice cake mix

Directions

Program the oven to 350°F.

Line a muffin tin with paper liners or cooking spray.

Combine all of the ingredients and bake 25 minutes.

Check for doneness with a toothpick in the center. If it comes out clean – it's done.

Enjoy when you just don't have time for the 'from scratch' recipe.

Conclusion

All bariatric surgeries can have some potential risks and side effects, and as we have already briefly discussed, gastric sleeve surgery is no exception. However, in comparison to other forms of bariatric surgery, gastric sleeve is by far more safe. It's one of the reasons why it's rapidly becoming one of the more popular weight loss surgeries.

In order to give you the most well rounded view of gastric sleeve surgery possible, we'll discuss the possible risks and side effects here.

Moderate Side Effects

-       Moderate side effects can be expected to happen in the days immediately following surgery, but these also go away very quickly and are not dangerous at all. Examples of moderate side effects include pain, bleeding, and swelling.

Severe Side Effects

-       Severe side effects are far less common for gastric sleeve surgery. Some potential complications include stomach acid leaking, inflammation in the stomach, or even bloating in the abdomen. Longer term severe side effects would include infections and pneumonia.

-       While it is a severe side effects, blood clots are extremely rare in patients who undergo gastric sleeve surgery. In fact, less than one percent of all gastric sleeve patients will ever develop blood clots.

-       Remember to take these potential side effects into consideration when you consider any type of bariatric surgery. Also remember that no two patients will ever experience the same combination or same level of risks at the same time. Next, we'll discuss some long term risks of the aftermath of gastric sleeve surgery that can possibly happen overtime.

Risks

-       The first risk that you can take with gastric sleeve surgery is possibly having an allergic reaction to the anesthesia or other medication.

-       Most of the other risks of gastric sleeve surgery would happen in the aftermath, mainly during the two week long recovery period. Examples can include developing infections in the incision area or in the bladder and kidneys, suffer from blood loss, damage to the intestines or organs in the stomach area, sutures becoming rejected, or the intestines becoming blocked.

One thing you have to be aware with gastric sleeve surgery risks is that the risks can develop over the course of several months following the surgery. The good news is that most of these risks can be prevented by simply following your surgeon's Directions, following your dieting regimen, and getting the necessary exercise.

The greatest possible risk of gastric sleeve surgery would be the stomach expanding. If you eat too much food, it can cause your stomach to expand and increase capacity. Remember that your stomach has been reduced by as much as eighty percent, so expanding your stomach beyond the twenty percent it would be after surgery can lead to some potential complications, such as developing malnutrition, lower vitamin levels, kidney stones, or gastritis.

All in all though, don't let these potential risks and side effects dishearten you from undergoing gastric sleeve surgery at all. The chance of you developing any of these risks during or following surgery are very minimal if you follow your doctor's Directions, and gastric sleeve surgery is regarded overall as being one of the safest weight loss surgeries available.

Last but not least, we'll discuss the new diet you'll have to embark on before and after surgery.

Dieting Before Surgery

-       Your stomach and liver are located very closely to one another. When the surgeon will get to your stomach to perform the surgery, they will need to retract your liver with a device to move it out of the way. The overwhelming majority of individuals who are obese will also have fatty liver disease, which is where fat cells will gather around the liver cells, and causes it to function improperly…not to mention increasing the size of it.

-       When the liver expands, it makes it much more difficult for the surgeon to get out of the way, which in turn makes it significantly more difficult for the actual operation and can lead to complications. Therefore, the goal of your diet before gastric sleeve surgery should be to lower the size of the liver via your diet as much as possible.

-       As a large liver will only increase your surgical risk, embarking on a healthy diet before surgery is very important to ensure that the operation proceeds as smoothly as it should. You'd be surprised to know that your liver will decrease in size very quickly if you can adhere to a strict diet in just two weeks before the date of the surgery.

-       Your doctor may recommend a different two week diet than the one we're going to discuss here, but this diet should serve as a golden rule (if you will call it that) for all pre-weight loss surgery diets. Begin by increasing your protein consumption by eating more lean meats, and lower your carbohydrate consumption. This means avoiding bread, pasta and rice. Finally, you'll need to eliminate all sugary foods completely. Candy, juice, soda, cake, you name it.

-       For breakfast, try consuming more protein shakes such as from a supplement store. The only thing to watch out for in these shakes is to make sure that there are no sugars in them. For lunch and dinner alike, focus on eating more vegetables and lean meats.

-       You can eat snacks throughout the day, but only ones that are healthy and low in carbs. Examples of this clued veggies, berries, nuts, and salads. It's also important that you stay hydrated throughout the days, so drinking plenty of water is critically important. An added benefit of water is that it will control the hunger you feel. Plus, it's common knowledge that water is good for you.

- In the three days before surgery, you will have to adhere to a strict liquid diet and stop drinking all beverages that are carbonated and/or have caffeine in them.Clear liquids that you can drink include protein shakes (though less shakes than you were consuming before), water, popsicles (provided they are sugar free), Jell-O, and broth.

- All in all, if you can adhere to this kind of strict surgery, the size of your liver should drastically decrease in the weeks before your surgery and the risk of developing any potential complications during surgery will dramatically decrease.

Dieting After Surgery

- At this point, you have completed the surgery and you may already be home following your stay in the hospital. However, now is no time to return to your previous eating habits. Whereas the previous diet you embarked on was designed to prevent complications from happening during your surgery by reducing the size of your liver, the new diet that you will embark on is focused on preventing the risk of complications after the surgery.

At times, this new diet may seem far more extreme than the previous diet, and even if you find yourself second guessing your decision to have gastric sleeve surgery, just know that this diet is essential to bringing your weight down and preventing the onset of risks. We'll go over what specific foods you can and cannot have for the weeks following your surgery and then beyond that.

- For the first week, you'll have to adhere to clear liquids only. Whereas before you spent two to three days with only clear liquids, you're now going to have to add seven days to that. Fortunately, the ghrelin hormone will be nearly eliminated at this point, so your desire to eat high amounts of 'normal foods' will be nearly eliminated as well. Foods you can eat during this time, provided they are all sugar free, include water, un-carbonated drinks, broth, decaf tea and coffee, jell-o, and popsicles. Specific foods that you should avoid include carbonated drinks, sweet drinks, non-decaf caffeine, and sugar.

- For the second week after surgery, you'll still have to adhere a liquid diet, but with less limitations than the clear liquid diet. For this week, you'll want to add more proteins to the mix. Examples of foods that you can eat during this time include protein powders mixed with liquid, sugar free ice cream, oatmeal, sugarless juices, creamy soups, non fat yogurts, soupy noodles, and sugar free pudding. While this diet definitely has less limitations than before, you can't get too overconfident at this point and eat foods you shouldn't be eating.

- Good news! For the third week after surgery, you'll be able to add some real foods to your diet instead of strictly liquids. However, you should still keep your intake of fats and sugars down if not avoiding them completely. For this week, focus on taking smaller bites and eating the individual bites more slowly, only trying one new food per meal (meaning you should not have two or more kinds of foods at the same meal), and continue to get plenty of protein. This is because you must give your body the time it needs to react to these 'new' foods; remember that's gone well over a month by now without the foods it is used to in taking and digesting. It will need more time to adjust fully.

- There are specific new foods that you can now add to your diet, as well as a few others that you should continue to avoid. New foods that you can add are protein shakes mixed with yogurt and non-fat milk, hummus, low fat cheese, mashed fruit, canned tuna or salmon, mayonnaise, steamed fish (as long as you chew well), scrambled eggs, soup, grounded beef, grounded chicken, soft cereals (tip: allow your cereal to sit in the milk to become soft), soft vegetables, soft cheese, almond milk, and coconut milk. None of these foods should be crunchy and you should remember to chew slowly with all of them.

Foods that you should continue to avoid in the third week are sugars, pasta, rice, bread, fibrous vegetables, and smoothies with high sugar levels.

- For the fourth week, you can continue to introduce more real foods that you're accustomed to. Remember though, your stomach is still very sensitive, and you aren't yet at the point where you can eat anything you want however you want. You still have to eat slowly, eat soft foods whenever possible, and only introduce one new food per meal.

During this time, you should continue consuming protein shakes, as they are one of your best sources of protein throughout this dieting process. You can introduce more fish, fruits, softened vegetables, chicken and beef. All of these foods should be as softened as much as possible and chewed thoroughly. You can also re-introduce potatoes to your diet (mashed, baked and sweetened alike) and cereal. You can also re-introduced caffeine products to your diet, but not to the point that it becomes a regular part of your diet. Be very discretionary as you add caffeine to your diet.

For the fourth week, you should focus primarily on eating three small meals throughout the day and getting plenty of water. But as long as your surgeon approves it, you should also be able to add snacks to your diet at this point. Examples of snacks that you can add include fresh fruit, small portions of baked or sweetened potatoes, small portions of oatmeal, one egg, a small portion of baby carrots, or a small portion of crackers.

Some foods you will have to continue to avoid. Most sodas, fried food, fibrous vegetables, candy and sugar, desserts, pasta, pizzas, whole milk, dairy in general, and nuts will all have to continue to be avoided in the fourth week of your diet.

- For the fifth week, your body will be able to tolerate more foods, but you could still feel an upset stomach at times. Continue to eat three small meals and remain fully hydrated throughout the day. Continue to take your prescribed medication and vitamins, and focus mainly on getting enough protein into your system (sixty grams at the least). Again, protein shakes are an excellent way to get plenty of protein in your system. You should also try to exercise more now, and your body should start to lose weight at a faster rate. Continue to adhere to a strict dieting plan, and when you do eat snacks, only eat from small portions.

Vegan Air Fryer Cookbook

Cook and Taste 50+ High-Protein Recipes. Kickstart Muscles and Body Transformation, Kill Hunger and Feel More Energetic

By

Sean Foster

Table of Contents

Introduction

To have a good, satisfying life, a balanced diet is important. Tiredness and susceptibility to illnesses, many severe, arise from a lifestyle so full of junk food. Our community, sadly, does not neglect unsafe choices. People turn to immoral practices in order to satisfy desire, leading to animal torture. Two of the key explanations that people adhere to vegetarianism, a vegan-based diet that often excludes animal foods such as cheese, beef, jelly, and honey, are fitness and animal welfare.

It's essential for vegetarians to get the most nutrients out of any food, and that's where frying using an air fryer shines. The air fryer cooking will maintain as many nutrients as possible from beans and veggies, and the gadget makes it incredibly simple to cook nutritious food.

Although there are prepared vegan alternatives, the healthier choice, and far less pricey, is still to prepare your own recipes. This book provides the very first moves to being a vegan and offers 50 quick breakfast recipes, sides, snacks, and much more, so you have a solid base on which to develop.

This book will teach you all you need to thrive, whether you are either a vegan and only need more meal choices or have just begun contemplating transforming your diet.

What is Cooking Vegan?

In recent decades, vegetarianism has become quite common, as individuals understand just how toxic the eating patterns of civilization have become. We are a society that enjoys meat, and, unfortunately, we go to dishonest measures to get the food we like. More citizens are choosing to give up beef and, unlike vegans, other livestock items due to various health issues, ethical issues, or both. Their diet moves to one focused on plants, whole grains, beans, fruit, seeds, nuts, and vegan varieties of the common dish.

What advantages would veganism have?

There are a lot of advantages to a diet away from all animal items. Only a few includes:

- Healthier hair, skin, and nails

- High energy

- Fewer chances of flu and cold

- Fewer migraines

- Increased tolerance to cancer

- Strengthened fitness of the heart

Although research has proven that veganism will contribute to reducing BMI, it must not be followed for the mere sake of weight reduction. "Vegan" does not indicate "lower-calorie," and if you wish to reduce weight, other healthier activities, including exercising and consuming water, can complement the diet.

Air Fryer

A common kitchen gadget used to create fried foods such as beef, baked goods and potato chips is an air fryer. It provides a crunchy, crisp coating by blowing hot air across the food. This also leads to a chemical reaction commonly known as the Maillard effect, which happens in the presence of heat in between reducing sugar and amino acid. This adds to shifts in food color and taste. Due to the reduced amount of calories and fat, air-fried items are marketed as a healthier substitute to deep-fried foods.

Rather than fully soaking the food in fat, air-frying utilizes just a teaspoon to create a flavor and feel equivalent to deep-fried foods.

The flavor and appearance of the fried food in the air are similar to the deep fryer outcomes: On the surface, crispy; from the inside, soft. You do need to use a limited amount of oil, though, or any at all (based on what you're baking). But indeed, contrary to deep frying, if you agree to use only 1-2 teaspoons of plant-based oil with spices and you stuck to air-frying vegetables rather than anything else, air frying is certainly a better option.

The secret to weight loss, decreased likelihood of cardiovascular illness and better long-term wellbeing as we mature is any gadget that assists you and your friends in your vegetarian game.

Air fryer's Working Process:

The air fryer is a worktop kitchen gadget that operates in the same manner as a traditional oven. To become acquainted with the operating theory of the traditional oven, you will need a little study. The air fryer uses rotating hot air to fry and crisp your meal, close to the convection oven. In a traditional convection oven, the airflow relies on revolving fans, which blast hot air around to produce an even or equalized temperature dispersal throughout the oven.

This is compared to the upward airflow of standard ovens, where the warm place is typically the oven's tip. And although the air fryer is not quite like the convection oven, it is a great approximation of it in the field of airflow for most components. The gadget has an air inlet at the top that lets air in and a hot air outlet at the side. All of these features are used to monitor the temperature within the air fryer. Temperatures will rise to 230 ° C, based on the sort of air fryer you're buying.

In conjunction with any grease, this hot air is used for cooking the food in the bowl within the device, if you like. Yes, if you want a taste of the oil, you should apply more oil. To jazz up the taste of the meal, simply add a little more to the blend. But the key concept behind the air fryer is to reduce the consumption of calories and fat without reducing the amount of taste.

Using air frying rather than deep frying saves between 70-80 calories, according to researchers. The growing success of recipes for air fryers is simply attributed to its impressive performance. It is simple to use and less time-consuming than conventional ovens.

This is more or less a lottery win for people searching for healthy alternative to deep-frying, as demonstrated by its widespread popularity in many homes today. In contrast to conventional ovens or deep frying, the air fryer creates crispy, crunchy, wonderful, and far fewer fatty foods in less duration. For certain individuals like us; this is what distinguishes air fryer recipes.

Tips for using an Air Fryer

1. The food is cooked easily. Air fried, unlike conventional cooking techniques, cut the cooking time a great deal. Therefore, to stop burning the food or getting a not-so-great flavor, it is best to hold a close eye on the gadget. Notice, remember that the smaller the food on the basket, the shorter the cooking period, which implies that the food cooks quicker.

2. You may need to reduce the temperature at first. Bear in mind that air fryers depend on the flow of hot air, which heats up rapidly. This ensures that it's better, to begin with, a low temperature so that the food cooks equally. It is likely that when the inside is already cooking, the exterior of the food is all cooked and begins to become dark or too dry.

3. When air fryers are in operation, they create some noise. If you are new to recipes for air fryers, you may have to realize that air fryers create noise while working. When it's in service, a whirring tone emanates from the device. However, the slight annoyance pales in contrast to the various advantages of having an air fryer.

4. Hold the grate within the container at all hours. As previously mentioned, the air fryer has a container inside it, where the food is put and permitted to cook. This helps hot air to flow freely around the food, allowing for even cooking.

5. Don't stuff the air fryer with so much food at once. If you plan to make a meal for one guy, with only one batch, you would most definitely be able to get your cooking right. If you're cooking for two or more individuals, you can need to plan the food in groups. With a 4 - 5 quart air fryer, you can always need to cook in groups, depending on the size and sort of air fryer you have. This not only means that your device works longer but also keeps

your food from cooking unevenly. You shouldn't have to turn the air fryer off as you pull out the basket since it simply turns off on its own until the basket is out. Often, make sure the drawer is completely retracted; otherwise, the fryer would not turn back on.

6. Take the basket out of the mix and mix the ingredients. You might need to move the food around or switch it over once every few minutes, based on the dish you're preparing and the time it takes to prepare your dinner.

The explanation for this is that even cooking can be done. Certain recipes involve the foods in the basket to shake and shuffle throughout the cooking phase. And an easy-to-understand checklist is given for each recipe to direct you thru the cycle.

7. The air fryer does not need cooking mist. It isn't needed. In order to prevent the urge to use non-stick frying spray in the container, you must deliberately take care of this. The basket is now coated with a non-stick covering, so what you need to do is fill your meal inside the container and push it back in.

Outcome

You can create nutritious meals very simply and fast, right in the comfort of your house. There are many excellent recipes for producing healthier meals and nutritious foods, which you can notice in the air fryer recipes illustrated in this book. However, you'll need to pay careful attention to the ingredients and know-how to easily use the air fryer to do this. To get straightforward guidance on installation and usage, you can need to refer to the company's manual.

CHAPTER 1: Breakfast Recipes

1. Toasted French toast

Preparation time: 2 minutes

Cooking time: 5 minutes

Servings: 1 people

Ingredients:

- ½ Cup of Unsweetened Shredded Coconut

- 1 Tsp. Baking Powder

- ½ Cup Lite Culinary Coconut Milk

- 2 Slices of Gluten-Free Bread (use your favorite)

Directions:

1. Stir together the baking powder and coconut milk in a large rimmed pot.

2. On a tray, layout your ground coconut.

3. Pick each loaf of your bread and dip it in your coconut milk for the very first time, and then pass it to the ground coconut, let it sit for a few minutes, then cover the slice entirely with the coconut.

4. Place the covered bread loaves in your air fryer, cover it, adjust the temperature to about 350 ° F and set the clock for around 4 minutes.

5. Take out from your air fryer until done, and finish with some maple syrup of your choice. French toast is done. Enjoy!

2. Vegan Casserole

Preparation time: 10-12 minutes

Cooking time: 15-20 minutes

Servings: 2-3 people

Ingredients:

- 1/2 cup of cooked quinoa

- 1 tbsp. of lemon juice

- 2 tbsp. of water

- 2 tbsp. of plain soy yogurt

- 2 tbsp. of nutritional yeast

- 7 ounces of extra-firm tofu about half a block, drained but not pressed

- 1/2 tsp. of ground cumin

- 1/2 tsp. of red pepper flakes

- 1/2 tsp. of freeze-dried dill

- 1/2 tsp. of black pepper

- 1/2 tsp. of salt

- 1 tsp. of dried oregano

- 1/2 cup of diced shiitake mushrooms

- 1/2 cup of diced bell pepper I used a combination of red and green

- 2 small celery stalks chopped

- 1 large carrot chopped

- 1 tsp. of minced garlic

- 1 small onion diced

- 1 tsp. of olive oil

Directions:

1. Warm the olive oil over medium-low heat in a big skillet. Add your onion and garlic and simmer till the onion is transparent (for about 3 to 6 minutes). Add your bell

pepper, carrot, and celery and simmer for another 3 minutes. Mix the oregano, mushrooms, pepper, salt, cumin, dill, and red pepper powder. Mix completely and lower the heat to low. If the vegetables tend to cling, stir regularly and add in about a teaspoon of water.

2. Pulse the nutritional yeast, tofu, water, yogurt, and some lemon juice in a food mixer until fluffy. To your skillet, add your tofu mixture. Add in half a cup of cooked quinoa. Mix thoroughly.

3. Move to a microwave-proof plate or tray that works for your air fryer basket.

4. Cook for around 15 minutes at about 350°F (or 18 to 20 minutes at about 330°F, till it turns golden brown).

5. Please take out your plate or tray from your air fryer and let it rest for at least five minutes before eating.

3. Vegan Omelet

Preparation time: 15 minutes

Cooking time: 16 minutes

Servings: 3 people

Ingredients:

- ½ cup of grated vegan cheese

- 1 tbsp. of water

- 1 tbsp. of brags

- 3 tbsp. of nutritional yeast

- ¼ tsp. of basil

- ¼ tsp. of garlic powder

- ¼ tsp. of onion powder

- ¼ tsp. of pepper

- ½ tsp. of cumin

- ½ tsp. of turmeric

- ¼ tsp. of salt

- ¼ cup of chickpea flour (or you may use any bean flour)

- ½ cup of finely diced veggies (like chard, kale, dried mushrooms, spinach, watermelon radish etc.)

- half a piece of tofu (organic high in protein kind)

Directions:

4. Blend all your ingredients in a food blender or mixer, excluding the vegetables and cheese.

5. Move the batter from the blender to a container and combine the vegetables and cheese in it. Since it's faster, you could use both hands to combine it.

6. Brush the base of your air fryer bucket with some oil.

7. Put a couple of parchment papers on your counter. On the top of your parchment paper, place a cookie cutter of your desire.

8. In your cookie cutter, push 1/6 of the paste. Then raise and put the cookie cutter on a different section of your parchment paper.

9. Redo the process till you have about 6 pieces using the remainder of the paste.

10. Put 2 or 3 of your omelets at the base of your air fryer container. Using some oil, brush the topsides of the omelets.

11. Cook for around 5 minutes at about 370 °, turn and bake for another 4 minutes or more if needed. And redo with the omelets that remain.

12. Offer with sriracha mayo or whatever kind of dipping sauce you prefer. Or use them for a sandwich at breakfast.

4. Waffles with Vegan chicken

Preparation time: 10 minutes

Cooking time: 15 minutes

Servings: 2 people

Ingredients:

Fried Vegan Chicken:

- ¼ to ½ teaspoon of Black Pepper

- ½ teaspoon of Paprika

- ½ teaspoon of Onion Powder

- ½ teaspoon of Garlic Powder

- 2 teaspoon of Dried Parsley

- 2 Cups of Gluten-Free Panko

- ¼ Cup of Cornstarch

- 1 Cup of Unsweetened Non-Dairy Milk

- 1 Small Head of Cauliflower

Yummy Cornmeal Waffles:

- ½ teaspoon of Pure Vanilla Extract

- ¼ Cup of Unsweetened Applesauce

- ½ Cup of Unsweetened Non-Dairy Milk

- 1 to 2 TB Erythritol (or preferred sweetener)

- 1 teaspoon Baking Powder

- ¼ Cup of Stoneground Cornmeal

- ⅔ Cup of Gluten-Free All-Purpose Flour

Toppings:

- Vegan Butter

- Hot Sauce

- Pure Maple Syrup

Directions:

For making your Vegan Fried Chicken:

1. Dice the cauliflower (you wouldn't have to be careful in this) into big florets and put it aside.

2. Mix the cornstarch and milk in a tiny pot.

3. Throw the herbs, panko, and spices together in a big bowl or dish.

4. In the thick milk mixture, soak your cauliflower florets, then cover the soaked bits in the prepared panko mix before putting the wrapped floret into your air fryer bucket.

5. For the remaining of your cauliflower, redo the same process.

6. Set your air fryer clock for around 15 minutes to about 400 ° F and let the cauliflower air fry.

For making you're Waffles:

1. Oil a regular waffle iron and warm it up.

2. Mix all your dry ingredients in a pot, and then blend in your wet ingredients until you have a thick mixture.

3. To create a big waffle, utilize ½ of the mixture and redo the process to create another waffle for a maximum of two persons.

To Organize:

1. Put on dishes your waffles, place each with ½ of the cooked cauliflower, now drizzle with the hot sauce, syrup, and any extra toppings that you want. Serve warm!

5. Tempeh Bacon

Preparation time: 15 minutes plus 2 hour marinating time

Cooking time: 10 minutes

Servings: 4 people

Ingredients:

- ½ teaspoon of freshly grated black pepper

- ½ teaspoon of onion powder

- ½ teaspoon of garlic powder

- 1 ½ teaspoon of smoked paprika

- 1 teaspoon of apple cider vinegar

- 1 tablespoon of olive oil (plus some more for oiling your air fryer)

- 3 tablespoon of pure maple syrup

- ¼ cup of gluten-free, reduced-sodium tamari

- 8 oz. of gluten-free tempeh

Directions:

1. Break your Tempeh cube into two parts and boil for about 10 minutes, some more if required. To the rice cooker bowl, add a cup of warm water. Then, put the pieces of tempeh into the steamer basket of the unit. Close the cover, push the button for heat or steam cooking (based on your rice cooker's type or brand), and adjust the steaming timer for around 10 minutes.

2. Let the tempeh cool completely before taking it out of the rice cooker or your steamer basket for around 5 minutes.

3. Now make the sauce while cooking the tempeh. In a 9" x 13" baking tray, incorporate all the rest of your ingredients and mix them using a fork. Then set it aside and ready the tempeh.

4. Put the tempeh steamed before and cooled on a chopping board, and slice into strips around 1/4' wide. Put each slice gently in the sauce. Then roll over each slice gently. Seal and put in the fridge for two to three hours or even overnight, rotating once or twice during the time.

5. Turn the bits gently one more time until you are about to create the tempeh bacon. And if you would like, you may spoon over any leftover sauce.

6. Put your crisper plate/tray into the air fryer if yours came with one instead of a built-in one. Oil the base of your crisper tray or your air fryer basket slightly with some olive oil or using an olive oil spray that is anti-aerosol.

7. Put the tempeh slices in a thin layer gently in your air fryer bucket. If you have a tiny air fryer, you will have to air fry it in two or multiple rounds. Air fry for around 10-15 minutes at about 325 ° F before the slices are lightly golden but not burnt. You

may detach your air fryer container to inspect it and make sure it's not burnt. It normally takes about 10 minutes.

6. Delicious Potato Pancakes

Preparation time: 5 minutes

Cooking time: 15 minutes

Servings: 4 people

Ingredients:

- black pepper according to taste

- 3 tablespoon of flour

- ¼ teaspoon of pepper

- ¼ teaspoon of salt

- ½ teaspoon of garlic powder

- 2 tablespoon of unsalted butter

- ¼ cup of milk

- 1 beaten egg

- 1 medium onion, chopped

Directions:

1. Preheat the fryer to about 390° F and combine the potatoes, garlic powder, eggs, milk, onion, pepper, butter, and salt in a small bowl; add in the flour and make a batter.

2. Shape around 1/4 cup of your batter into a cake.

3. In the fryer's cooking basket, put the cakes and cook for a couple of minutes.

4. Serve and enjoy your treat!

CHAPTER 2: Air Fryer Main Dishes

1. Mushroom 'n Bell Pepper Pizza

Preparation time: 5 minutes

Cooking time: 10 minutes

Servings: 10 people

Ingredients:

- salt and pepper according to taste

- 2 tbsp. of parsley

- 1 vegan pizza dough

- 1 shallot, chopped

- 1 cup of oyster mushrooms, chopped

- ¼ red bell pepper, chopped

Directions:

1. Preheat your air fryer to about 400°F.

2. Cut the pie dough into small squares. Just set them aside.

3. Put your bell pepper, shallot, oyster mushroom, and parsley all together into a mixing dish.

4. According to taste, sprinkle with some pepper and salt.

5. On top of your pizza cubes, put your topping.

6. Put your pizza cubes into your air fryer and cook for about 10 minutes.

2. Veggies Stuffed Eggplants

Preparation time: 5 minutes

Cooking time: 14 minutes

Servings: 5 people

Ingredients:

- 2 tbsp. of tomato paste

- Salt and ground black pepper, as required

- ½ tsp. of garlic, chopped

- 1 tbsp. of vegetable oil

- 1 tbsp. of fresh lime juice

- ½ green bell pepper, seeded and chopped

- ¼ cup of cottage cheese, chopped

- 1 tomato, chopped

- 1 onion, chopped

- 10 small eggplants, halved lengthwise

Directions:

1. Preheat your air fryer to about 320°F and oil the container of your air fryer.

2. Cut a strip longitudinally from all sides of your eggplant and scrape out the pulp in a medium-sized bowl.

3. Add lime juice on top of your eggplants and place them in the container of your Air Fryer.

4. Cook for around a couple of minutes and extract from your Air Fryer.

5. Heat the vegetable oil on medium-high heat in a pan and add the onion and garlic.

6. Sauté for around 2 minutes and mix in the tomato, salt, eggplant flesh, and black pepper.

7. Sauté and add bell pepper, tomato paste, cheese, and cilantro for roughly 3 minutes.

8. Cook for around a minute and put this paste into your eggplants.

9. Shut each eggplant with its lids and adjust the Air Fryer to 360°F.

10. Organize and bake for around 5 minutes in your Air Fryer Basket.

11. Dish out on a serving tray and eat hot.

3. Air-fried Falafel

Preparation time: 10 minutes

Cooking time: 25 minutes

Servings: 6 people

Ingredients:

- Salt and black pepper according to taste

- 1 teaspoon of chili powder

- 2 teaspoon of ground coriander

- 2 teaspoon of ground cumin

- 1 onion, chopped

- 4 garlic cloves, chopped

- Juice of 1 lemon

- 1 cup of fresh parsley, chopped

- ½ cup of chickpea flour

Directions:

1. Add flour, coriander, chickpeas, lemon juice, parsley, onion, garlic, chili, cumin, salt, turmeric, and pepper to a processor and mix until mixed, not too battery; several chunks should be present.

2. Morph the paste into spheres and hand-press them to ensure that they are still around.

3. Spray using some spray oil and place them in a paper-lined air fryer bucket; if necessary, perform in groups.

4. Cook for about 14 minutes at around 360°F, rotating once mid-way through the cooking process.

5. They must be light brown and crispy.

4. Almond Flour Battered Wings

Preparation time: 10 minutes

Cooking time: 25 minutes

Servings: 4 people

Ingredients:

- Salt and pepper according to taste

- 4 tbsp. of minced garlic

- 2 tbsp. of stevia powder

- 16 pieces of vegan chicken wings

- ¾ cup of almond flour

- ¼ cup of butter, melted

Directions:

1. Preheat your air fryer for about 5 minutes.

2. Mix the stevia powder, almond flour, vegan chicken wings, and garlic in a mixing dish. According to taste, sprinkle with some black pepper and salt.

3. Please put it in the bucket of your air fryer and cook at about 400°F for around 25 minutes.

4. Ensure you give your fryer container a shake midway through the cooking process.

5. Put in a serving dish after cooking and add some melted butter on top. Toss it to coat it completely.

5. Spicy Tofu

Preparation time: 5 minutes

Cooking time: 13 minutes

Servings: 3 people

Ingredients:

- Salt and black pepper, according to taste

- 1 tsp. of garlic powder

- 1 tsp. of onion powder

- 1½ tsp. of paprika

- 1½ tbsp. of avocado oil

- 3 tsp. of cornstarch

- 1 (14-ounces) block extra-firm tofu, pressed and cut into ¾-inch cubes

Directions:

1. Preheat your air fryer to about 390°F and oil the container of your air fryer with some spray oil.

2. In a medium-sized bowl, blend the cornstarch, oil, tofu, and spices and mix to cover properly.

3. In the Air Fryer basket, place the tofu bits and cook for around a minute, flipping twice between the cooking times.

4. On a serving dish, spread out the tofu and enjoy it warm.

6. Sautéed Bacon with Spinach

Preparation time: 5 minutes

Cooking time: 9 minutes

Servings: 2 people

Ingredients:

- 1 garlic clove, minced

- 2 tbsp. of olive oil

- 4-ounce of fresh spinach

- 1 onion, chopped

- 3 meatless bacon slices, chopped

Directions:

1. Preheat your air fryer at about 340° F and oil the air fryer's tray with some olive oil or cooking oil spray.

2. In the Air Fryer basket, put garlic and olive oil.

3. Cook and add in the onions and bacon for around 2 minutes.

4. Cook and mix in the spinach for approximately 3 minutes.

5. Cook for 4 more minutes and plate out in a bowl to eat.

7. Garden Fresh Veggie Medley

Preparation time: 5 minutes

Cooking time: 15 minutes

Servings: 4 people

Ingredients:

- 1 tbsp. of balsamic vinegar

- 1 tbsp. of olive oil

- 2 tbsp. of herbs de Provence

- 2 garlic cloves, minced

- 2 small onions, chopped

- 3 tomatoes, chopped

- 1 zucchini, chopped

- 1 eggplant, chopped

- 2 yellow bell peppers seeded and chopped

- Salt and black pepper, according to taste.

Directions:

1. Preheat your air fryer at about 355° F and oil up the air fryer basket.

2. In a medium-sized bowl, add all the ingredients and toss to cover completely.

3. Move to the basket of your Air Fryer and cook for around 15 minutes.

4. After completing the cooking time, let it sit in the air fryer for around 5 minutes and plate out to serve warm.

8. Colorful Vegetable Croquettes

Preparation time: 5 minutes

Cooking time: 10 minutes

Servings: 4 people

Ingredients:

- 1/2 cup of parmesan cheese, grated

- 2 eggs

- 1/4 cup of coconut flour

- 1/2 cup of almond flour

- 2 tbsp. of olive oil

- 3 tbsp. of scallions, minced

- 1 clove garlic, minced

- 1 bell pepper, chopped

- 1/2 cup of mushrooms, chopped

- 1/2 tsp. of cayenne pepper

- Salt and black pepper, according to taste.

- 2 tbsp. of butter

- 4 tbsp. of milk

- 1/2 pound of broccoli

Directions:

1. Boil your broccoli in a medium-sized saucepan for up to around 20 minutes. With butter, milk, black pepper, salt, and cayenne pepper, rinse the broccoli and mash it.

2. Add in the bell pepper, mushrooms, garlic, scallions, and olive oil and blend properly. Form into patties with the blend.

3. Put the flour in a deep bowl; beat your eggs in a second bowl; then put the parmesan cheese in another bowl.

4. Dip each patty into your flour, accompanied by the eggs and lastly the parmesan cheese, push to hold the shape.

5. Cook for around 16 minutes, turning midway through the cooking period, in the preheated Air Fryer at about 370° F. Bon appétit!

9. Cheesy Mushrooms

Preparation time: 3 minutes

Cooking time: 8 minutes

Servings: 4 people

Ingredients:

- 1 tsp. of dried dill
- 2 tbsp. of Italian dried mixed herbs
- 2 tbsp. of olive oil
- 2 tbsp. of cheddar cheese, grated
- 2 tbsp. of mozzarella cheese, grated
- Salt and freshly ground black pepper, according to taste
- 6-ounce of button mushrooms stemmed

Directions:

Preheat the air fryer at around 355° F and oil your air fryer basket.

In a mixing bowl, combine the Italian dried mixed herbs, mushrooms, salt, oil, and black pepper and mix well to cover.

In the Air Fryer bucket, place the mushrooms and cover them with some cheddar cheese and mozzarella cheese.

To eat, cook for around 8 minutes and scatter with dried dill.

10. Greek-style Roasted Vegetables

Preparation time: 10 minutes

Cooking time: 25 minutes

Servings: 3 people

Ingredients:

- 1/2 cup of Kalamata olives, pitted

- 1 (28-ounce) canned diced tomatoes with juice

- 1/2 tsp. of dried basil

- Sea salt and freshly cracked black pepper, according to taste

- 1 tsp. of dried rosemary

- 1 cup of dry white wine

- 2 tbsp. of extra-virgin olive oil

- 2 bell peppers, cut into 1-inch chunks

- 1 red onion, sliced

- 1/2 pound of zucchini, cut into 1-inch chunks

- 1/2 pound of cauliflower, cut into 1-inch florets

- 1/2 pound of butternut squash, peeled and cut into 1-inch chunks

Directions:

1. Add some rosemary, wine, olive oil, black pepper, salt, and basil along with your vegetables toss until well-seasoned.

2. Onto a lightly oiled baking dish, add 1/2 of the canned chopped tomatoes; scatter to fill the base of your baking dish.

3. Add in the vegetables and add the leftover chopped tomatoes to the top. On top of tomatoes, spread the Kalamata olives.

4. Bake for around 20 minutes at about 390° F in the preheated Air Fryer, turning the dish midway through your cooking cycle. Serve it hot and enjoy it!

11. Vegetable Kabobs with Simple Peanut Sauce

Preparation time: 10 minutes

Cooking time: 30 minutes

Servings: 4 people

Ingredients:

- 1/3 tsp. of granulated garlic

- 1 tsp. of dried rosemary, crushed

- 1 tsp. of red pepper flakes, crushed

- Sea salt and ground black pepper, according to your taste.

- 2 tbsp. of extra-virgin olive oil

- 8 small button mushrooms, cleaned

- 8 pearl onions, halved

- 2 bell peppers, diced into 1-inch pieces

- 8 whole baby potatoes, diced into 1-inch pieces

Peanut Sauce:

- 1/2 tsp. of garlic salt

- 1 tbsp. of soy sauce

- 1 tbsp. of balsamic vinegar

- 2 tbsp. of peanut butter

Directions:

1. For a few minutes, dunk the wooden chopsticks in water.

2. String the vegetables onto your chopsticks; drip some olive oil all over your chopsticks with the vegetables on it; dust with seasoning.

3. Cook for about 1 minute at 400°F in the preheated Air Fryer.

Peanut Sauce:

1. In the meantime, mix the balsamic vinegar with some peanut butter, garlic salt and some soy sauce in a tiny dish. Offer the kabobs with a side of peanut sauce. Eat warm!

12. Hungarian Mushroom Pilaf

Preparation time: 10 minutes

Cooking time: 50 minutes

Servings: 4 people

Ingredients:

- 1 tsp. of sweet Hungarian paprika

- 1/2 tsp. of dried tarragon

- 1 tsp. of dried thyme

- 1/4 cup of dry vermouth

- 1 onion, chopped

- 2 garlic cloves

- 2 tbsp. of olive oil

- 1 pound of fresh porcini mushrooms, sliced

- 2 tbsp. of olive oil

- 3 cups of vegetable broth

- 1 ½ cups of white rice

Directions:

1. In a wide saucepan, put the broth and rice, add some water, and bring it to a boil.

2. Cover with a lid and turn the flame down to a low temperature and proceed to cook for the next 18 minutes or so. After cooking, let it rest for 5 to 10 minutes, and then set aside.

3. Finally, in a lightly oiled baking dish, mix the heated, fully cooked rice with the rest of your ingredients.

4. Cook at about 200° degrees for around 20 minutes in the preheated Air Fryer, regularly monitoring to even cook.

5. In small bowls, serve. Bon appétit!

13. Chinese cabbage Bake

Preparation time: 15 minutes

Cooking time: 35 minutes

Servings: 4 people

Ingredients:

- 1 cup of Monterey Jack cheese, shredded

- 1/2 tsp. of cayenne pepper

- 1 cup of cream cheese

- 1/2 cup of milk

- 4 tbsp. of flaxseed meal

- 1/2 stick butter

- 2 garlic cloves, sliced

- 1 onion, thickly sliced

- 1 jalapeno pepper, seeded and sliced

- Sea salt and freshly ground black pepper, according to taste.

- 2 bell peppers, seeded and sliced

- 1/2 pound of Chinese cabbage, roughly chopped

Directions:

1. Heat the salted water in a pan and carry it to a boil. For around 2 to 3 minutes, steam the Chinese cabbage. To end the cooking process, switch the Chinese cabbage to cold water immediately.

2. Put your Chinese cabbage in a lightly oiled casserole dish. Add in the garlic, onion, and peppers.

3. Next, over low fire, melt some butter in a skillet. Add in your flaxseed meal steadily and cook for around 2 minutes to create a paste.

4. Add in the milk gently, constantly whisking until it creates a dense mixture. Add in your cream cheese. Sprinkle some cayenne pepper, salt, and black pepper. To the casserole tray, transfer your mixture.

5. Cover with some Monterey Jack cheese and cook for about 2 minutes at around 390° F in your preheated Air Fryer. Serve it warm.

14. Brussels sprouts With Balsamic Oil

Preparation time: 5 minutes

Cooking time: 15 minutes

Servings: 4 people

Ingredients:

- 2 tbsp. of olive oil

- 2 cups of Brussels sprouts, halved

- 1 tbsp. of balsamic vinegar

- ¼ tsp. of salt

Directions:

1. For 5 minutes, preheat your air fryer.

2. In a mixing bowl, blend all of your ingredients to ensure the zucchini fries are very well coated. Put the fries in the basket of an air fryer.

3. Close it and cook it at about 350°F for around 15 minutes.

15. Aromatic Baked Potatoes with Chives

Preparation time: 15 minutes

Cooking time: 45 minutes

Servings: 2 people

Ingredients:

- 2 tbsp. of chives, chopped

- 2 garlic cloves, minced

- 1 tbsp. of sea salt

- 1/4 tsp. of smoked paprika

- 1/4 tsp. of red pepper flakes

- 2 tbsp. of olive oil

- 4 medium baking potatoes, peeled

Directions:

1. Toss the potatoes with your seasoning, olive oil, and garlic.

2. Please put them in the basket of your Air Fryer. Cook at about 400° F for around 40 minutes just until the potatoes are fork soft in your preheated Air Fryer.

3. Add in some fresh minced chives to garnish. Bon appétit!

16. Easy Vegan "chicken"

Preparation time: 10 minutes

Cooking time: 20 minutes

Servings: 4 people

Ingredients:

- 1 tsp. of celery seeds

- 1/2 tsp. of mustard powder

- 1 tsp. of cayenne pepper

- 1/4 cup of all-purpose flour

- 1/2 cup of cornmeal

- 8 ounces of soy chunks

- Sea salt and ground black pepper, according to taste.

Directions:

1. In a skillet over medium-high flame, cook the soya chunks in plenty of water. Turn off the flame and allow soaking for several minutes. Drain the remaining water, wash, and strain it out.

2. In a mixing bowl, combine the rest of the components. Roll your soy chunks over the breading paste, pressing lightly to stick.

3. In the slightly oiled Air Fryer basket, place your soy chunks.

4. Cook at about 390° for around 10 minutes in your preheated Air Fryer, rotating them over midway through the cooking process; operate in batches if required. Bon appétit!

17.Paprika Vegetable Kebab's

Preparation time: 10 minutes

Cooking time: 20 minutes

Servings: 4 people

Ingredients:

- 1/2 tsp. of ground black pepper

- 1 tsp. of sea salt flakes

- 1 tsp. of smoked paprika

- 1/4 cup of sesame oil

- 2 tbsp. of dry white wine

- 1 red onion, cut into wedges

- 2 cloves garlic, pressed

- 1 tsp. of whole grain mustard

- 1 fennel bulb, diced

- 1 parsnip, cut into thick slices

- 1 celery, cut into thick slices

Directions:

1. Toss all of the above ingredients together in a mixing bowl to uniformly coat. Thread the vegetables alternately onto the wooden skewers.

2. Cook for around 15 minutes at about 380° F on your Air Fryer grill plate.

3. Turn them over midway during the cooking process.

4. Taste, change the seasonings if needed and serve steaming hot.

18. Spiced Soy Curls

Preparation time: 5 minutes

Cooking time: 10 minutes

Servings: 2 people

Ingredients:

- 1 tsp. of poultry seasoning

- 2 tsp. of Cajun seasoning

- ¼ cup of fine ground cornmeal

- ¼ cup of nutritional yeast

- 4 ounces of soy curls

- 3 cups of boiling water

- Salt and ground white pepper, as needed

Directions:

1. Dip the soy curls for around a minute or so in hot water in a heat-resistant tub.

2. Drain your soy coils using a strainer and force the excess moisture out using a broad spoon.

3. Mix the cornmeal, nutritional yeast, salt, seasonings, and white pepper well in a mixing bowl.

4. Transfer your soy curls to the bowl and coat well with the blend. Let the air-fryer temperature to about 380° F. Oil the basket of your air fryers.

5. Adjust soy curls in a uniform layer in the lined air fryer basket. Cook for about 10 minutes in the air fryer, turning midway through the cycle.

6. Take out the soy curls from your air fryer and put them on a serving dish. Serve it steaming hot.

19. Cauliflower & Egg Rice Casserole

Preparation time: 5 minutes

Cooking time: 15 minutes

Servings: 4 people

Ingredients:

- 2 eggs, beaten

- 1 tablespoon of soy sauce

- Salt and black pepper according to taste.

- ½ cup of chopped onion

- 1 cup of okra, chopped

- 1 yellow bell pepper, chopped

- 2 teaspoon of olive oil

Directions:

1. Preheat your air fryer to about 380° F. Oil a baking tray with spray oil. Pulse the cauliflower till it becomes like thin rice-like capsules in your food blender.

2. Now add your cauliflower rice to a baking tray mix in the okra, bell pepper, salt, soy sauce, onion, and pepper and combine well.

3. Drizzle a little olive oil on top along with the beaten eggs. Put the tray in your air fryer and cook for about a minute. Serve it hot.

20. Hollandaise Topped Grilled Asparagus

Preparation time: 2 minutes

Cooking time: 15 minutes

Servings: 6 people

Ingredients:

- A punch of ground white pepper
- A pinch of mustard powder
- 3 pounds of asparagus spears, trimmed
- 3 egg yolks
- 2 tbsp. of olive oil
- 1 tsp. of chopped tarragon leaves
- ½ tsp. of salt
- ½ lemon juice
- ½ cup of butter, melted
- ¼ tsp. of black pepper

Directions:

1. Preheat your air fryer to about 330° F. In your air fryer, put the grill pan attachment.

2. Mix the olive oil, salt, asparagus, and pepper into a Ziploc bag. To mix all, give everything a quick shake. Load onto the grill plate and cook for about 15 minutes.

3. In the meantime, beat the lemon juice, egg yolks, and salt in a double boiler over a moderate flame until velvety.

4. Add in the melted butter, mustard powder, and some white pepper. Continue whisking till the mixture is creamy and thick. Serve with tarragon leaves as a garnish.

5. Pour the sauce over the asparagus spears and toss to blend.

21. Crispy Asparagus Dipped In Paprika-garlic Spice

Preparation time: 2 minutes

Cooking time: 15 minutes

Servings: 5 people

Ingredients:

- ¼ cup of almond flour

- ½ tsp. of garlic powder

- ½ tsp. of smoked paprika

- 10 medium asparagus, trimmed

- 2 large eggs, beaten

- 2 tbsp. of parsley, chopped

- Salt and pepper according to your taste

Directions:

1. For about 5 minutes, preheat your air fryer.

2. Mix the almond flour, garlic powder, parsley, and smoked paprika in a mixing dish. To taste, season with some salt and black pepper.

3. Soak your asparagus in the beaten eggs, and then dredge it in a combination of almond flour.

4. Put in the bowl of your air fryer. Close the lid. At about 350°F, cook for around a minute.

22. Eggplant Gratin with Mozzarella Crust

Preparation time: 10 minutes

Cooking time: 30 minutes

Servings: 2 people

Ingredients:

- 1 tablespoon of breadcrumbs

- ¼ cup of grated mozzarella cheese

- Cooking spray

- Salt and pepper according to your taste

- ¼ teaspoon of dried marjoram

- ¼ teaspoon of dried basil

- 1 teaspoon of capers

- 1 tablespoon of sliced pimiento-stuffed olives

- 1 clove garlic, minced

- ⅓ cup of chopped tomatoes

- ¼ cup of chopped onion

- ¼ cup of chopped green pepper

- ¼ cup of chopped red pepper

Directions:

1. Put the green pepper, eggplant, onion, red pepper, olives, tomatoes, basil marjoram, garlic, salt, capers, and pepper in a container and preheat your air fryer to about 300° F.

2. Lightly oil a baking tray with a spray of cooking olive oil.

3. Fill your baking with the eggplant combination and line it with the vessel.

4. Place some mozzarella cheese on top of it and top with some breadcrumbs. Put the dish in the frying pan and cook for a few minutes.

23. Asian-style Cauliflower

Preparation time: 10 minutes

Cooking time: 25 minutes

Servings: 4 people

Ingredients:

- 2 tbsp. of sesame seeds

- 1/4 cup of lime juice

- 1 tbsp. of fresh parsley, finely chopped

- 1 tbsp. of ginger, freshly grated

- 2 cloves of garlic, peeled and pressed

- 1 tbsp. of sake

- 1 tbsp. of tamari sauce

- 1 tbsp. of sesame oil

- 1 onion, peeled and finely chopped

- 2 cups of cauliflower, grated

Directions:

1. In a mixing bowl, mix your onion, cauliflower, tamari sauce, sesame oil, garlic, sake, and ginger; whisk until all is well integrated.

2. Air-fry it for around a minute at about 400° F.

3. Pause your Air Fryer. Add in some parsley and lemon juice.

4. Cook for an extra 10 minutes at about 300° degrees F in the air fryer.

5. In the meantime, in a non-stick pan, toast your sesame seeds; swirl them continuously over medium-low heat. Serve hot on top of the cauliflower with a pinch of salt and pepper.

24. Two-cheese Vegetable Frittata

Preparation time: 15 minutes

Cooking time: 35 minutes

Servings: 2 people

Ingredients:

- ⅓ cup of crumbled Feta cheese

- ⅓ cup of grated Cheddar cheese

- Salt and pepper according to taste

- ⅓ cup of milk

- 4 eggs, cracked into a bowl

- 2 teaspoon of olive oil

- ¼ lb. of asparagus, trimmed and sliced thinly

- ¼ cup of chopped chives

- 1 small red onion, sliced

- 1 large zucchini, sliced with a 1-inch thickness

- ⅓ cup of sliced mushrooms

Directions:

1. Preheat your air fryer to about 380° F. Set aside your baking dish lined with some parchment paper. Put salt, milk, and pepper into the egg bowl; whisk evenly.

2. Put a skillet on the stovetop over a moderate flame, and heat your olive oil. Add in the zucchini, asparagus, baby spinach, onion, and mushrooms; stir-fry for around 5 minutes. Transfer the vegetables into your baking tray, and finish with the beaten egg.

3. Put the tray into your air fryer and finish with cheddar and feta cheese.

4. For about 15 minutes, cook. Take out your baking tray and add in some fresh chives to garnish.

25.Rice & Beans Stuffed Bell Peppers

Preparation time: 10 minutes

Cooking time: 15 minutes

Servings: 5 people

Ingredients:

- 1 tbsp. of Parmesan cheese, grated

- ½ cup of mozzarella cheese, shredded

- 5 large bell peppers, tops removed and seeded

- 1½ tsp. of Italian seasoning

- 1 cup of cooked rice

- 1 (15-ounces) can of red kidney beans, rinsed and drained

- 1 (15-ounces) can of diced tomatoes with juice

- ½ small bell pepper, seeded and chopped

Directions:

1. Combine the tomatoes with juice, bell pepper, rice, beans, and Italian seasoning in a mixing dish. Using the rice mixture, fill each bell pepper uniformly.

2. Preheat the air fryer to 300° F. Oil the basket of your air fryer with some spray oil. Put the bell peppers in a uniform layer in your air fryer basket.

3. Cook for around 12 minutes in the air fryer. In the meantime, combine the Parmesan and mozzarella cheese in a mixing dish.

4. Remove the peppers from the air fryer basket and top each with some cheese mix. Cook for another 3 -4 minutes in the air fryer

5. Take the bell peppers from the air fryer and put them on a serving dish. Enable to cool slowly before serving. Serve it hot.

26.Parsley-loaded Mushrooms

Preparation time: 5 minutes

Cooking time: 15 minutes

Servings: 2 people

Ingredients:

- 2 tablespoon of parsley, finely chopped

- 2 teaspoon of olive oil

- 1 garlic clove, crushed

- 2 slices white bread

- salt and black pepper according to your taste

Directions:

1. Preheat the air fryer to about 360° F. Crush your bread into crumbs in a food blender. Add the parsley, garlic, and pepper; blend with the olive oil and mix.

2. Remove the stalks from the mushrooms and stuff the caps with breadcrumbs. In your air fryer basket, position the mushroom heads. Cook for a few minutes, just until golden brown and crispy.

27. Cheesy Vegetable Quesadilla

Preparation time: 2 minutes

Cooking time: 15 minutes

Servings: 1 people

Ingredients:

- 1 teaspoon of olive oil

- 1 tablespoon of cilantro, chopped

- ½ green onion, sliced

- ¼ zucchini, sliced

- ¼ yellow bell pepper, sliced

- ¼ cup of shredded gouda cheese

Directions:

1. Preheat your air fryer to about 390° F. Oil a basket of air fryers with some cooking oil.

2. Put a flour tortilla in your air fryer basket and cover it with some bell pepper, Gouda cheese, cilantro, zucchini, and green onion. Take the other tortilla to cover and spray with some olive oil.

3. Cook until slightly golden brown, for around 10 minutes. Cut into 4 slices for serving when ready. Enjoy!

28.Creamy 'n Cheese Broccoli Bake

Preparation time: 10 minutes

Cooking time: 30 minutes

Servings: 2 people

Ingredients:

- 1/4 cup of water

- 1-1/2 teaspoons of butter, or to taste

- 1/2 cup of cubed sharp Cheddar cheese

- 1/2 (14 ounces) can evaporate milk, divided

- 1/2 large onion, coarsely diced

- 1 tbsp. of dry bread crumbs, or to taste

- salt according to taste

- 2 tbsp. of all-purpose flour

- 1-pound of fresh broccoli, coarsely diced

Directions:

1. Lightly oil the air-fryer baking pan with cooking oil. Add half of the milk and flour into a pan and simmer at about 360° F for around 5 minutes.

2. Mix well midway through the cooking period. Remove the broccoli and the extra milk. Cook for the next 5 minutes after fully blending.

3. Mix in the cheese until it is fully melted. Mix the butter and bread crumbs well in a shallow tub. Sprinkle the broccoli on top.

4. At about 360° F, cook for around 20 minutes until the tops are finely golden brown. Enjoy and serve warm.

29. Sweet & Spicy Parsnips

Preparation time: 12 minutes

Cooking time: 44 minutes

Servings: 6 people

Ingredients:

- ¼ tsp. of red pepper flakes, crushed

- 1 tbsp. of dried parsley flakes, crushed

- 2 tbsp. of honey

- 1 tbsp. of n butter, melted

- 2 pounds of a parsnip, peeled and cut into 1-inch chunks

- Salt and ground black pepper, according to your taste.

Directions:

1. Let the air-fryer temperature to about 355° F. Oil the basket of your air fryers. Combine the butter and parsnips in a big dish.

2. Transfer the parsnip pieces into the lined air fryer basket arranges them in a uniform layer. Cook for a few minutes in the fryer.

3. In the meantime, combine the leftover ingredients in a large mixing bowl.

4. Move the parsnips into the honey mixture bowl after around 40 minutes and toss them to coat properly.

5. Again, in a uniform layer, organize the parsnip chunks into your air fryer basket.

6. Air-fry for another 3-4 minutes. Take the parsnip pieces from the air fryer and pass them onto the serving dish. Serve it warm.

30. Zucchini with Mediterranean Dill Sauce

Preparation time: 20 minutes

Cooking time: 60 minutes

Servings: 4 people

Ingredients:

- 1/2 tsp. of freshly cracked black peppercorns

- 2 sprigs thyme, leaves only, crushed

- 1 sprig rosemary, leaves only, crushed

- 1 tsp. of sea salt flakes

- 2 tbsp. of melted butter

- 1 pound of zucchini, peeled and cubed

For your Mediterranean Dipping:

- 1 tbsp. of olive oil

- 1 tbsp. of fresh dill, chopped

- 1/3 cup of yogurt

- 1/2 cup of mascarpone cheese

Directions:

1. To start, preheat your Air Fryer to 350° F. Now, add ice cold water to the container with your potato cubes and let them sit in the bath for about 35 minutes.

2. Dry your potato cubes with a hand towel after that. Whisk together the sea salt flakes, melted butter, thyme, rosemary, and freshly crushed peppercorns in a mixing container. This butter/spice mixture can be rubbed onto the potato cubes.

3. In the cooking basket of your air fryer, air-fry your potato cubes for around 18 to 20 minutes or until cooked completely; ensure you shake the potatoes at least once during cooking to cook them uniformly.

4. In the meantime, by mixing the rest of the ingredients, create the Mediterranean dipping sauce. To dip and eat, serve warm potatoes with Mediterranean sauce!

31. Zesty Broccoli

Preparation time: 10 minutes

Cooking time: 15 minutes

Servings: 4 people

Ingredients:

- 1 tbsp. of butter

- 1 large crown broccoli, chopped into bite-sized pieces

- 1 tbsp. of white sesame seeds

- 2 tbsp. of vegetable stock

- ½ tsp. of red pepper flakes, crushed

- 3 garlic cloves, minced

- ½ tsp. of fresh lemon zest, grated finely

- 1 tbsp. of pure lemon juice

Directions:

1. Preheat the Air fryer to about 355° F and oil an Air fryer pan with cooking spray. In the Air fryer plate, combine the vegetable stock, butter, and lemon juice.

2. Move the mixture and cook for about 2 minutes into your Air Fryer. Cook for a minute after incorporating the broccoli and garlic.

3. Cook for a minute with lemon zest, sesame seeds, and red pepper flakes. Remove the dish from the oven and eat immediately.

32. Chewy Glazed Parsnips

Preparation time: 15 minutes

Cooking time: 44 minutes

Servings: 6 people

Ingredients:

- ¼ tsp. of red pepper flakes, crushed

- 1 tbsp. of dried parsley flakes, crushed

- 2 tbsp. of maple syrup

- 1 tbsp. of butter, melted

- 2 pounds of parsnips, skinned and chopped into 1-inch chunks

Directions:

1. Preheat the Air fryer to about 355° F and oil your air fryer basket. In a wide mixing bowl, combine the butter and parsnips and toss well to cover. Cook for around 40 minutes with the parsnips in the Air fryer basket.

2. In the meantime, combine in a wide bowl the rest of your ingredients. Move this mix to your basket of the air fryer and cook for another 4 minutes or so. Remove the dish from the oven and eat promptly.

33. Hoisin-glazed Bok Choy

Preparation time: 5 minutes

Cooking time: 10 minutes

Servings: 4 people

Ingredients:

- 1 tbsp. of all-purpose flour

- 2 tbsp. of sesame oil

- 2 tbsp. of hoisin sauce

- 1/2 tsp. of sage

- 1 tsp. of onion powder

- 2 garlic cloves, minced

- 1 pound of baby Bok choy, roots removed, leaves separated

Directions:

1. In a lightly oiled Air Fryer basket, put the onion powder, garlic, Bok Choy, and sage. Cook for around 3 minutes at about 350° F in a preheated Air Fryer.

2. Whisk together the sesame oil, hoisin sauce, and flour in a deep mixing dish. Drizzle over the Bok choy with the gravy. Cook for an extra minute. Bon appétit!

34. Green Beans with Okra

Preparation time: 10 minutes

Cooking time: 20 minutes

Servings: 2 people

Ingredients:

- 3 tbsp. of balsamic vinegar

- ¼ cup of nutritional yeast

- ½ (10-ounces) of bag chilled cut green beans

- ½ (10-ounces) of bag chilled cut okra

- Salt and black pepper, according to your taste.

Directions:

1. Preheat your Air fryer to about 400° F and oil the air fryer basket.

2. In a wide mixing bowl, toss together the salt, green beans, okra, vinegar, nutritional yeast, and black pepper.

3. Cook for around 20 minutes with the okra mixture in your Air fryer basket. Dish out into a serving plate and eat warm.

35. Celeriac with some Greek Yogurt Dip

Preparation time: 12 minutes

Cooking time: 25 minutes

Servings: 2 people

Ingredients:

- 1/2 tsp. of sea salt

- 1/2 tsp. of ground black pepper, to taste

- 1 tbsp. of sesame oil

- 1 red onion, chopped into 1 1/2-inch piece

- 1/2 pound of celeriac, chopped into 1 1/2-inch piece

Spiced Yogurt:

- 1/2 tsp. of chili powder

- 1/2 tsp. of mustard seeds

- 2 tbsp. of mayonnaise

- 1/4 cup of Greek yogurt

Directions:

1. In the slightly oiled cooking basket, put the veggies in one uniform layer. Pour sesame oil over the veggies.

2. Season with a pinch of black pepper and a pinch of salt. Cook for around 20 minutes at about 300° F, tossing the basket midway through your cooking cycle.

3. In the meantime, whisk all the leftover ingredients into the sauce. Spoon the sauce over the veggies that have been cooked. Bon appétit!

36. Wine & Garlic Flavored Vegetables

Preparation time: 7-10 minutes

Cooking time: 15 minutes

Servings: 4 people

Ingredients:

- 4 cloves of garlic, minced
- 3 tbsp. of red wine vinegar
- 1/3 cup of olive oil
- 1 red onion, diced
- 1 package frozen diced vegetables
- 1 cup of baby Portobello mushrooms, diced
- 1 tsp. of Dijon mustard
- 1 ½ tbsp. of honey
- Salt and pepper according to your taste
- ¼ cup of chopped fresh basil

Directions:

1. Preheat the air fryer to about 330° F. In the air fryer, put the grill pan attachment.

2. Combine the veggies and season with pepper, salt, and garlic in a Ziploc container. To mix all, give everything a strong shake. Dump and cook for around 15 minutes on the grill pan.

3. Additionally, add the remainder of the ingredients into a mixing bowl and season with some more salt and pepper. Drizzle the sauce over your grilled vegetables.

37. Spicy Braised Vegetables

Preparation time: 10 minutes

Cooking time: 25 minutes

Servings: 4 people

Ingredients:

- 1/2 cup of tomato puree

- 1/4 tsp. of ground black pepper

- 1/2 tsp. of fine sea salt

- 1 tbsp. of garlic powder

- 1/2 tsp. of fennel seeds

- 1/4 tsp. of mustard powder

- 1/2 tsp. of porcini powder

- 1/4 cup of olive oil

- 1 celery stalk, chopped into matchsticks

- 2 bell peppers, deveined and thinly diced

- 1 Serrano pepper, deveined and thinly diced

- 1 large-sized zucchini, diced

Directions:

1. In your Air Fryer cooking basket, put your peppers, zucchini, sweet potatoes, and carrot.

2. Drizzle with some olive oil and toss to cover completely; cook for around 15 minutes in a preheated Air Fryer at about 350°F.

3. Make the sauce as the vegetables are frying by quickly whisking the remaining ingredients (except the tomato ketchup). Slightly oil up a baking dish that fits your fryer.

4. Add the cooked vegetables to the baking dish, along with the sauce, and toss well to cover.

5. Turn the Air Fryer to about 390° F and cook for 2-4 more minutes with the vegetables. Bon appétit!

CHAPTER 3: Air Fryer Snack Side Dishes and Appetizer Recipes

1. Crispy 'n Tasty Spring Rolls

Preparation time: 5 minutes

Cooking time: 15 minutes

Servings: 4 people

Ingredients:

- 8 spring roll wrappers

- 1 tsp. of nutritional yeast

- 1 tsp. of corn starch + 2 tablespoon water

- 1 tsp. of coconut sugar

- 1 tbsp. of soy sauce

- 1 medium carrot, shredded

- 1 cup of shiitake mushroom, sliced thinly

- 1 celery stalk, chopped

- ½ tsp. of ginger, finely chopped

Directions:

1. Mix your carrots, celery stalk, soy sauce, coconut sugar, ginger, and nutritional yeast with each other in a mixing dish.

2. Have a tbsp. of your vegetable mix and put it in the middle of your spring roll wrappers.

3. Roll up and secure the sides of your wraps with some cornstarch.

4. Cook for about 15 minutes or till your spring roll wraps is crisp in a preheated air fryer at 200F.

2. Spinach & Feta Crescent Triangles

Preparation time: 10 minutes

Cooking time: 20 minutes

Servings: 4 people

Ingredients:

- ¼ teaspoon of salt

- 1 teaspoon of chopped oregano

- ¼ teaspoon of garlic powder

- 1 cup of crumbled feta cheese

- 1 cup of steamed spinach

Directions:

1. Preheat your air fryer to about 350 F, and then roll up the dough over a level surface that is gently floured.

2. In a medium-sized bowl, mix the spinach, feta, salt, oregano, and ground garlic cloves. Split your dough into four equal chunks.

3. Split the mix of feta/spinach among the four chunks of dough. Fold and seal your dough using a fork.

4. Please put it on a baking tray covered with parchment paper, and then put it in your air fryer.

5. Cook until nicely golden, for around 1 minute.

3. Healthy Avocado Fries

Preparation time: 5 minutes

Cooking time: 20 minutes

Servings: 2 people

Ingredients:

- ¼ cup of aquafaba

- 1 avocado, cubed

- Salt as required

Directions:

1. Mix the aquafaba, crumbs, and salt in a mixing bowl.

2. Preheat your air fryer to about 390°F and cover the avocado pieces uniformly in the crumbs blend.

3. Put the ready pieces in the cooking bucket of your air fryer and cook for several minutes.

4. Twice-fried Cauliflower Tater Tots

Preparation time: 5 minutes

Cooking time: 16 minutes

Servings: 12 people

Ingredients:

- 3 tbsp. Of oats flaxseed meal + 3 tbsp. of water)

- 1-pound of cauliflower, steamed and chopped

- 1 tsp. of parsley, chopped

- 1 tsp. of oregano, chopped

- 1 tsp. of garlic, minced

- 1 tsp. of chives, chopped

- 1 onion, chopped

- 1 flax egg (1 tablespoon 3 tablespoon desiccated coconuts)

- ½ cup of nutritional yeast

- salt and pepper according to taste

- ½ cup of bread crumbs

Directions:

1. Preheat your air fryer to about 390 degrees F.

2. To extract extra moisture, place the steamed cauliflower onto a ring and a paper towel.

3. Put and mix the remainder of your ingredients, excluding your bread crumbs, in a small mixing container.

4. Use your palms, blend it until well mixed and shapes into a small ball.

5. Roll your tater tots over your bread crumbs and put them in the bucket of your air fryer.

6. For a minute, bake. Raise the cooking level to about 400 F and cook for the next 10 minutes.

5. Cheesy Mushroom & Cauliflower Balls

Preparation time: 10 minutes

Cooking time: 50 minutes

Servings: 4 people

Ingredients:

- Salt and pepper according to taste

- 2 sprigs chopped fresh thyme

- ¼ cup of coconut oil

- 1 cup of Grana Padano cheese

- 1 cup of breadcrumbs

- 2 tablespoon of vegetable stock

- 3 cups of cauliflower, chopped

- 3 cloves garlic, minced

- 1 small red onion, chopped

- 3 tablespoon of olive oil

Directions:

1. Over moderate flame, put a pan. Add some balsamic vinegar. When the oil is heated, stir-fry your onion and garlic till they become transparent.

2. Add in the mushrooms and cauliflower and stir-fry for about 5 minutes. Add in your stock, add thyme and cook till your cauliflower has consumed the stock. Add pepper, Grana Padano cheese, and salt.

3. Let the mix cool down and form bite-size spheres of your paste. To harden, put it in the fridge for about 30 minutes.

4. Preheat your air fryer to about 350°F.

5. Add your coconut oil and breadcrumbs into a small bowl and blend properly.

6. Take out your mushroom balls from the fridge, swirl the breadcrumb paste once more, and drop the balls into your breadcrumb paste.

7. Avoid overcrowding, put your balls into your air fryer's container and cook for about 15 minutes, flipping after every 5 minutes to ensure even cooking.

8. Serve with some tomato sauce and brown sugar.

6. Italian Seasoned Easy Pasta Chips

Preparation time: 5 minutes

Cooking time: 10 minutes

Servings: 2 people

Ingredients:

- 2 cups of whole wheat bowtie pasta
- 1 tbsp. of olive oil
- 1 tbsp. of nutritional yeast
- 1 ½ tsp. of Italian seasoning blend
- ½ tsp. of salt

Directions:

1. Put the accessory for the baking tray into your air fryer.
2. Mix all the ingredients in a medium-sized bowl, offer it a gentle stir.
3. Add the mixture to your air fryer basket.
4. Close your air fryer and cook at around 400°degrees F for about 10 minutes.

7. Thai Sweet Potato Balls

Preparation time: 10 minutes

Cooking time: 50 minutes

Servings: 4 people

Ingredients:

- 1 cup of coconut flakes

- 1 tsp. of baking powder

- 1/2 cup of almond meal

- 1/4 tsp. of ground cloves

- 1/2 tsp. of ground cinnamon

- 2 tsp. of orange zest

- 1 tbsp. of orange juice

- 1 cup of brown sugar

- 1 pound of sweet potatoes

Directions:

1. Bake your sweet potatoes for around 25 to 30 minutes at about 380° F till they become soft; peel and mash them in a medium-sized bowl.

2. Add orange zest, orange juice, brown sugar, ground cinnamon, almond meal, cloves, and baking powder. Now blend completely.

3. Roll the balls around in some coconut flakes.

4. Bake for around 15 minutes or until fully fried and crunchy in the preheated Air Fryer at about 360° F.

5. For the rest of the ingredients, redo the same procedure. Bon appétit!

8. Barbecue Roasted Almonds

Preparation time: 5 minutes

Cooking time: 20 minutes

Servings: 6 people

Ingredients:

- 1 tbsp. of olive oil

- 1/4 tsp. of smoked paprika

- 1/2 tsp. of cumin powder

- 1/4 tsp. of mustard powder

- 1/4 tsp. of garlic powder

- Sea salt and ground black pepper, according to taste

- 1 ½ cups of raw almonds

Directions:

1. In a mixing pot, mix all your ingredients.

2. Line the container of your Air Fryer with some baking parchment paper. Arrange the covered almonds out in the basket of your air fryer in a uniform layer.

3. Roast for around 8 to 9 minutes at about 340°F, tossing the bucket once or twice. If required, work in groups.

4. Enjoy!

9. Croissant Rolls

Preparation time: 2 minutes

Cooking time: 6 minutes

Servings: 8 people

Ingredients:

- 4 tbsp. of butter, melted

- 1 (8-ounces) can croissant rolls

Directions:

1. Adjust the air-fryer temperature to about 320°F. Oil the basket of your air fryers.

2. Into your air fryer basket, place your prepared croissant rolls.

3. Airs fry them for around 4 minutes or so.

4. Flip to the opposite side and cook for another 2-3 minutes.

5. Take out from your air fryer and move to a tray.

6. Glaze with some melted butter and eat warm.

10. Curry' n Coriander Spiced Bread Rolls

Preparation time: 5 minutes

Cooking time: 15 minutes

Servings: 5 people

Ingredients:

- salt and pepper according to taste

- 5 large potatoes, boiled

- 2 sprigs, curry leaves

- 2 small onions, chopped

- 2 green chilies, seeded and chopped

- 1 tbsp. of olive oil

- 1 bunch of coriander, chopped

- ½ tsp. of turmeric

- 8 slices of vegan wheat bread, brown sides discarded

- ½ tsp. of mustard seeds

Directions:

1. Mash your potatoes in a bowl and sprinkle some black pepper and salt according to taste. Now set aside.

2. In a pan, warm up the olive oil over medium-low heat and add some mustard seeds. Mix until the seeds start to sputter.

3. Now add in the onions and cook till they become transparent. Mix in the curry leaves and turmeric powder.

4. Keep on cooking till it becomes fragrant for a couple of minutes. Take it off the flame and add the mixture to the potatoes.

5. Mix in the green chilies and some coriander. This is meant to be the filling.

6. Wet your bread and drain excess moisture. In the center of the loaf, put a tbsp. of the potato filling and gently roll the bread so that the potato filling is fully enclosed within the bread.

7. Brush with some oil and put them inside your air fryer basket.

8. Cook for around 15 minutes in a preheated air fryer at about 400°F.

9. Ensure that the air fryer basket is shaken softly midway through the cooking period for an even cooking cycle.

11. Scrumptiously Healthy Chips

Preparation time: 5 minutes

Cooking time: 10 minutes

Servings: 2 people

Ingredients:

- 2 tbsp. of olive oil

- 2 tbsp. of almond flour

- 1 tsp. of garlic powder

- 1 bunch kale

- Salt and pepper according to taste

Directions:

1. For around 5 minutes, preheat your air fryer.

2. In a mixing bowl, add all your ingredients, add the kale leaves at the end and toss to completely cover them.

3. Put in the basket of your fryer and cook until crispy for around 10 minutes.

12. Kid-friendly Vegetable Fritters

Preparation time: 5 minutes

Cooking time: 20 minutes

Servings: 4 people

Ingredients:

- 2 tbsp. of olive oil

- 1/2 cup of cornmeal

- 1/2 cup of all-purpose flour

- 1/2 tsp. of ground cumin

- 1 tsp. of turmeric powder

- 2 garlic cloves, pressed

- 1 carrot, grated

- 1 sweet pepper, seeded and chopped

- 1 yellow onion, finely chopped

- 1 tbsp. of ground flaxseeds

- Salt and ground black pepper, according to taste

- 1 pound of broccoli florets

Directions:

1. In salted boiling water, blanch your broccoli until al dente, for around 3 to 5 minutes. Drain the excess water and move to a mixing bowl; add in the rest of your ingredients to mash the broccoli florets.

2. Shape the paste into patties and position them in the slightly oiled Air Fryer basket.

3. Cook for around 6 minutes at about 400° F, flipping them over midway through the cooking process; if needed, operate in batches.

4. Serve hot with some Vegenaise of your choice. Enjoy it!

13. Avocado Fries

Preparation time: 10 minutes

Cooking time: 50 minutes

Servings: 4 people

Ingredients:

- 2 avocados, cut into wedges

- 1/2 cup of parmesan cheese, grated

- 2 eggs

- Sea salt and ground black pepper, according to taste.

- 1/2 cup of almond meal

- 1/2 head garlic (6-7 cloves)

Sauce:

- 1 tsp. of mustard

- 1 tsp. of lemon juice

- 1/2 cup of mayonnaise

Directions:

1. On a piece of aluminum foil, put your garlic cloves and spray some cooking spray on it. Wrap your garlic cloves in the foil.

2. Cook for around 1-2 minutes at about 400°F in your preheated Air Fryer. Inspect the garlic, open the foil's top end, and keep cooking for an additional 10-12 minutes.

3. Once done, let them cool for around 10 to 15 minutes; take out the cloves by pressing them out of their skin; mash your garlic and put them aside.

4. Mix the salt, almond meal, and black pepper in a small dish.

5. Beat the eggs until foamy in a separate bowl.

6. Put some parmesan cheese in the final shallow dish.

7. In your almond meal blend, dip the avocado wedges, dusting off any excess.

8. In the beaten egg, dunk your wedges; eventually, dip in some parmesan cheese.

9. Spray your avocado wedges on both sides with some cooking oil spray.

10. Cook for around 8 minutes in the preheated Air Fryer at about 395° F, flipping them over midway thru the cooking process.

11. In the meantime, mix the ingredients of your sauce with your cooked crushed garlic.

12. Split the avocado wedges between plates and cover with the sauce before serving. Enjoy!

14. Crispy Wings with Lemony Old Bay Spice

Preparation time: 10 minutes

Cooking time: 25 minutes

Servings: 4 people

Ingredients:

- Salt and pepper according to taste

- 3 pounds of vegan chicken wings

- 1 tsp. of lemon juice, freshly squeezed

- 1 tbsp. of old bay spices

- ¾ cup of almond flour

- ½ cup of butter

Directions:

1. For about 5 minutes, preheat your air fryer. Mix all your ingredients in a mixing dish, excluding the butter. Put in the bowl of an air fryer.

2. Preheat the oven to about 350°F and bake for around 25 minutes. Rock the fryer container midway thru the cooking process, also for cooking.

3. Drizzle with some melted butter when it's done frying. Enjoy!

15.Cold Salad with Veggies and Pasta

Preparation time: 30 minutes

Cooking time: 1 hour 35 minutes

Servings: 12 people

Ingredients:

- ½ cup of fat-free Italian dressing

- 2 tablespoons of olive oil, divided

- ½ cup of Parmesan cheese, grated

- 8 cups of cooked pasta

- 4 medium tomatoes, cut in eighths

- 3 small eggplants, sliced into ½-inch thick rounds

- 3 medium zucchinis, sliced into ½-inch thick rounds

- Salt, according to your taste.

Directions:

1. Preheat your Air fryer to about 355° F and oil the inside of your air fryer basket. In a dish, mix 1 tablespoon of olive oil and zucchini and swirl to cover properly.

2. Cook for around 25 minutes your zucchini pieces in your Air fryer basket. In another dish, mix your eggplants with a tablespoon of olive oil and toss to coat properly.

3. Cook for around 40 minutes your eggplant slices in your Air fryer basket. Re-set the Air Fryer temperature to about 320° F and put the tomatoes next in the ready basket.

4. Cook and mix all your air-fried vegetables for around 30 minutes. To serve, mix in the rest of the ingredients and chill for at least 2 hours, covered.

16. Zucchini and Minty Eggplant Bites

Preparation time: 15 minutes

Cooking time: 35 minutes

Servings: 8 people

Ingredients:

- 3 tbsp. of olive oil

- 1 pound of zucchini, peeled and cubed

- 1 pound of eggplant, peeled and cubed

- 2 tbsp. of melted butter

- 1 ½ tsp. of red pepper chili flakes

- 2 tsp. of fresh mint leaves, minced

Directions:

1. In a large mixing container, add all of the ingredients mentioned above.

2. Roast the zucchini bites and eggplant in your Air Fryer for around 30 minutes at about 300° F, flipping once or twice during the cooking cycle. Serve with some dipping sauce that's homemade.

17.Stuffed Potatoes

Preparation time: 15 minutes

Cooking time: 31 minutes

Servings: 4 people

Ingredients:

- 3 tbsp. of canola oil

- ½ cup of Parmesan cheese, grated

- 2 tbsp. of chives, chopped

- ½ of brown onion, chopped

- 1 tbsp. of butter

- 4 potatoes, peeled

Directions:

1. Preheat the Air fryer to about 390° F and oil the air fryer basket. Coat the canola oil on the potatoes and place them in your Air Fryer Basket.

2. Cook for around 20 minutes before serving on a platter. Halve each potato and scrape out the middle from each half of it.

3. In a frying pan, melt some butter over medium heat and add the onions. Sauté in a bowl for around 5 minutes and dish out.

4. Combine the onions with the middle of the potato, chives and half of the cheese. Stir well and uniformly cram the onion potato mixture into the potato halves.

5. Top and layer the potato halves in your Air Fryer basket with the leftover cheese. Cook for around 6 minutes before serving hot.

18. Paneer Cutlet

Preparation time: 5 minutes

Cooking time: 15 minutes

Servings: 1 people

Ingredients:

- ½ teaspoon of salt

- ½ teaspoon of oregano

- 1 small onion, finely chopped

- ½ teaspoon of garlic powder

- 1 teaspoon of butter

- ½ teaspoon of chai masala

- 1 cup of grated cheese

Directions:

1. Preheat the air fryer to about 350° F and lightly oil a baking dish. In a mixing bowl, add all ingredients and stir well. Split the mixture into cutlets and put them in an oiled baking dish.

2. Put the baking dish in your air fryer and cook your cutlets until crispy, around a minute or so.

19. Spicy Roasted Cashew Nuts

Preparation time: 10 Minutes

Cooking time: 20 Minutes

Servings: 4

Ingredients:

- 1/2 tsp. of ancho chili powder

- 1/2 tsp. of smoked paprika

- Salt and ground black pepper, according to taste

- 1 tsp. of olive oil

- 1 cup of whole cashews

Directions:

1. In a mixing big bowl, toss all your ingredients.

2. Line parchment paper to cover the Air Fryer container. Space out the spiced cashews in your basket in a uniform layer.

3. Roast for about 6 to 8 minutes at 300 degrees F, tossing the basket once or twice during the cooking process. Work in batches if needed. Enjoy!

CHAPTER 4: Deserts

1. Almond-apple Treat

Preparation time: 5 minutes

Cooking time: 15 minutes

Servings: 4 people

Ingredients:

- 2 tablespoon of sugar
- ¾ oz. of raisins
- 1 ½ oz. of almonds

Directions:

1. Preheat your air fryer to around 360° F.
2. Mix the almonds, sugar, and raisins in a dish. Blend using a hand mixer.
3. Load the apples with a combination of the almond mixture. Please put them in the air fryer basket and cook for a few minutes. Enjoy!

2. Pepper-pineapple With Butter-sugar Glaze

Preparation time: 5 minutes

Cooking time: 10 minutes

Servings: 2 people

Ingredients:

- Salt according to taste.
- 2 tsp. of melted butter
- 1 tsp. of brown sugar

- 1 red bell pepper, seeded and julienned

- 1 medium-sized pineapple, peeled and sliced

Directions:

1. To about 390°F, preheat your air fryer. In your air fryer, put the grill pan attachment.

2. In a Ziploc bag, combine all ingredients and shake well.

3. Dump and cook on the grill pan for around 10 minutes to ensure you turn the pineapples over every 5 minutes during cooking.

3. True Churros with Yummy Hot Chocolate

Preparation time: 10 minutes

Cooking time: 25 minutes

Servings: 3 people

Ingredients:

- 1 tsp. of ground cinnamon

- 1/3 cup of sugar

- 1 tbsp. of cornstarch

- 1 cup of milk

- 2 ounces of dark chocolate

- 1 cup of all-purpose flour

- 1 tbsp. of canola oil

- 1 tsp. of lemon zest

- 1/4 tsp. of sea salt

- 2 tbsp. of granulated sugar

- 1/2 cup of water

Directions:

1. To create the churro dough, boil the water in a pan over a medium-high flame; then, add the salt, sugar, and lemon zest and fry, stirring continuously, until fully dissolved.

2. Take the pan off the heat and add in some canola oil. Stir the flour in steadily, constantly stirring until the solution turns to a ball.

3. With a broad star tip, pipe the paste into a piping bag. In the oiled Air Fryer basket, squeeze 4-inch slices of dough. Cook for around 6 minutes at a temperature of 300° F.

4. Make the hot cocoa for dipping in the meantime. In a shallow saucepan, melt some chocolate and 1/2 cup of milk over low flame.

5. In the leftover 1/2 cup of milk, mix the cornstarch and blend it into the hot chocolate mixture. Cook for around 5 minutes on low flame.

6. Mix the sugar and cinnamon; roll your churros in this combination. Serve with a side of hot cocoa. Enjoy!

Conclusion

These times, air frying is one of the most common cooking techniques and air fryers have become one of the chef's most impressive devices. In no time, air fryers can help you prepare nutritious and tasty meals! To prepare unique dishes for you and your family members, you do not need to be a master in the kitchen.

Everything you have to do is buy an air fryer and this wonderful cookbook for air fryers! Soon, you can make the greatest dishes ever and inspire those around you.

Cooked meals at home with you! Believe us! Get your hands on an air fryer and this handy set of recipes for air fryers and begin your new cooking experience. Have fun!

Keto Bread Machine Cookbook 2021 with Pictures

Choose between 25+ Keto Hands-Off Recipes and Bake Homemade Bread that Make Everyone Envy

By

Sean Foster

Table of Contents

Introduction

Bread is the most prominent food in almost every household around the globe. Bread is commonly a product of baking consists of numerous kinds of doughs, buns, and crusts. Usually, all kinds of bread dough are made from flour, yeast, and water in different shapes, methods, and flavors. The main process evolves around mixing and blending until they turned into a rigid paste or dough and then baked into a bread, loaf, or bun form afterward.

If we go through history, we will see that bread is one of the oldest food made and consumed by human beings since the beginning of agriculture. It plays a noteworthy role in religious rituals and cultural life, and language. Bread has a lot of significant roles as a meal around the world. It is consumed differently in different cultures, most often as a side meal, snacks, breakfast, lunch, or dinner or even combined as an important ingredient in different food/cuisine preparations.

Freshly homemade bread is one of the most satisfying things to eat and make. Although because of hectic life routines and busy schedules, most people have never even tried making homemade bread in their lives. But a lot has begun to change with the arrival of automatic bread machines you can easily make bread at the convenience of your home without spending a lot of time.

One of the best things about making your homemade bread is that you can always opt for healthy ingredients; unlike bread, you buy from outside when you make homemade fresh bread. You can always customize your list of ingredients, be it nuts of your choice, almond or coconut flour, gluten-free bread, nutritional yeast, or any other sort of restrictive ingredients.

Now the main question arises what a bread machine is? How does the bread machine work? How many kinds of bread can you make with a bread machine? Or is the bread machine worth buying?

An automatic home appliance for turning uncooked ingredients into dough or baked bread is called a bread machine. A bread machine is made up of a baking pan, built-in paddles at the bottom of the pan seated in a small oven center. The bread machine usually comes up with a small built-in screen called a control panel. You can adjust your choice of preferences while baking bread using settings input via the control panel.

Usually, the different bread machine comes up with different instructions. It may take some time to read the full instructions of your machine. But you will get a whole idea about the operating, cleaning, and safety features of the machine. Besides operating and other options manual will also provide a selection of recipes that are tested. If you are new to breadmaking, these recipes particularly are an excellent way to start.

The traditional order of ingredients starts with liquids and finishes with the dry ingredients, the fat, and then the yeast, though there may be some exceptions. The yeast is held away from the fluids not to activate until it starts to knead.

There are many different programs for producing many different styles of the loaf for most bread makers. Using various types of flour and varying the other ingredients, you can produce white bread, pizza whole meal, or special loaves. On its display screen, you can see the numerous choices this beadmaker offers (from the top: basic, whole meal, multigrain, French, pizza, cake, dough, and bake only). You put a slightly different mix into the tin at the beginning for different breads and choose a different program from the show. The bread machine can automatically manage various kneading, growing and baking times, and so on. You can use the bread machine to make different kinds of dough by choosing the dough cycle option from the control panel then baking it in the oven in any shape or form you like. From bun to baguettes, to pizza pull-apart, if you prefer a particular shape or bread style.

Nowadays bread machine is a very helpful and essential tool for most busy people. It has transformed baking bread into a hand-off process. From kneading to baking, the bread machine does all the job. Just measure and put all the ingredients in the baking pan, close the lid, start the button, and you are done. It feels magical if you own a bread machine. Without any extra effort, you can enjoy fresh homemade bread any day or at any time of the week, and it is worth investing your money in.

Chapter 1: Bread Machine Breakfast Recipes

1.1 Simple Flaxseed Keto Bread

Total time of cooking

3 hours 10 minute

Servings

5

Nutrition facts

Calories 263 (for two slices)

Fat 18g

Protein 12g

Net carbs 4g

fiber 10g

total carbs 14g

Ingredients:

This is the list of ingredients required to make simple flaxseeds keto bread.

- 1 cup of almond flour
- 1/4 cup of brown flaxseeds
- 1/3 cup of coconut flour
- 1 teaspoon of active dry yeast
- 2 tablespoons of psyllium husk powder
- 1/2 teaspoon of baking soda
- 1/2 teaspoon of salt
- 3 egg whites
- 1 whole egg
- 1 cup of warm water
- 1 teaspoon of olive oil

Instructions:

Follow the instructions mentioned below to make flaxseeds keto bread.

1. Sift the flour first to remove lumps.
2. First, add warm water to the bread machine pan, and sprinkle active dry yeast on top .
3. Wait for the yeast to activate.
4. Approximately After 5 minutes, add all the other ingredients into the bread machine pan.

5. Press the basic cycle option from your bread machine and choose medium crust.

6. When baking is finished, wait for few minutes before you remove bread from the pan.

7. slice and enjoy

1.2 Keto Coconut white bread (grain, gluten, and sugarfree)

Total time of cooking

3 hours 50 minutes

Servings

20 servings

Nutrition facts

Calories 56 (per serving)

Fat 4g

Protein 2.4g

Net carbs 1.2g

Ingredients:

Here is the list of ingredients required to make keto coconut white bread.

- 1 1/2 (180g) cups of almond flour

- 7 large eggs at room temperature

- 3 tablespoon (43 g) of apple cider vinegar

- 3.75 tablespoon (33g) of finely grounded psyllium husk powder

- 4 teaspoon (12g) of instant yeast

- 1 1/2 (360g) of lukewarm water

- 4 teaspoon (18g) of baking powder

- 1 teaspoon of salt

- 3 tablespoon (45g) of olive or coconut oil optional

Instructions:

Follow the instructions mentioned below to make keto coconut white bread.

1. Assemble all the ingredients.

2. Place the kneading paddles in the bread machine pan.

3. Follow your bread machine recommended order and add all of the above ingredients. Sprinkle yeast on top of the ingredients to ensure that it does not come into contact with other liquid ingredients.

4. Choose gluten-free and medium crust in the settings press the start button.

5. When the baking time is over, click the stop button.

6. Remove the baking pan from the bread machine to cool down for a while before removing the bread.

7. After a while, when it is cooled down, give your baking pan a toss and slightly remove bread from the pan.

8. bread is ready to serve.

1.3 Light and fluffy keto flaxseed buns

Total time of cooking

55 minutes

Servings

4 servings

Nutrition facts

Calories 232 (per serving)

Fat 11.9g

Protein 10.6g

Fiber 13.6g

Net carbs 2.1

Total carbs 15.7g

Ingredients:

Here is the list of ingredients required to make light and fluffy keto flaxseed buns.

- 1 1/4 (150g) cups of golden grounded flaxseeds

- 4 large egg whites or 2 whole egg at room temperature

- 2 tablespoon (28 g) of apple cider vinegar

- 1 teaspoon of psyllium powder

- 1/4 to 1 teaspoon of salt

- 2 teaspoon (8g) of baking powder

- 50 ml/0.2 cup of hot boiling water

Instructions:

Follow the instructions mentioned below to make light and fluffy keto flaxseed buns

1. Assemble all the ingredients.

2. As recommended by your bread machine, add all of the above ingredients. Add water, apple cider vinegar, golden flaxseeds grounded, psyllium powder, eggs, baking powder, and salt.

3. Choose the dough cycle option from the settings and press the start button.

4. When the dough cycle is over, click the stop button.

5. Remove the dough from the bread pan and divide the dough into 90 g portions each evenly. You will have more buns if you will make smaller portions.

6. Turn on the oven. At 350 F or 180 C, preheat your oven.

7. As the dough is sticky, so make sure to wet your hands before shaping it into balls. Now make balls and place them over a baking tray lined with parchment paper.

8. Sprinkle the top of the bun with seeds or herbs of your choice.

9. Place the baking tray in the oven. And bake for around 30 minutes or until golden brown. Touch and see if buns feel light and hollow upon touching it's done.

10. Remove from oven and serve.

1.4 Keto banana almond bread

Total time of cooking

4 hours

Servings

12 servings

Nutrition facts

Calories 173 (per serving)

Fiber 2.5g

Protein 3.9g

Net carbs 2.3g

Fat 14.9g

Ingredients:

Here is the list of ingredients required to make keto banana almond bread.

- 3/4 (84g) cups of coconut flour

- 1/2 (120ml) cups of heavy whipping cream at room temperature

- 1/2 cup + 1 tablespoon (130g) melted unsalted butter at room temperature

- 5 large eggs at room temperature

- 1/2 (100g) cup of granulated sweetener

- 2 teaspoons (10 ml) of banana extract

- 1/4 teaspoon (1g) of salt

- 2 teaspoons (8g) of baking powder

- 1 teaspoon (3g) of ground cinnamon

- 1 teaspoon (5ml) of vanilla extract

- 1 cup of chopped almonds

Instructions:

Follow the instructions mentioned below to make keto banana almond bread.

1. Assemble all the ingredients.

2. As suggested by your bread machine, add all of the above ingredients in the bread machine baking pan except almonds.

3. Check dough after 5 minutes. If required, add 1 to 2 tbsp of water or flour according to the consistency of the dough.

4. When the machine beep, add almonds 5 to 10 minutes before the kneading cycle completes.

5. Choose the baking option according to the instructions of your bread machine.

6. Select the loaf size and crust color from the bread machine settings.

7. Once the baking is completed, transfer the bread into the oven rack and let it cool down for some time.

8. Cut into slices, top up with your favorite keto low carb syrup and enjoy.

1.5 Easy Keto Egg Loaf(How to make a keto French toast from an egg loaf)

Total time of cooking

55 minutes

Servings

4

Nutrition facts

Calories 232(per slice for egg loaf only)

Protein 5.7g

Net carbs 2.5g

Fat 20.6g

Ingredients:

Here is the list of ingredients required to make keto egg loaf.

- 4 tablespoons of melted butter

- 1/4 cup of coconut flour

- 4 whole eggs

- 8 oz cream cheese

- 3 tablespoons of any sweetener of your choice

- 1/4 cup of heavy whipping cream

- 2 teaspoons of baking powder

- 1 teaspoon of vanilla extract

- 1 teaspoon of cinnamon powder

Ingredients for keto French toast egg dip:

- 2 medium-sized eggs

- 1/2 tablespoon or 8 grams of unsweetened vanilla almond milk

- 1/2 tablespoon or 8 grams of keto maple syrup

- pinch of cinnamon powder

Instructions:

Follow the instructions mentioned below to make keto egg loaf

1. Put all the egg loaf ingredients in the bread machine pan, select the dough option from your bread machine menu and press the start button. After five minutes, check the dough if water or flour is needed.

2. Lined loaf pan with parchment paper, pour the egg loaf mixture into loaf pan and even out the top surface of egg loaf with a spatula's help.

3. Bake an egg loaf at 350 f for around 45 minutes or check with a toothpick.

4. Remove the loaf from the pan.

5. Before cutting it into slices, let the bread cool down on the baking rack for a while.

Instructions to make French toast egg dip

6. Take a small-size mixing bowl and break two medium eggs in it.

7. Add 1/2 tablespoon of unsweetened vanilla almond milk, 1/2 tablespoon of keto maple syrup, and a pinch of powdered cinnamon. Whisk with a fork until eggs are fully combined with other ingredients.

8. Dip the bread slices one by one into egg dip from both sides.

9. Turn on the stove and place the pan over medium heat, coat it with baking spray and cook bread from both sides until crispy or golden brown.

10. Serve your French toast with fruits and keto maple syrup.

1.6 Low Carb Keto Bagels

Total time of cooking

45 minutes

Servings

8

Nutrition facts

Calories 298(per bagel)

Protein 18g

Net carbs 5g

Fat 23g

Ingredients:

Here is the list of ingredients required to make keto bagels.

- 3 cups of shredded mozzarella cheese

- 2 oz cream cheese

- 3 large eggs (reserved one egg for egg wash)

- 1 1/3 cup of almond flour

- 1 tablespoon of baking powder

- for topping sesame seeds cheese or bagel seasoning (optional)

Instructions:

Follow the method mentioned below to make low-carb keto bagels.

1.Assemble all the ingredients.

2.In a safe microwave bowl, melt together mozzarella and cream cheese in 30 second intervals. Check after every 30 seconds, stir until cheese is completely melted. You can also melt cheese in a double boiler over the burner.

3.Now, place all the ingredients, including melted cheese, in the bread machine pan, select dough from settings, and press the start button.

4. Once the dough cycle is finished, take the dough out of the bread machine. The dough will be very adhering, which is ok.

5. Wrap pastry board with plastic wrap. Coat your hands with oil, and divide your dough into 8 equal sections. Now roll each dough section on the pastry board to make 1-inch thick dough ropes. The plastic wrap will prevent your dough from sticking to the board.

6. Make the circle shape with a 1-inch thick rope and pinch the ends shut.

7. Place bagels carefully on a baking sheet lined with parchment paper .place each bagel from a distance of 1 inch at least.

8. Now coat the top surface of bagels with an egg wash at this stage. If you want to add any bagel toppings, you can.

9. In a preheated oven, bake the bagels in the middle rack of the oven for around 14 to 15 minutes or until it turns golden brown.

10. Before removing it from the baking tray, allow the bagels to cool down.

1.7 Keto Raspberry and Lemon Loaf(grain, sugar, and gluten-free)

Total time of cooking

4 hours

Servings

12

Nutrition facts

Calories 166 (per slice)

Protein 5.7g

Fiber 2.5g

Net carbs 2.8g

Fat 14.7g

Ingredients:

Here is the list of ingredients required to make keto raspberry and lemon loaf.

- 4 tablespoons of sour cream

- 4 tablespoons of melted butter

- 2 whole eggs

- 200 grams of almond flour

- 1.5 teaspoon of baking powder

- 1 teaspoon of lemon essence/extract.

- 1 teaspoon of vanilla extract

- 1/4 cup of sugar substitute

- 100 grams of raspberries halved

Instructions:

Follow the method mentioned below to make keto raspberry and lemon loaf.

1.Assemble all the ingredients.

2.In the bread machine pan, add all the ingredients except raspberries and select the basic setting for bread and medium crust color, press start.

3.Prior to 5 minutes before the kneading cycle finishes, add raspberries(your machine will beep as a signal).

4.Bread machine will beep once the baking is done.

5.Remove bread pan from baking machine. Turn the bread pan upside down, give it a toss to remove bread easily place on baking rack let it cool down for few minutes before slicing.

6.serve.

1.8 Keto Peanut Butter Donut Recipe(grain, sugar, and gluten-free)

Total time of cooking

45 minutes

Servings

8

Nutrition facts

Calories 175 (per donut)

Protein 7g

Carbs 5g

Fiber 2g

Net carbs 3

Fat 14g

Ingredients:

Here is the list of ingredients required to make a keto peanut butter donut recipe.

- 1 and 1/4 cup of almond flour

- 1/2 cup of sugar substitute

- 1/3 cup and 2 tablespoons of unsweetened vanilla almond milk

- 5 tablespoons of no sugar added peanut butter

- 2 large eggs

- 1 teaspoon of baking powder

- 1/2 teaspoon of vanilla extract

- pinch of salt

For donut glaze

- 4 tablespoons of powdered peanut butter

- 3/4 tablespoon of confectioners' sugar

- 2 1/2 tablespoon of water

Instructions:

Follow the method mentioned below to make keto peanut butter donuts.

1.Assemble all the ingredients.

2.In the bread machine pan, add all the ingredients except unsweetened vanilla almond milk in the order mentioned by your bread machine – select the dough option from the control panel and press the start button.

3.Place dough in a large mixing bowl and add 1/3 cup of unsweetened vanilla almond milk. Fold it in the batter until it combines with dough and pourable batter forms.

4.Coat a donut pan with baking spray and pour the batter into the donut tray.

5.Place donut pan in the oven bake at 350 f for around 15 to 16 minutes.

6.Remove the donut pan out of the oven and let them cool down for few minutes.

Instructions for donut glaze:

1.For a donut glaze, add powdered peanut butter, confectioner sugar, and water in a bowl.

2.Mix well until a thick peanut butter glaze starts to form.

3.Add glaze layer on a donut.

4.Add toppings of your choice over donut glaze (you can use crushed peanuts or no-sugar-added chocolate chips.

1.9 Easy and Yummy Keto Blueberry Bread

Total time of cooking

5 hours

Servings

6

Nutrition facts

Calories 216 (per slice)

Protein 6g

Sugar 1g

Carbs 6g

Fiber 2g

Net carbs 4g

Fat 20g

Ingredients:

Here is the list of ingredients required to make a keto blueberry bread

- 1 cup of almond flour blanched

- 1/3 cup of blueberries

- 1/4 cup of coconut oil softened

- 2 large eggs at room temperature

- 1/2 cup of erythritol

- 2 tablespoons of canned coconut milk

- 1 teaspoon of vanilla extract

- 2 teaspoon bread machine yeast

Instructions:

Follow the method mentioned below to make keto blueberry bread.

1.Assemble all the ingredients.

2.In the bread machine pan, add all the ingredients except blueberries in the order mentioned by your bread machine.

3.Choose a basic cycle and medium crust from the settings.

4.Add blueberries when the bread machine beep, around five minutes before kneading completes.

5.Let it bake until the machine beeps.

6.When done, take out bread from the baking pan carefully and let it cool completely before serving.

7.slice and enjoy.

1.10 Low-Carb Keto Chocolate Breakfast Loaf

Total time of cooking

2 hours 40 minutes

Servings

12

Nutrition facts

Calories 133 (per slice)

Protein 4g

Carbs 5.5g

Fiber 3g

Net carbs 2.5g

Fat 10.5g

Ingredients:

Here is the list of ingredients required to make a low-carb keto chocolate breakfast loaf.

- 6 tablespoons of salted butter

- 4 eggs large

- 1/3 cup heaping full fat sour cream

- 1 1/3 cup almond flour

- 2/3 cup of sugar substitute

- 1/4 cup cocoa powder(unsweetened)

- 1 teaspoon vanilla extract

- 2 1/2 tablespoon keto chocolate chips

- 2 teaspoon instant yeast

Instructions:

Follow the method mentioned below to make low-carb keto chocolate breakfast loaf.

1.Add all the ingredients except chocolate chips to the bread machine pan. Follow the order recommended by your bread machine.

2.choose dough cycle from the settings panel. start press.

3.Add chocolate chips five minutes before the kneading cycle completes. (when the machine beeps as a signal).

4.When the dough cycle ends, remove the dough from the bread machine pan.

5.Coat loaf pan with baking spray and line with parchment paper.

6.Evenly spread the dough into the loaf pan and sprinkle keto chocolate chips at the surface of the loaf.

7.Bake it for around 50 minutes at 350 f in the preheated oven.

8.Insert a toothpick to check if your loaf is raw or done if it comes out clean, your loaf is done.

9.Cool it for a while before slicing.

1.11 Keto Rye Bread

Total time of cooking

2 hours 40 minutes

Servings

18

Nutrition facts

Calories 107 (per slice)

Protein 9.4g

Carbs 1.94g

Fiber 1.66g

Net carbs 7.44g

Fat 5g

Ingredients:

Here is the list of ingredients required to make keto rye bread.

- 1/2 cup of oat fiber

- 2 eggs beaten (at room temperature)

- 1.25 cups of vital wheat gluten

- 1 cup of warm, strong coffee

- 2/3 cup of flaxseed meal

- 2 tablespoons of unsweetened cocoa powder

- 2 tablespoons of erythritol powdered sweetener

- 2 tablespoons of butter(at room temperature)

- 1 tablespoon of caraway and 1 tablespoon of dill seeds

- 1 tablespoon active dry yeast

- 1 teaspoon honey

- 1 teaspoon pink Himalayan salt

- 1/2 teaspoon xanthan gum

Instructions:

Follow the method mentioned below to make keto rye bread.

1.Grab your container out of your bread machine.

2.Add all the ingredients (warm coffee, eggs, oat fiber, flaxseed meal, vital wheat gluten, add salt, erythritol, honey, xanthan gum, and butter around the outside edge of bread container not directly in the middle)now add active dry yeast, make a hole in the middle of dry ingredients, and add active dry yeast in the middle of the little hole to make sure the yeast does not come in contact with liquid ingredients. At the top of the mixture, add cocoa powder, caraway seeds, and dill seeds.

3.Put back the container in the bread machine, close the lid, and select basic white bread settings and dark crust from your machine control panel.

4.When the bread is done, remove it from the pan and cool it for a while on the oven rack.

5. slice and enjoy.

1.12 Soft And Fluffy Keto Walnut And Chocolate bread

Total time of cooking

2 hours 10 minutes

Servings

21

Nutrition facts

Calories 66 (per slice)

Protein 3g

Net carbs 1g

Fat 4.4g

Ingredients:

Here is the list of ingredients required to make walnut and chocolate bread.

- 3/4 cup of coconut flour

- 3/4 golden flaxseed grounded(use coffee bean grinder or multi grinder to make powder)

- 1/2 cup of erythritol

- 1/2 cup of dark chocolate (melted)

- 1/2 cup chopped walnuts(reserved half for topping and half for bread)

- 1 cup of hot water

- 3 tablespoons of psyllium husk powder(grounded in finer texture)

- 3 tablespoons of apple cider vinegar

- 9 large egg whites

- 3 teaspoons of baking powder

- 1 teaspoon of salt

Instructions:

Follow the method mentioned below to make keto walnut and chocolate bread.

1.Assemble all the ingredients.

2.Add all the ingredients except walnuts to the bread machine container in the order suggested by your bread machine.

3.Choose basic dough settings and press the start button. After kneading for few minutes, check the consistency of the dough and add one tablespoon of water or flour if required.

4.Five minutes prior to the last kneading, when the machine beeps, add walnuts.

5.Remove the dough from the pan when the kneading cycle ends.

6.Warmed up your oven at 350 f or 180 c.

7.Coat 8x4 pan lined at the bottom with parchment paper with baking spray. Spread the dough evenly.

8.Coat the top of the bread with chopped walnuts.

9.Bake for around 60 minutes in the preheated oven.

10.Place a wooden skewer in bread to check if it comes out clean it is done.

11.Cool it down on the oven rack before slicing.

12.Serve and enjoy.

1.13 Best Keto Coffee Cake

Total time of cooking

2 hours

Servings

16

Nutrition facts

Calories 167 (per slice)

Protein 3g

Net carbs 2g

Fat 16g

Total carbs 3g

Sugar 1g

Ingredients:

Here is the list of ingredients required to make keto coffee cake.

For the coffee cake batter:

- 1 1/2 cup of almond flour

- 1/2 cup of any keto sweetener

- 1/4 cup of heavy cream or coconut cream

- 1/3 cup of unsweetened almond milk

- 1/2 cup of melted butter or coconut oil

- 4 medium eggs at room temperature

- 2 tablespoons of coconut flour

- 2 teaspoons of baking powder

- 1/4 teaspoon of salt

- 2 teaspoons of vanilla extract

For the crumb topping:

- 1 cup of almond flour

- 1/2 cup of keto powdered sweetener

- 1/4 cup of soft butter or coconut oil

- 1/2 cup of nuts of your choice

- 1 teaspoon of ground cinnamon powder

For the cinnamon sugar:

- 1/4 cup of powdered sweetener

- 1 tablespoon of almond flour

- 1 teaspoon of ground cinnamon powder

For the sugar-free glaze:

- 1/3 cup of powdered erythritol

- 4 to 5 tablespoons of heavy cream

- 1 teaspoon of vanilla extract

Instructions:

Follow the method mentioned below to make keto coffee cake

1.Assemble all the ingredients.

2.Add all the ingredients of the coffee cake batter mentioned in the list into the bread machine container and select dough cycle.

3.During kneading, check the dough add water or flour if required according to the consistency of the dough.

4.When the machine beeps. Remove the dough from the bread machine.

5.At 350 f or 180 c preheat your oven.

6.For Crumb Topping:

Combine all of the crumb topping ingredients with the help of a fork until the mixture becomes crumbly.

7.For Cinnamon Sugar:

Take a bowl and mix together almond flour, ground cinnamon powder, and sweetener. Keep it aside.

8.Line a 9x9 inches square cake pan with parchment paper.

9.For assembling the first spread half of the cake batter to the pan. Now add a layer of cinnamon sugar and then again spread the remaining cake batter. Over the top of the cake, evenly spread crumb mixture.

10.Place the baking pan in preheated oven and bake for around 35 to 40 minutes or until of cake is golden browned.

11.Now, prepare a sugar-free glaze. Mix all the ingredients to make a sugar-free glaze until the glaze thickens, and powdered erythritol is dissolved.

12.Cut the cake into 16 slices and drizzle the glaze over the top of the coffee cake.

13.Serve and enjoy.

1.14 Easy And Tasty Keto Yogurt Cake

Total time of cooking

2 hours 55 minutes

Servings

12

Nutrition facts

Calories 188(per serving)

Protein 7g

Carbs 6g

Fat 16g

Fiber 4g

Ingredients:

Here is the list of ingredients for yogurt bread.

- 2 cups of almond flour

- 1 cup of Greek yogurt

- 1/2 cup of granulated erythritol

- 1/3 cup of melted unsalted butter

- 3 large eggs

- 2 tablespoons of coconut flour

- 1 1/2 tablespoon of lemon juice

- 1 tablespoon of lemon zest

- 2 teaspoons of bread machine yeast

For glaze:

- 1/2 cup of powdered erythritol

- 2 to 3 tablespoons of water

- 1 tablespoon of lemon juice

Instructions:

Follow the method mentioned below to make keto yogurt bread.

1.Assemble all the ingredients.

2.In the bread maker pan, add all the ingredients of lemon bread and choose basic bread and medium crust from the control panel to start the machine.

3.Check the consistency of dough during kneading. If needed, add two tablespoons of water.

4.When the baking cycle ends, place bread on a cooling rack.

5.For the glaze, add powdered erythritol and lemon juice, and water into the bowl mix until all ingredients are well combined.

6.Slice the cooled bread and top up with glaze.

Chapter 2: Bread Machine Lunch Recipes

2.1 Keto Low Carb Naan Flatbread

Total time of cooking

40 minutes

Servings

3

Nutrition facts

Calories 530 (per flatbread naan)

Protein 28g

Carbs 6g

Fat 41g

Fiber 2g

Ingredients:

Here is the list of ingredients required to make keto low carb naan flatbread.

- 1 1/2 and another 1/4 cup of almond flour blanched

- 1 1/2 cups of shredded mozzarella full fat

- 2/3 cup of protein powder unflavored

- 1 egg beaten

- 1 1/2 tablespoons of full-fat sour cream

- 1 teaspoon of baking powder

- pinch of salt

Instructions:

Follow the method mentioned below to make keto low carb naan flatbread.

1.Assemble all the ingredients.

2.In a microwave-proof bowl, add mozzarella and sour cream and melt in 30 seconds of intervals until both ingredients are fully melted down.

3.Place all the ingredients in the bread machine container and select the dough cycle. After five minutes of kneading, check the dough consistency. If needed, add water or flour.

4.When the dough cycle finishes, remove the dough from the container and let the dough rest for 15 to 20 minutes.

5.Once the dough has rested, divide your dough into three portions equally and add water into your hands to prevent dough from sticking into your fingers.

6.Shape each ball into round flat naan bread.

7.On a baking sheet lined with parchment paper and place your naan bread dough and bake for 7 to 8 minutes and grill for 1 to 2 minutes from both sides in the oven until golden brown color develops on the top of flatbread naan.

8.Serve fresh and enjoy.

2.2 Tasty And Delicious Keto Gingerbread Cake

Total time of cooking

3 hours

Servings

16

Nutrition facts

Calories 287 (per slice)

Protein 9.3g

Net carbs 4.3g

Fat 26.4g

Ingredients:

Here is the list of ingredients required to make keto gingerbread cake.

- 3 cups of almond flour

- 1/2 cup of keto brown sugar

- 2 to 3 tablespoons of ginger

- 1 tablespoon of ground cinnamon

- 3 teaspoons of baking powder

- 1 teaspoon of baking soda

- 1 teaspoon of ground cloves

- 1 teaspoon of salt

- 1 teaspoon of ground nutmeg

- 6 eggs

- 300 ml of whipping cream

- 60 g of melted butter

- 1 cup of chopped walnuts

- 1/4 cup sugar-free maple syrup (optional)

Instructions:

Follow the method mentioned below to make keto gingerbread cake.

1.Assemble all the ingredients.

2. Into bread machine container add all the wet ingredients and on top add dry ingredients except walnuts. Select a simple setting for dough. At nut signal, add walnuts five minutes before the last kneading period completes.

3.Select the cake option from settings, choose the medium crust, and press start.

4.When baking finishes, remove the cake from the pan and let it cool down for a while.

5.Slice and sprinkle powdered sweetener on the top of the cake.

2.3 Easy Keto Sourdough Bread Rolls Recipe

Total time of cooking

2 hours

Servings

8

Nutrition facts

Calories 263 (per bread roll)

Protein 12g

Net carbs 2g

Fat 20g

Fiber 10g

Carbs 12g

Ingredients:

Here is the list of ingredients required to make keto sourdough bread rolls.

- 1 1/2 cups of almond flour

- 1/2 cup of coconut flour

- 1/2 cup of flax meal

- 1/2 cup of apple cider vinegar

- 1/3 cup of psyllium husk

- 3/4 cup of egg whites

- 3/4 cup of buttermilk

- 1/2 cup of warm water

- 1 scoop of keto unflavored whey protein

- 2 whole eggs

- 3 tablespoons of melted butter

- 2 teaspoon of instant yeast

- 1 teaspoon of Italian seasoning

- 1 teaspoon of kosher salt

Instructions:

Follow the method mentioned below to make keto sourdough bread rolls.

1.In your bread machine container, add all the ingredients and select dough cycle from your bread machine control panel, and press start.

2.Check Dough during kneading. Add water or flour if required according to the consistency of the Dough.

3.when the kneading cycle finished. Remove Dough from bread machine container.

4.Preheat oven at 350 f.

5.Line a baking sheet with parchment paper.

6.Divide Dough into eight pieces and make small loaves/rolls using your hands.

7.With a sharp knife, mark cuts on the top of each roll. Bake for 35 minutes or until each bread roll turned golden brown.

8.Then remove the baking sheet from the oven and brush the top of each bread roll with melted butter, and sprinkle Italian seasoning on the bread roll as well.

9.Place back again in the oven for 2 to 3 minutes under the grill until rolls turned deep golden brown from the top in color. (keep checking them during grill, so they

don't burn)

10.Serve fresh and enjoy.

2.4 Keto Fathead Cinnamon Rolls

Total time of cooking

1 hour 45 minutes

Servings

5

Nutrition facts

Calories 290 (per cinnamon roll)

Protein 13g

Net carbs 5g

Fat 24g

Fiber 4g

Carbs 9g

Ingredients:

Here is the list of ingredients required to make keto fathead cinnamon rolls.

- 1 3/4 cups of almond flour(superfine)

- 3/4 cup of mozzarella cheese

- 3 tablespoons of coconut flour

- 3 tablespoons of confectioners erythritol

- 4oz cream cheese

- 1 large egg

- 2 teaspoons of instant yeast

Ingredients for cinnamon roll filling:

- 3 tablespoons of granulated erythritol

- 1 tablespoon of cinnamon powder

- 1 tablespoon of melted butter

Ingredients for icing:

- 1/4 cup of erythritol

- 1 tablespoon of vanilla almond milk

Instructions:

Follow the method mentioned below to make fathead cinnamon rolls.

1.Assemble all the ingredients.

2.Microwave cream cheese and mozzarella cheese in the microwave-proof bowl until melted.

3.Put all the ingredients of a cinnamon roll dough, including melted cheese mixture, into the bread machine container(first liquids, then dry ingredients on the top). Select dough cycle and press the start button.

4..Once the dough cycle ends, remove the dough from the container and place it on a floured surface and knead it with your hands for few minutes.

5.Use your hands to work with dough. Press out dough into an oval shape, do not use a rolling pin; otherwise, the dough will stick to the pin.

6.Make sure your dough is about 1/4 inch thick and 16 inches long. Now coat the top of the dough first with the melted butter and sprinkle granulated erythritol and cinnamon powder all over the dough. Now roll up the dough and cut it into five equal-sized pieces.

7.Leave rolls for 20 minutes to let them rise a bit.

8.Grease Parchment paper-lined baking sheet with baking spray.

9.At 350 f degrees, bake for around 20 minutes or until golden brown.

10.Remove rolls from the oven and let them cool down for few minutes.

11.Make icing for rolls. Take a bowl and add confectioners erythritol and almond milk and mix until dissolved.

12.Coat cinnamon rolls with icing and enjoy.

2.5 Mini Crispy Crust Keto Quiche With Filling

Total time of cooking

1 hour 15 minutes

Servings

6

Nutrition facts

Calories 470 (per slice)

Protein 14.5g

Net carbs 5.5g

Fat 44.2g

Fiber 4.2g

Carbs 9.7g

Ingredients:

Here is the list of ingredients required to make keto quiche crust.

- 1/4 cup of Coconut flour
- 1/4 cup of almond flour
- 1/3 cup of cold butter
- 1 large egg
- 1/2 teaspoon of salt

Ingredients for egg mixture:

- 3/4 cup of whipping cream
- 4 large eggs
- 1/2 teaspoon of black pepper
- 1/2 teaspoon of salt

Ingredients for filling:

- Mozzarella cheese
- Smoked salmon
- Dill for garnishing

Instructions:

Follow the method mentioned below to make keto quiche crust.

1. Assemble all the ingredients of the crust.

2. Add all the ingredients mentioned above for quiche crust in the bread machine pan.

3. Close the lid, choose dough cycle, and press the start button.

4.When the kneading period ends, remove the dough, make a ball out of the dough with your hands. wrap the dough with foil, flatten it and freeze it for around 15 minutes.

5.Take out the dough from the freezer after 15 minutes and divide it into six equal portions.

6.Grease mini pie pan with butter.

7.Shape pie dough using your hands.

8.To avoid air bubbles, prick holes with a fork.

9.Again, freeze for 15 minutes.

10.After 15 minutes, bake for 15 to 16 mins at 350 f or 180 c if the dough's center rises during baking. Press down with the back of the spoon.

For egg mixture:

11.In a bowl, add all ingredients of the egg mixture mentioned above and whisk until well mixed.

Assembling:

12.Place cheese and smoked salmon into the baked crust.

13.Pour the egg mixture on top, garnish with dill.

14.Bake for 20 minutes at 350 f or 180 c.

2.6 Keto Garlic Bread

Total time of cooking

3 hours

Servings

12

Nutrition facts

Calories 309 (per slice)

Protein 9g

Net carbs 5.5g

Fat 29g

Carbs 5g

Ingredients:

Here is the list of ingredients required to make keto garlic bread.

- 2 1/2 cups of Almond flour

- 1 1/2 cups of egg whites

- 2/3 cup of melted butter

- 1 1/2 tablespoon bread machine yeast

- 1 teaspoon of salt

Ingredients for topping:

- 1/2 cup of melted butter

- 1 tablespoon of dried parsley

- 2 teaspoons of garlic powder

Instructions:

Follow the method mentioned below to make keto garlic bread.

1. Assemble all the ingredients of the crust.

2. Add all the garlic bread items to the bread machine container — liquid ingredients on the bottom and dry ingredients on top. Just be careful to keep the yeast away from the liquid by putting yeast on top of dry ingredients.

3. Select basic bread cycle and medium crust from the settings panel and press the start button.

4.When baking is finished, remove bread from the pan and let it cool completely on the oven rack.

5.Cut down into 12 equal pieces.

6.For the topping, in a boiler, mix together butter, parsley, and garlic powder.

7.Spread topping on the bread evenly.

8.Again, place in the oven and broil for few minutes to crisp up the bread.

9.Serve.

2.7 Keto Coconut Crust Pizza (Eggless)

Total time of cooking

1 hour

Servings

10

Nutrition facts

Calories 74 (per slice)

Protein 2.6g

Net carbs 0.8g

Fat 5.8g

Ingredients:

Here is the list of ingredients required to make keto coconut crust pizza.

- 1/2 cup of coconut flour

- 1/2 cup of grounded golden flaxseeds or flaxseed meal

- 2 tablespoons of olive oil

- 2 tablespoons of finely grounded psyllium husk

- 1 tablespoon of Italian seasoning

- 2 teaspoons of active dry yeast

- 1/2 teaspoon of salt

- 240 ml hot or boiling water

Ingredients for pizza sauce:

- 200g canned peeled tomatoes

- 2 to 3 tablespoons of tomatoes paste

- 2 tablespoons olive oil

- 2 to 3 teaspoons salt

- 1 teaspoon dry basil

- 1 teaspoon onion powder

- 1 teaspoon dried parsley

- 1 teaspoon garlic powder

- 1 teaspoon black pepper

- 1 teaspoon oregano

(Blend all the ingredients, until smooth paste/sauce is formed)

Ingredients for topping:

- 180g vegan cheese

- 3 to 4 sliced button mushrooms

- 4 to 5 sliced black olives

- tricolor capsicum (cut into strips)

- chopped parsley for garnishing

Instructions:

Follow the method mentioned below to make keto coconut crust pizza.

1.Assemble all the ingredients of the crust.

2.In bread machine container, add yeast and hot water together and mix and let it sit for 10 minutes, so the yeast dissolves in water and becomes creamy in texture.

3.After 10 minutes, add olive oil, coconut flour, flaxseeds, psyllium husk, Italian seasoning, and salt.

4.Close the lid: select dough cycle, and press the start button.

5.Remove dough from the bread machine. Spread out in greased pizza pan.

6.Cover with cloth or towel and set aside for around 25 minutes for rising.

7.Prick holes with a fork to release air bubbles during bake for around 15 to 20 minutes on the lowest rack of your oven at 350 f or 180 c, then flip over the side and bake for another 5 minutes.

8.Remove pizza from the oven, spread the pizza sauce, then add vegan cheese and all other ingredients mentioned in the topping list.

9.Bake again for 10 minutes on the middle rack of the oven.

10.Remove the pizza from the oven. When it's done, sprinkle chopped parsley all over the pizza.

11.Make slices with a pizza cutter and serve.

2.8 Tasty And Easy Keto Cornbread

Total time of cooking

1 hour 10 minutes

Servings

12

Nutrition facts

Calories 254 (per serving)

Protein 8.4g

Carbs 6g

Fat 22.7g

Fiber 3g

Ingredients:

Here is the list of ingredients required to make keto cornbread.

- 2 cups of almond flour

- 1 cup of shredded cheddar cheese

- 1/2 cup of melted butter

- 1/4 cup of coconut flour

- 1/4 cup of sour cream

- 2/3 can of baby corn roughly chopped

- 3 large eggs

- 2 1/2 teaspoons of instant yeast

- 1 teaspoon of pink Himalayan salt

- 25 drops of liquid stevia

Instructions:

Follow the method mentioned below to make keto coconut crust pizza.

1.Assemble all the ingredients of the crust.

2.In the bread machine pan, add all the ingredients except baby corn, starting with liquid ingredients first and dry ingredients in the last).close the lid and select dough cycle. Add water or flour if required during kneading.

3.When the machine beeps, five minutes before final kneading begins, add chopped baby corn.

4.Remove dough from the pan. Spread in a casserole dish.

5.Bake for around 40 to 42 minutes in the preheated oven at 350 f.

6.Allow to cool down for few minutes before slicing.

7.Serve and enjoy.

2.9 Keto Tomato And Parmesan buns

Total time of cooking

1 hour 40 minutes

Servings

5

Nutrition facts

Calories 261 (per bun)

Protein 14.5g

Net carbs 4.9g

Fat 18.9g

Fiber 8.3g

Ingredients:

Here is the list of ingredients required to make keto tomato and parmesan buns.

- 1/2 cup of coconut flour

- 3/4 cup of almond flour

- 1/4 cup flax meal

- 1/3 cup chopped sun-dried tomatoes

- 2/3 cup of parmesan cheese

- 2 1/2 tablespoons of psyllium husk powder

- 2 tablespoons of sesame seeds

- 2 teaspoon of active dry yeast

- 1 teaspoon cream of tartar

- 1/2 teaspoon of salt

- 1 cup boiling water

- 3 large egg whites

- 1 whole egg

Instructions:

Follow the method mentioned below to make keto tomato and parmesan buns.

1.Add all the ingredients in the bread machine container except sun-dried tomato. Start with liquid ingredients first, and then add all the dry ingredients with yeast on top. Make sure yeast does not come in contact with liquid.

2.Select dough from the control panel and start the machine.

3.Remove dough from the bread machine and divide into five equal parts. Make balls with the help of your hands.

4.Place them with a 2 to 3 inches gap (buns will grow in size once baked) on a non-stick Baking sheet .let it rise for around 25 minutes. Sprinkle sesame seeds all over the bun.

5.At 350 f in the preheated oven, bake for 35 to 40 minutes.

6.Remove once done and cool on a baking rack before serving.

2.10 Eggless Keto Focaccia

Total time of cooking

1 hour 45 minutes

Servings

25

Nutrition facts

Calories 105 (per serving)

Protein 2.1g

Net carbs 1.6g

Fat 8.9g

Ingredients:

Here is the list of ingredients required to make an eggless keto focaccia recipe

- 2 1/2 cups of almond flour

- 1/3 cup of golden flaxseeds

- 1/2 cup of coconut flour

- 2 cups of hot boiling water

- 5 tablespoons of psyllium husk powder

- 2 teaspoons of bread machine yeast

- 1 teaspoon of salt

For oil mixture:

- 1/2 cup of olive oil extra virgin

- 3 to 4 cloves garlic (minced)

- 1 teaspoon of dried or fresh thyme

- 1 teaspoon of dried or fresh thyme

- 1/2 teaspoon of black pepper

- 1/2 teaspoon of salt

Instructions:

Follow the method mentioned below to make eggless keto focaccia.

1.Turn on your stove and cook all the items mentioned in the list for oil mixture in a small pot over low to medium heat and until garlic turns brown, then turn off the stove. Keep two tablespoons of oil mixture for greasing the baking pan, two tablespoons to brush the dough's top, and remaining to add in the dough.

2.In the bread machine pan, add all the ingredients of focaccia mentioned in the list of ingredients above, including the remaining oil mixture. And start the dough cycle when the dough cycle ends. Remove the dough from the pan.

3.With two tablespoons of oil mixture, brush the bottom of a deep-dish pizza pan. Spread the dough into a pan, flatten the dough using your hands. make as many dimples as you like with your fingers on the dough.

4.With two tablespoons of the reserved oil, brush the top of the dough.

5.Sprinkle some flaky salt and some fresh thyme and rosemary on top(optional).

6.At 350 f preheated oven bake for about 30 to 40 minutes on lowest rack.

7.Turn off the oven once ready and for around 30 minutes, let it sit in the oven to dry.

8.Once completely cool, cut into small squares and enjoy.

2.11 Keto Fathead Dough Stuffed Sausage Buns

Total time of cooking

1 hour

Servings

6

Nutrition facts

Calories 363(per serving)

Protein 19g

fiber 1g

Carbs 3g

Fat 30g

Ingredients:

Here is the list of ingredients required to make keto fathead dough stuffed sausage buns.

For fathead dough:

- 1 oz of cream cheese

- 3/4 cup of almond flour

- 1.5 cup of mozzarella cheese

- 12 oz ground breakfast sausage(pre-seasoned)

- 1 large egg

- 1 1/2 teaspoons of instant yeast

Instructions:

Follow the method mentioned below to make keto fathead dough stuffed sausage buns.

1.Assemble all the ingredients.

2.Melt cream cheese and mozzarella cheese in the microwave for 30 seconds.

3.In the bread machine pan, add all the ingredients except sausages, choose dough cycle, and press start.

4.When the dough cycle completes, take out the dough from the bread machine pan.

5.Warm up your oven at 400 F.

6.Turn on the stove and preheat a pan to medium-high heat.

7.Cut pre-seasoned sausage into six pieces equally, add to the hot pan and cook. Once cooked, set aside and let them cool down.

8.Divide your dough into six equal balls. Use your hands to flatten out each ball or either roll it. Place cooked sausage in the middle of the dough, wrap it, and make a ball with your hands. Repeat the procedure with all other dough balls.

9.On a baking sheet lined with parchment paper, place sausage balls, put seam side down.

10.Bake for around 15 to 20 minutes or until golden browned.

11.Serve.

2.12 Keto Chicken Pot Pie Turnover bread

Total time of cooking

1 hour 15 minutes

Servings

9

Nutrition facts

Calories 589(per serving)

Protein 37.9g

Net carbs 9.6g

Fat 45.7g

Ingredients:

Here is the list of ingredients required to make keto chicken pot pie turnover bread.

Ingredients for dough:

- 3 cups of almond flour

- 7 cups of mozzarella cheese

- 2 eggs

- 1 tablespoon of water

- 2 teaspoon of xanthan gum

- 2 teaspoon of instant yeast

Ingredients for pot pie mixture:

- 1/2 cup of diced onion

- 3 cups of shredded cooked chicken

- 1/2 cup red onion diced

- 1 cup chicken broth

- 3 tablespoons of freshly chopped parsley

- 1 tablespoon of coconut flour

- 8 oz mushrooms chopped

- 4 oz cream cheese

- 1 teaspoon thyme

- 3 minced garlic cloves

Instructions:

Follow the method mentioned below to make keto chicken pot pie turnover bread.

1.Assemble all the ingredients.

2.Add all the ingredients of dough mentioned in the list in the bread machine pan, close the lid, choose dough cycle, and start the machine.

3.Take the dough out of the bread machine when kneading finishes. Cover with a kitchen towel for around 20 to 25 minutes and let it rise.

4.Turn on the stove over medium-high heat melt butter in a large pan.

5.Add onion and cook for five minutes until it softens. Now add mushrooms, garlic, and thyme, sprinkle pepper and salt and cook for 5 minutes more until mushroom becomes tender.

6.Add coconut flour, whisk in the broth and proceed to cook for 3 to 5 minutes until the mixture thickens. Add chicken and turn the heat to low.

7.Add cream cheese and cook until cream cheese is fully melted. Add parsley and sprinkle salt. Remove from the stove and turn off the heat, and let it cool down.

8.To ensure all ingredients are fully combined, knead the dough with your hands.

9.Lay down parchment paper on a floured surface, place dough over it, put another parchment paper on top, and roll dough with a rolling pin into a rectangular shape (dough should be around 1/4 inches thick). Cut edges of the dough to form a perfect rectangular shape using a knife or pizza cutter. Cut further into nine tiny rectangles.

10.Place a spoonful of chicken pot pie mixture into each rectangle and fold over. Repeat the same procedure with other rectangles.

11.With egg brush, the tops of turnover bread.

12.Place turnovers in a non-stick baking sheet and bake for 20 minutes at 375 f degrees.

13.Serve and enjoy.

2.13 Keto Pecan Chocolate Pie

Total time of cooking

2 hour 15 minutes

Servings

8

Nutrition facts

Calories 504(per serving)

Protein 11g

Carbs 11g

Fat 49g

Fiber 7g

Ingredients:

Here is the list of ingredients required to make keto pecan chocolate pie.

For the sweet pie crust:

- 1.25 cups of almond flour

- 1/4 cup of cream cheese

- 3 tablespoons of unsalted butter

- 2 tablespoons of coconut flour

- 1 beaten egg

- 1/2 teaspoon of xanthan gum

- 1 teaspoon of instant yeast

- 1/4 pink Himalayan salt

- 15 drops of stevia

For the chocolate pie filling:

- 1 cup of heavy whipping cream

- 1 cup of raw chopped pecans

- 1/4 cup of butter

- 3 eggs large (room temperature)

- 4 oz unsweetened chocolate chopped

- 2 tablespoons of erythritol

- 1 teaspoon of vanilla extract

- 1/4 teaspoon of pink salt

- 1/4 teaspoon liquid stevia

Instructions:

Follow the method mentioned below to make keto chocolate pie.

1. Add all the sweet pie crust ingredients to the bread machine container. Select the dough cycle press the start button.

2. When kneading completes, remove dough from pan, make a ball of dough seal in plastic wrap, and freeze for at least 20 minutes.

3. Take out the dough after 20 minutes from the freezer. Place dough between two parchment papers, roll out the dough using a rolling pin, spread on the greased pie pan, flatten dough with your fingers, and prick holes using a fork in the crust.

4. Freeze again for 15 minutes.

5. At 350 F/180 C preheated oven, bake for 15 minutes or until it turns light brown.

6. Once done, allow the crust to cool down. Meanwhile, make the chocolate pie filling.

7. On a double boiler, heat butter, and heavy cream until it completely melts down, remove from the boiler and add the chocolate mix well until it turns smooth in texture. Add vanilla extract, erythritol, stevia, and salt and mix well until dissolved.

8. In a separate bowl, whisk eggs, add them into the chocolate mixture, and mix until completely blends.

9. Spread pecans on the bottom layer of cooled pie. Then pour the chocolate mixture on top and bake again for 20 minutes.

10. Before serving, let the tart cool for a while.

11. Before eating, sprinkle with unsweetened cocoa powder or powdered erythritol.

2.14 Starbucks Inspired Keto Poppy Seeds And Lemon Loaf

Total time of cooking

3 hour 40 minutes

Servings

12

Nutrition facts

Calories 201(per serving)

Protein 9g

Carbs 6g

Fat 17g

Fiber 3g

Ingredients:

Here is the list of ingredients required to make poppy seeds and lemon loaf.

- 2 1/8 cups of almond flour

- 1/2 cup of any sweetener

- 6 eggs large

- 3 tablespoons of unsalted melted butter

- 2 tablespoons of poppy seeds

- 2 tablespoons of lemon juice

- 1 1/2 heaping tablespoons of lemon zest

- 1 1/2 bread machine yeast

For Glaze:

- 1/2 cup of erythritol(powdered)

- 1 to 2 tablespoons of water

- 1 tablespoon of lemon juice

Instructions:

Follow the method mentioned below to make poppy seeds and lemon bread.

1.Combine all the ingredients in the bread machine container in the order suggested by your bread maker.

2.Pick basic bread and medium crust from the options of the bread machine control panel. And press the start button.

3.Check during kneading. Add two tablespoons of water if needed.

4.When baking finishes, remove bread from the bread machine container.

5.Leave it for 15 minutes to cool down before slicing.

6.For Glaze add lemon juice and erythritol to a bowl and slowly add water mix until fully incorporated.

7.Spread the Glaze over cooled bread slices and enjoy.

Chapter 3: Bread Machine Dinner Recipes

3.1 Keto Garlic Flatbread

Total time of cooking

1 hour 20 minutes

Servings

8

Nutrition facts

Calories 134(per serving)

Protein 7.7g

Net carbs 2.1g

Fat 9.9g

Ingredients:

Here is the list of ingredients required to make keto garlic flatbread.

Ingredients for dough:

- 1/2 cup of grated mozzarella cheese

- 1/2 cup of ground almonds or milled linseed

- 1 cup of courgette grated

- 1/3 cup of coconut flour

- 3 large eggs

- 1 1/2 teaspoons of bread machine yeast

- 1 teaspoon of garlic powder

- 1 teaspoon of mixed herbs

- 1 teaspoon of baking powder

- 1/4 teaspoon of xanthan gum

- 1/4 teaspoon of salt

For the garlic butter:

- 2 tablespoons of butter melted

- 1 to 2 garlic cloves (minced)

Instructions:

Follow the method mentioned below to make keto garlic flatbread.

1. Assemble all the ingredients.

2. Place keto garlic flatbread ingredients in the bread machine container, choose dough cycle, and start the machine. After five minutes of kneading, check the dough's consistency add one to two tablespoons of water if required.

3.Take out the dough from the bread machine once the dough cycle finishes. Grease your non-stick round pizza pan and spread the dough. Flatten the dough using your hands. leave it for 10 minutes to rise.

4.Place the baking pan in 350 degrees preheated oven and bake for around 25 to 30 minutes or until flatbread turns light golden brown.

5.Turn on your stove at low, medium heat. In a pan, heat butter first, then add minced garlic and cook until garlic turns nut brown.

6.Spread garlic butter mixture over the top of flatbread and brush evenly all over the baked flatbread.

7.Cut flatbread into eight slices and serve.

3.2 Simple And Tasty Keto Zucchini Bread

Total time of cooking

3 hours 20 minutes

Servings

14

Nutrition facts

Calories 186(per serving)

Protein 8.3g

Net carbs 2.7g

Fat 15.1g

Ingredients:

Here is the list of ingredients required to make keto zucchini bread.

- 1 1/2 cups of grated zucchini(courgette)

- 1/2 cup of ground almonds

- 3/4 cup of melted unsalted butter

- 2/3 cup of grated mozzarella cheese

- 2/3 cup of coconut flour

- 5 eggs large

- 2 teaspoons of bread machine yeast

- 1 teaspoon of dried oregano

- 1/2 teaspoon of xanthan gum

- 1/2 teaspoon of salt

Instructions:

Follow the method mentioned below to make keto zucchini bread.

1. Assemble all the ingredients.

2. Remove the Bread machine container. Add all the ingredients of zucchini keto bread to the container. Place the container into the bread machine, close the lid, select basic bread cycle and medium crust, and press the start button.

3. Check the dough consistency. After five minutes, add two tablespoons of water if required.

4. When the Baking period is finished. Remove the bread from the pan and place it into the cooling rack for some time.

5. Cut into slices and serve.

3.3 Low Carb Keto Pumpkin Spice Bread

Total time of cooking

3 hours

Servings

12

Nutrition facts

Calories 191(per serving)

Protein 7g

Net carbs 4g

Fat 16g

Total carbs 7g

Ingredients:

Here is the list of ingredients required to make pumpkin bread.

- 2 cups of almond flour

- 3/4 cup pumpkin puree

- 3/4 cup of erythritol

- 5 medium-sized eggs

- 4 tablespoons of softened butter

- 3 tablespoons of heavy whipping cream

- 2 tablespoons of coconut flour

- 3 teaspoons of pumpkin pie spice

- 1 1/2 teaspoons of instant yeast

- 1 teaspoon vanilla extract

Instructions:

Follow the method mentioned below to make keto pumpkin bread.

1.In a Bread machine container, add all the ingredients(liquids first followed by the dry ingredients in the end).

2.Select basic bread settings, medium crust, and loaf size. Start the machine.

3.After 5 minutes of mixing check dough, add 2 to 3 tablespoons of water required.

4.Once baking is done. Shift bread to a cooling rack and let it cool down completely.

5.Cut into 12 equal slices and serve.

3.4 Tasty And Easy Keto Olive Bread

Total time of cooking

2 hours

Servings

16

Nutrition facts

Calories 93(per serving)

Protein 3.5g

Net carbs 1.7g

Fat 6.4g

Ingredients:

Here is the list of ingredients required to make keto olive bread.

- 1 cup of hot water

- 3/4 cup of coconut flour

- 3 whole eggs

- 3/4 cup of golden flaxseed

- 3/4 cup of black olives(cut in small cubes)

- 3 tablespoons of psyllium husk (finely grounded)

- 3 tablespoons of apple cider vinegar

- 2 tablespoons of olive oil

- 2 teaspoons of instant yeast

- 1 teaspoon of salt

- 1 teaspoon of basil

- 1 teaspoon of ground oregano

- 1 teaspoon of thyme

- 1/2 teaspoon of garlic powder

Instructions:

Follow the method mentioned below to make keto olive bread.

1.Follow the order recommended by your bread maker, except olives add all the ingredients to the pan.

2.Choose your bread maker dough settings.

3.Five minutes before the last kneading cycle when the machine beeps, add olives

4.when the dough is formed, remove it from the bread machine.

5.Spread the dough evenly in the loaf pan lined with parchment paper.

6.Bake at 350 f at the middle rack of the preheated oven for 40 minutes .

7.Cooldown for sometime before slicing.

3.5 Classic Keto Meatloaf Recipe

Total time of cooking

2 hours 30 minutes

Servings

14

Nutrition facts

Calories 245(per serving)

Protein 13g

Net carbs 2g

Fat 19g

fiber 1g

Ingredients:

Here is the list of ingredients required to make keto meatloaf.

For meatloaf:

- 2 lbs ground beef

- 1 cup of almond flour

- 2 eggs large

- 1/2 chopped onion

- 4 garlic cloves (minced)

- 1 teaspoon of salt

- 1 teaspoon instant yeast

- 1/4 teaspoon of black pepper

For meatloaf sauce:

- 1/2 of cup tomato sauce (sugar-free)

- 2 tablespoons of mustard

- 2 tablespoons of vinegar

- 2 tablespoons of sweetener

- 2 tablespoons of olive oil

- 2 tablespoons of Worcestershire sauce

Instructions:

Follow the method mentioned below to make keto meatloaf.

1.Assemble all the ingredients.

2.In the bread machine container, add the eggs, almond flour, ground beef, garlic cloves, onion, black, salt, and instant yeast. Close the lid and select the dough option from the bread machine control panel.

2.During kneading, check the dough's consistency if required, add 2 to 3 tablespoons of water.

3.Turn off the bread machine once the dough cycle completes. Transfer the loaf mixture to a non-stick loaf pan.

4.Bake at 350 F/180 C for 35 minutes in the preheated oven.

5.Add all the ingredients in a medium mixing bowl mentioned in the list for meatloaf sauce. mix until combine .

6.Spread sauce evenly over top of the meatloaf. And bake for 40 minutes more.

7.Let it cool down for 15 minutes before serving.

3.6 Classic Keto Cheese Bread

Total time of cooking

4 hours

Servings

16

Nutrition facts

Calories 88(per serving)

Protein 3.25g

Carbs 2.25g

Fat 7.5g

fiber 0.3g

Ingredients:

Here is the list of ingredients required to make keto classic cheese bread.

- 1/4 cup of melted butter

- 1/2 cup of peanut flour

- 4 large egg yolks

- 5 oz cream cheese

- 2 tablespoons of golden monk fruit sweetener

- 1 teaspoon bread machine yeast

- 1 teaspoon Himalayan salt

- 1 teaspoon vanilla extract

Instructions:

Follow the method mentioned below to make keto classic cheese bread.

1.In order suggested by your bread maker. Add all the ingredients into the bread machine container (liquid ingredients first, then dry ingredients).

2.Choose basic bread settings and light crust also loaf size.

3.Start the machine check the dough during the kneading period. If needed, add two to three tablespoons of water.

4.Once baking is finished. Turn off the machine and let bread rest for few minutes.

5.Place bread on a cooling rack and leave it for 10 to 15 minutes.

6.Cut into 16 slices and enjoy.

3.7 Easy Keto Dinner Buns Low Carb

Total time of cooking

1 hour 50 minutes

Servings

8

Nutrition facts

Calories 170(per serving)

Protein 7g

Net Carbs 2g

Fat 13g

Ingredients:

Here is the list of ingredients required to make keto dinner buns.

- 1 1/4 cups of almond flour

- 1 cup of hot water

- 3 egg whites

- 5 tablespoons of psyllium husk powder

- 2 tablespoons of sesame seeds

- 2 teaspoons of bread machine yeast

- 2 teaspoons of vinegar

- 1/2 teaspoon of rock salt

Instructions:

Follow the method mentioned below to make keto dinner buns.

1.In order suggested by your bread maker. Add water, vinegar, egg whites, almond flour, psyllium husk powder, rock salt, and yeast(liquid ingredients first, then dry ingredients).

2.Choose dough cycle and start the machine.

3.Take out the dough from the pan once the dough cycle ends.

4.Divide dough into eight equal portions. And make balls with your hands. to prevent dough from sticking your hands, wet your hands a little before doing this.

5.Leave them for around 20 minutes to let them rise in size.

6.Place buns in a parchment paper-lined baking sheet with a 2 to 3 inches gap.

7.On top of each bun, sprinkle white and black sesame seeds.

8.Put in the oven preheated oven for 50 to 55 minutes at 350 F/ 180 C.

9.Let it cool down before eating.

3.8 Delicious And Easy Keto Tahini Almond Bread

Total time of cooking

2 hour 50 minutes

Servings

10

Nutrition facts

Calories 160(per serving)

Protein 7.3g

Carbs 0.6g

Fat 13.5g

Ingredients:

Here is the list of ingredients required to make tahini bread.

- 1 cup of tahini

- 1/2 cup of almond flour

- 2 large size eggs

- 1 1/2 tablespoons of lemon juice

- 2 teaspoons of chia seeds

- 1 teaspoon of vanilla extract

- 1 teaspoon of instant yeast

- 1 teaspoon of salt

Instructions:

Follow the method mentioned below to make tahini almond bread.

1. Add eggs, lemon juice, vanilla extract, tahini, almond flour, chia seeds, yeast, and salt into your bread machine container.

2.Close the bread machine's lid, pick the basic bread settings and medium crust, press the start button.

3.Once the bread is baked, let it rest few minutes in the bread machine.

4.Remove the bread from bread machine and transfer to oven rack for cooling purpose.

5.Once the bread is cooled down, slice and serve.

3.9 Keto Low Carb Savory Pie-Salmon Quiche

Total time of cooking

2 hour 20 minutes

Servings

10

Nutrition facts

Calories 320.42(per serving)

Protein 15.95g

Total Carbs 6.98g

Fat 25.54g

Fiber 3.02g

Sugar 1.4g

Ingredients:

Here is the list of ingredients required to make keto low-carb savory pie.

For the savory pie crust:

- 3/4 cup of almond flour

- 3 tablespoons of coconut flour

- 1/3 cup of sesame seeds

- 3 tablespoons of olive oil

- 3 to 4 tablespoons of water

- 1 egg large

- 2 teaspoons of instant yeast

- 1/2 teaspoon of salt

For quiche filling:

- 8 oz salmon

- 1/2 cup of whipping cream

- 1/2 cup of shredded cheese

- 1/4 cup of parmesan

- 4 eggs

- 1 chopped small onion

- 1 chopped green onion

- 2 1/2 tablespoons of butter

- 1 1/2 tablespoons of fresh dill or parsley

- 1/4 teaspoon ground black pepper

- 1 teaspoon salt

Instructions:

Follow the method mentioned below to make keto low-carb savory pie.

1. Add all the savory pie crust ingredients to the bread machine container. Select the dough cycle press the start button.

2.When kneading completes, remove dough and spread on the greased pie pan, flatten dough with your fingers and prick holes using a fork in the crust.

3.At 350 F/180 C preheated oven, bake for 15 minutes or until it turns light brown.

4.Once done, allow the crust to cool down. Meanwhile, make salmon quiche filling.

5.On a medium heat pan, sauté onion in butter until it softens.

6.In a separate bowl, add eggs, whipping cream, cheese, pepper, and salt, whisk until well mixed.

7.On baked crust, first spread cooked onion and fresh parsley/dill, .then add salmon and egg mixture on top.

8.Bake again for 35 to 40 minutes.

9.Allow the salmon quiche to cool for 10 minutes before serving.

10.Serve with fresh cream or salad.

3.10 Keto Fathead Stuffed Pizza Buns

Total time of cooking

1 hour 30 minutes

Servings

4

Nutrition facts

Calories 443(per serving)

Protein 26g

Total Carbs 10g

Fat 34g

Fiber 2g

Ingredients:

Here is the list of ingredients required to make keto fathead stuffed pizza buns.

For fathead dough:

- 1 1/2 cups of shredded mozzarella (melted)

- 3 eggs (1 for egg wash,2 for dough)

- 3/4 cup of almond flour

- 5 tablespoons of cream cheese (melted)

- 2 teaspoons of instant yeast

- 2 teaspoons of xanthan gum

- pinch of salt

For the stuffed filling:

- 1/4 cup cheddar or mozzarella cheese

- 4 tablespoons of cooked Italian sausage

- 8 slices of pepperoni

- 2 tablespoons of feta cheese

For garnishing:

- 1/4 cup of shredded parmesan

- 1 tablespoon of butter

- 1 teaspoon of Italian seasoning

Instructions:

Follow the method mentioned below to make keto fathead pizza buns.

1. Assemble all the ingredients.

2. In the bread machine container, add all the ingredients of fathead pizza dough in the order suggested by your bread machine: select dough cycle and press start. During kneading, checks dough consistency if required, add two tablespoons of water.

3. When the machine beeps, remove dough from the pan and knead with wet hands for few minutes. Divide the dough into four equal balls.

4. Flatten all four dough balls with a rolling pin, fill in the stuffed filling ingredients in the center of each ball and close the ball with your hands.

5. Brush each ball with egg wash, place stuffed pizza buns on a non-stick baking sheet and bake for 25 to 30 minutes on the middle rack of the oven at 350 F/180 C.

6. Mix Italian seasoning with melted butter and brush over the top of each bun. Sprinkle parmesan cheese over the pizza buns and serve.

3.11 Keto Onion And Cheese Bread Low Carb

Total time of cooking

3 hour 10 minutes

Servings

23

Nutrition facts

Calories 75(per serving)

Protein 7.5g

Net Carbs 1.5g

Fat 7g

Fiber 1g

Ingredients:

Here is the list of ingredients required to make keto onion and cheese bread.

- 2 cups of almond flour

- 1.5 cups of shredded cheese

- 1/4 cup of chopped green onions

- 1 cup of water

- 1/4 cup of sour cream

- 1/2 chopped small onion

- 4 scoops of unflavored whey powder

- 1 chopped shallot

- 3 minced garlic cloves

- 2 teaspoon of instant yeast

- 1 teaspoon of chili flakes

- 1 teaspoon of xanthan gum

- 1/2 teaspoon of salt

- 1/2 teaspoon of pepper

Instructions:

Follow the method mentioned below to make keto onion and cheese bread.

1.Put all the onion and cheese bread ingredients into the bread machine pan in the order suggested by your bread maker. Do not add onions and shallot Close down the lid of the machine, select simple bread settings and choose medium crust, and start the machine.

2.When the machine beeps for extra ingredients, add onions and shallot.

3.When done, remove baked bread from the pan and let it cool down.

4.Once cooled, cut into slices and enjoy.

3.12 Keto Pesto Chicken Cheese Pizza

Total time of cooking

1 hour

Servings

8

Nutrition facts

Calories 387(per slice)

Protein 27.2g

Net Carbs 5.1g

Fat 28.9g

Ingredients:

Here is the list of ingredients required to make keto pesto chicken cheese pizza.

- 1 1/2 cups of almond flour

- 1 egg

- 3 1/2 cups of shredded mozzarella

- 2 tablespoons of olive oil

- 2 to 3 tablespoons of water

- 1 1/2 teaspoons of dry yeast

- 1 teaspoon of xanthan gum

- 1 teaspoon of salt

For topping:

- 3/4 cup of shredded chicken

- 1/2 cups of shredded mozzarella

- 6 cherry tomatoes

- 3 tablespoons of pesto

- 2 tablespoons of sliced roasted bell pepper

- 1 1/2 tablespoons of keto garlic sauce

- 4 oz sliced mozzarella

Instructions:

Follow the method mentioned below to make keto pesto chicken cheese pizza.

1.Meltdown 3 1/2 cups of mozzarella cheese in a microwave oven.

2.Place water, olive oil, egg, mozzarella cheese, almond flour, xanthan gum, salt, and yeast on top of dry ingredients into the machine pan.

3.Pick dough cycle from settings and start the machine.

4.When the kneading procedure is done, remove it from the machine, roll it out with a rolling pin, and spread it into greased pizza sheet.

5.Cover the pizza pan and leave it for 25 minutes to rise.

6.Spread pesto and garlic sauce evenly on the top of the pizza crust.

7.Top up with chicken, tomatoes, bell pepper, shredded cheese, and sliced mozzarella.

8.Bake for 20 minutes at 380 F preheated oven until the crust turns golden brown, and cheese melts down.

9.Make eight slices with a pizza cutter and serve.

3.13 Classic Keto Baguette With Garlic Butter

Total time of cooking

1 hour 50 minutes

Servings

32

Nutrition facts

Calories 27(For 2 baguettes, per serving)

Protein 1.2g

Net Carbs 0.4g

Total Fat 1.4g

Ingredients:

Here is the list of ingredients required to make a classic keto baguette with garlic butter.

For Baguettes dough:

- 1 cup hot water

- 3/4 cup of coconut flour

- 3/4 cup of golden flaxseed (make a powder using seeds grinder)

- 6 large egg whites

- 3 tablespoons of apple cider vinegar

- 3 tablespoons of psyllium husk

- 2 teaspoons of instant yeast

- 1/2 teaspoon of salt

For the garlic butter:

- 1/2 cup of softened butter

- 1/4 cup of any cheese of your choice

- 4 tablespoons of minced garlic

- 1 1/2 teaspoon of parsley

(Mix them all in a bowl)

Instructions:

Follow the method mentioned below to make a keto baguette.

1.Gather all the ingredients.

2.Place all the ingredients for the baguette in the bread machine container, start the machine and choose the dough cycle.

3.Once done, place your dough into a floured surface and knead for few minutes, divide into two portions and make two 9" inches long dough.

4.On the baking sheet, place both doughs. Mark diagonal cuts on the top of the dough.

5.For about 45 to 50 minutes, bake at 350 F/180 C preheated oven.

6.Place baguettes on the wire rack for cooling.

7.Cut each baguette into slices and spread garlic bread before serving.

8.Enjoy

3.14 Tasty Cheese And Garlic Pull-Apart Keto Bread

Total time of cooking

1 hour 25 minutes

Servings

10

Nutrition facts

Calories 302(per serving)

Protein 16g

Carbs 6g

Fat 10g

Fiber 3g

Ingredients:

Here is the list of ingredients required to make cheese and garlic pull-apart bread.

- 1 1/3 cups of almond flour

- 3 cups of grated mozzarella cheese

- 1 cup of grated cheddar cheese

- 1/4 cups of sliced green onion

- 2 medium-sized eggs

- 2 garlic cloves

- 4 tablespoons of salted butter

- 2 tablespoons of warm water

- 2 tablespoons of chives

- 2 teaspoons of dried yeast

- 2 teaspoons of inulin

- 2 teaspoons of xanthan gum

- 1 teaspoon of salt

- pinch of pepper

Instructions:

Follow the method mentioned below to make cheese and garlic pull-apart bread.

1.In a microwave-safe bowl, mix cheese and butter until completely melts.

2.Combine inulin, yeast, and warm water in a bread machine container, leave it for 15 to 20 minutes and let it proof.

3.Now, on top of the yeast mixture, add almond flour, salt, xanthan gum, pour eggs followed by melted cheese and butter mixture, choose dough cycle and start the machine.

4.Once kneading is over. Transfer the dough into a bowl and cover with a kitchen cloth to rise for 20 minutes.

5.Knead the dough with hands for a while, roll out into a rectangular shape on the floured surface.

6.Spread over the cheddar, cheese, garlic, green onions, chive, salt, and pepper.

7.Make a large scroll , rolling the dough from one end to the other.

8.Slit the dough at an angle(approx 3/4 of the way through) with kitchen scissors. Twist each portion of the dough oppositely from the previous one. To overlap the portions and form more of an oval shape. Press the dough together.

9.Place at the greased non-stick baking sheet and leave for 20 minutes.

10.Bake your pull-apart bread for 25 to 30 minutes at 350 F/180 C preheated oven.

11.Allow cooling first for 10 to 15 minutes.

12.Serve on a platter and enjoy.

3.15 Low Carb Keto Spinach Bread

Total time of cooking

3 hour 5 minutes

Servings

8

Nutrition facts

Calories 345(per serving)

Protein 13g

Carbs 7g

Fat 31g

Fiber 4g

Ingredients:

Here is the list of ingredients required to make spinach bread.

- 1 3/4 cups of almond flour

- 1 cup of cheddar cheese

- 1 cup of spinach finely chopped

- 2 eggs large

- 7 tablespoons of melted butter

- 1 tablespoon of rosemary chopped

- 2 clove of garlic finely chopped

- 2 teaspoons of instant yeast

- 1/2 teaspoon of salt

Instructions:

Follow the method mentioned below to make spinach bread.

1.Combine all the ingredients.

2.Put all the ingredients except spinach into your bread maker in the order recommended by your bread machine.

3.Pick bread cycle and medium crust from your bread maker settings panel and start the machine.

4.Check after 5 minutes of kneading. Add two tablespoons of water if needed.

5.At nut signals, add spinach to the mixture.

6.When the bread cycle completes, Remove and allow to cool down for a while.

7.Slice and serve.

3.16 Keto Mexican Jalapeno Cornbread

Total time of cooking

1 hour 15 minutes

Servings

8

Nutrition facts

Calories 412(per serving)

Protein 13g

Carbs 6g

Fat 40g

Fiber 3g

Ingredients:

Here is the list of ingredients for Mexican jalapeno cornbread.

- 2 cups of almond flour

- 1 cup of grated cheddar cheese

- 1 cup of heavy cream

- 1/4 cup of melted butter

- 4 large beaten eggs

- 3 tablespoons of diced jalapenos

- 1 teaspoon of instant yeast

- 1/2 teaspoon of salt

Instructions:

Follow the method mentioned below to make Mexican jalapeno cornbread.

1.Assemble all the ingredients.

2.In the bread maker pan, add all the ingredients except jalapenos, select dough cycle, and start the machine. Check after few minutes if needed, add two tablespoons of water.

3.When the machine beeps five minutes before the last kneading, add jalapenos.

4.Warm up your oven at 350 F.

5.Spray 8 inches oven-safe iron skillet.

6.Place your dough batter into an iron skillet and bake for around 30 minutes.

7.Remove from oven once done, cut in 8 slices, and serve.

Conclusion

The bread machine is such a blessing in the shape of an appliance to get your hands on. The more you play with it and bake new things, the more you can create magic with it and never want to get away with the feeling of how it saves your time and energy and why you always want one in your kitchen.

Practice makes things perfect, so do not hesitate to experiment. You may not master the art of making bread and using a bread machine in just one day. However, you can kick start your learning journey with ample bread recipes combined in this cookbook. Regardless of your expertise in making different kinds of bread and operating a bread machine. Buying and starting with a cookbook will reveal a world of new recipes to you.

Keto Air Fryer Cookbook with Pictures

Cook and Taste Tens of Low-Carb Fried Recipes. Shed Weight, Kill Hunger, and Regain Confidence Living the Keto Lifestyle

By

Sean Foster

Table of Contents

Introduction

An air-fryer is a modern kitchen device that cooks food instead of using oil by blowing extremely hot air around it. It provides a low-fat variant of food that in a deep fryer will usually be fried. Consequently, fatty foods such as French fries, fried chicken, and onion rings are usually prepared with no oil or up to 80% less fat relative to traditional cooking techniques.

If you already have an air fryer, you probably know that it's a futuristic gadget designed to save time and help make your life easier. You'll be eager to hear about how soon you'll be addicted to using your air fryer for cooking almost any meal if you've still not taken the jump. What is so unique about air frying, though?

The air fryer will substitute your deep fryer, microwave, oven, and dehydrator and cook tasty meals uniformly in a very small amount of time. Your air fryer is a show stopper if you're trying to help your friends with nutritious food but do not have much time.

With your progress on the ketogenic diet, an air fryer will also aid. The fast cooking time it offers is one of the main advantages of air frying. When you are starving and limited on resources, this is extremely helpful, a formula for cheating on your keto diet. Simple planning of nutritious meals is also linked to long-term progress on a keto diet. That's why during your keto trip, your air fryer can be your best buddy and support you to stay on track, even on days when time is limited for you.

The Air Fryer offers fried foods and nutritious meals, helping you eliminate the calories that come with fried foods and providing you the crunchiness, taste, and flavor you love. By blowing very hot air (up to 400 ° F) uniformly and rapidly around a food ingredient put in an enclosed room, this household appliance works. The heat renders the food part on the outside crispy and brittle, but it is warm and moist on the inside. You can use an air fryer on pretty much everything. You should barbecue, bake and roast in addition to frying. Its choice of cooking choices allows it simpler at any time of the day to eat any food.

Cooking using an Air Fryer

It is as simple to cook with an air fryer as using an oven. Anyone may do it, and then you'll wish that you had turned to this brilliant cooking process earlier after only a few tries. This section will outline air frying choices, optimize your cooking period and juiciness, clarify how to make your air fryer clean and offer some gadgets that will make sure that your air frying experience is even simpler and more pleasant.

Although the fundamentals of using an air fryer would be discussed in this section, the first phase is studying the guide that comes along with the air fryer. Almost all air fryers are distinct, and there are several different versions of the industry with the recent spike in device demand. Knowing how to thoroughly operate your particular air fryer is the secret to victory and can familiarize you with debugging concerns as well as protection features.

Until first use, reading through the guide and washing every component with soft, soapy water can make you feel prepared to release your cooking finesse!

Why Use It:

Air frying is widely common because it enables you to cook tasty meals easily and uniformly with very small quantity of oil and very little energy. Here are only a handful of reasons to turn to air frying:

Quick cleanup: You would certainly stain your cooker with every cooking process, but with the smaller frying region of the air fryer and portable basket, comprehensive cleanup is a breeze!

Cooks faster: By rotating heated air throughout the cooking compartment, air frying operates. This contributes to quick and even frying, using a portion of your oven's resources. You can set most air fryers to an extreme temperature of around 350-400°F. Because of which, in an air fryer, you can cook just about everything you can create in a microwave.

Low-Fat Food: The most important feature of the air fryer is the usage of hot-air airflow to cook food products from all directions, removing the need for gasoline. This makes it easier for individuals on a reduced-fat diet to eat deliciously balanced meals safely.

Highly Safe: While tossing chicken or any other ingredients into the deep fryer, do you know how extra cautious you have to be? As it is still really hot, you want to be sure that the hot oil does not spill and damage your face. You wouldn't have to think about brunette skin from hot oil spillage with your air fryer.

Multifunctional Use: Since it can cook many dishes at once, the air fryer helps you multitask. It is your all-in-one gadget that can barbecue, bake, fry and roast the dishes you need! For separate work, you no longer require several appliances.

Healthier Foods: Air fryers are built to operate without fattening oils and up to 80 percent less fat to create healthier foods. This makes it possible to lose weight because you can also enjoy your fried dishes while retaining calories and saturated fat. Through utilizing this appliance, making the transition to a healthy existence is more feasible. The scent that comes with deep-fried items, which also hangs in the room even many hours after deep frying, is also eliminated from your house.

Selecting a Custom Air Fryer:

The dual most significant aspects to concentrate on are scale/size and heat range when picking an air fryer. In general, quart scale air fryers are calculated and vary from around 1.2 quarts size to about 10 quarts or even more. You may be drawn in at a minimum a 5.3-quart fryer which may be used to wonderfully roast a whole chicken if you are trying to prepare meals to serve a group, but if you require a tiny machine owing to the minimal counter room and you are preparing for just one or two, you can certainly crisp up those Fries with a much minor air fryer.

And for the range of temperatures available, many air fryers encourage you to dry out foods and, for a prolonged period, you can fry them at extremely low heat, say about 120 ° F. You'll want to ensure the air fryer takes the necessary cooking power and heat range, based on the functions you use.

Accessories

The cooking chamber of your air fryer is essentially just a wide, open room for the warm air to move. It is a big bonus because it offers you the opportunity to integrate into your kitchen some different accessories. These devices increase the amount of dishes that you can produce using your air fryer and start opening choices that you might never have known was feasible. Below are few of the popular gadgets.

Parchment: In specific, precut parchment may be useful while baking with your air fryer to make cleaning much simpler. Similarly, for quick steaming, you will find parchment paper with precut holes.

Pizza pan: Indeed, using the air fryer, you can make a pizza, and this book contains many recipes for various kinds of keto-friendly pizzas. This is a fantastic alternative to still have the desired form quickly.

Cupcake pan: It typically comes with several tiny cups, and the 5.3-quart size air fryer takes up the whole chamber. For cupcakes, muffins, or even egg plates, these flexible cups are fine. You can still use single silicone baking containers if you would not want to go this path.

Cake pan: For your air fryer, you will find specially designed cake pans that fit perfectly into the inner pot. They even come with a built-in handle so that when your cakes are finished baking, you can quickly take them out.

Skewer rack: This is identical to a holder made of aluminum, except it has built-in skewers of metal that make roasting kebabs a breeze.

Metal holder: To add a layer to your cooking plate, this round rack is used so that you can optimize room and cook several items simultaneously. When you cook meat and vegetables and don't want to stop to cook to get going on the other, this is especially helpful.

How to clean an Air Fryer

Make sure that the air fryer is cold and unhooked before washing it. To wash the air fryer slate, you'll need to follow the steps below:

1. Separate your air fryer plate from its foundation. Fill a tub of worm water and soap for your pan. Let the plate sit in warm water and soap mix for about 10 minutes with your frying bucket inside.
2. Using a brush or sponge, thoroughly clean the bucket.
3. Lift the basket from the frying pan and clean the underneath and exterior surfaces.
4. Now use the same brush or sponge to clean your air-fryer plate.
5. Allow all to air-dry completely and transfer to the foundation of the air fryer.

Simply scrub the exterior with a wet cloth to disinfect the exterior of your air fryer. Then, before starting your next cooking experience, make sure all parts are in there right places.

Keto Diet

A relatively moderate-protein, low-carb, and elevated diet that help the body sustain itself without using sugars or high amounts of carbs is the keto diet or keto. When the system is low on glucose (sugar), ketones are formed by a mechanism called ketosis in the liver from food metabolism. This diet will contribute to some lower blood sugar, weight loss, balanced insulin levels, plus managed cravings, with diligent monitoring, imaginative meals, and self-control.

Your body takes some carbohydrates as you consume high-carb nutrition and converts them into energy to fuel itself. Your liver instead burns fat as you leave out the carbohydrates. A ketogenic régime usually limits carbohydrates to about 0-50 grams a day.

Tips for Usage:

- Preheat your fryer before use
- Always cook in batches. Do not overcrowd your fryer
- Space Your Foods evenly when added to the air fryer
- Keep It Dry
- Use spray oil to oil your food

CHAPTER 1: Breakfast Recipes

If you set your air fryer to work, simple and healthy low-carb breakfasts will soon be the rule in your home! These meals will boot the day in a nutritious way without robbing you of days that should be full of savory fun! It can be not easy to make a nourishing meal for oneself or relatives while you're trying to get out of the house in time. The easiest choice might be to catch a granola bar or microwave pastry, but it will quickly contribute to thoughts of shame and guilt and extreme malnutrition at noon.

This section's meals are full and keto-approved, making you improve your mornings and all your days. Get prepared in a snap for nutritious meals that can be created using your air fryer. You can make meals in advance, such as Cheese Balls, and Sausage and you can put dishes in the air fryer to get ready until you get dressed, such as Quick and Simple Bacon Strips, you'll want to have begun frying your breakfasts earlier!

1. Loaded Cauliflower Breakfast Bake

Preparation time: 15 minutes

Cooking time: 20 minutes

Servings: 4 people

Ingredients:

- 12 slices sugar-free bacon, cooked and crumbled
- 2 scallions, sliced on the bias
- 8 tablespoons full-fat sour cream
- 1 medium avocado, peeled and pitted
- 1 cup shredded medium Cheddar cheese
- 11/2 cups chopped cauliflower
- 1/4 cup heavy whipping cream
- 6 large eggs

Directions:

1. Mix the eggs and milk in a medium dish. Pour it into a circular 4-cup baking tray.
2. Add and blend the cauliflower, and cover it with cheddar. Put your dish in the air-fryer bowl.
3. Change the temperature and set the timer to about 320°F for around 20 minutes.
4. The eggs will be solid once fully baked, and the cheese will be golden brown. Slice it into 4 bits.
5. Cut the avocado and split the bits equally. Put two teaspoons of sliced scallions, sour cream, and crumbled bacon on top of each plate.

2. Scrambled Eggs

Preparation time: 5 minutes

Cooking time: 20 minutes

Servings: 2 people

Ingredients:

- 1/2 cup shredded sharp Cheddar cheese
- 2 tablespoons unsalted butter, melted
- 4 large eggs

Directions:

1. Crack the eggs into a round 2-cup baking pan and whisk them. Put the tray in the air-fryer container.

2. Change the temperature settings and set the timer to about 400°F for around 10 minutes.

3. Mix the eggs after about 5 minutes and add some cheese and butter. Let it cook for another 3 minutes and mix again.

4. Give an extra 2 minutes to finish frying or remove the eggs from flame if they are to your preferred taste.

5. For fluffing, use a fork. Serve it hot.

3. "Hard-Boiled" Eggs

Preparation time: 2 minutes

Cooking time: 20 minutes

Servings: 4 people

Ingredients:

- 1 cup water
- 4 large eggs

Directions:

1. Put the eggs in a heat-proof 4-cup round baking tray and pour some water over your eggs. Put the tray in the air-fryer basket.

2. Set the air fryer's temperature to about 300 ° F and set the clock for about 18-minute.

3. In the fridge, store boiled eggs before ready to consume or peel and serve warmly.

4. Breakfast Stuffed Poblanos

Preparation time: 20 minutes

Cooking time: 15 minutes

Servings: 5 people

Ingredients:

- 1/2 cup full-fat sour cream

- 8 tablespoons shredded pepper jack cheese
- 4 large poblano peppers
- 1/4 cup canned diced tomatoes and green chilies, drained
- 4 ounces full-fat cream cheese, softened
- 4 large eggs
- 1/2 pound spicy ground pork breakfast sausage

Directions:

1. Crumble and brown the cooked sausage in a large skillet over medium-low heat until no red exists. Take the sausage from the skillet and clean the oil. Crack your eggs in the skillet, scramble, and simmer until they are no longer watery.

2. In a wide bowl, add the fried sausage and add in cream cheese. Mix the sliced tomatoes and chilies. Gently fold the eggs together.

3. Cut a 4-5-inch gap at the top of each poblano, separating the white layer and seeds with a tiny knife. In four portions, divide the filling and gently scoop into each pepper. Cover each with 2 teaspoons of cheese from the pepper jack.

4. Drop each pepper into the container of the air fryer.

5. Change the temperature and set the timer to about 350 °F for around 15 minutes.

6. The peppers will be tender, and when prepared, the cheese will be golden brown. Serve instantly with sour cream on top.

5. Cheesy Cauliflower Hash Browns

Preparation time: 20 minutes

Cooking time: 12 minutes

Servings: 4 people

Ingredients:

- 1 cup shredded sharp Cheddar cheese
- 1 large egg
- 1 (12-ounce) steamer bag cauliflower

Directions:

1. Put the bag in the oven and cook as per the directions in the box. To extract excess moisture, leave to cool fully and place cauliflower in a cheesecloth or paper towel and squeeze.

2. Add the cheese and eggs and mash the cauliflower using a fork.

3. Cut a slice of parchment to match the frame of your air fryer. Take 1/4 of the paste and make it into a hash-brown patty shape and mold it. Put it on the parchment and, into your air fryer basket, if required, running in groups.

4. Change the temperature and set the clock to about 400°F for around 12 minutes.

5. Halfway into the cooking process, turn your hash browns. They will be nicely browned when fully baked. Instantly serve.

6. Egg, Cheese, and Bacon Roll-Ups

Preparation time: 20 minutes

Cooking time: 20 minutes

Servings: 4 people

Ingredients:

*   1/2 cup mild salsa for dipping
*   1 cup shredded sharp Cheddar cheese

- 12 slices sugar free bacon
- 6 large eggs
- 1/2 medium green bell pepper, seeded and chopped
- 1/4 cup chopped onion
- 2 tablespoons unsalted butter

Directions:

1. Melt the butter in a small skillet over medium flame. Add the pepper and onion to the skillet and sauté until aromatic, around 3 minutes, and your onions are transparent.

2. In a shallow pot, whisk the eggs and dump them into a skillet. Scramble the pepper and onion with the eggs once fluffy and fully fried after 5 minutes. Remove from the flame and set aside.

3. Put 3 strips of bacon beside each other on the cutting board, overlapping about 1/4. Place 1/4 cup of scrambled eggs on the side nearest to you in a pile and scatter 1/4 cup of cheese on top of your eggs.

4. Wrap the bacon around the eggs securely and, if needed, protect the seam using a toothpick. Put each wrap into the container of the air fryer.

5. Switch the temperature to about 350 ° F and set the clock for around 15 minutes. Midway through the cooking time, turn the rolls.

6. When fully fried, the bacon would be brown and tender. For frying, serve immediately with some salsa.

7. Pancake

Preparation time: 10 minutes

Cooking time: 7 minutes

Servings: 4 people

Ingredients:

- 1/2 teaspoon ground cinnamon

- 1/2 teaspoon vanilla extract
- 1/2 teaspoon unflavored gelatin
- 1 large egg
- 2 tablespoons unsalted butter, softened
- 1/2 teaspoon baking powder
- 1/4 cup powdered erythritol
- 1/2 cup blanched finely ground almond flour

Directions:

1. Combine the erythritol, almond flour, and baking powder in a wide pot. Add some egg, butter, cinnamon, gelatin, and vanilla. Place into a rectangular 6-inch baking tray.
2. Place the tray in the container of your air fryer.
3. Change the temperature to about 300 °F and set the clock for 7 minutes.
4. A toothpick can pop out dry when the dessert is fully baked. Split the cake into four servings and eat.

8. Lemon Poppy Seed Cake

Preparation time: 10 minutes

Cooking time: 14 minutes

Servings: 6 people

Ingredients:

- 1 teaspoon poppy seeds
- 1 medium lemon
- 1 teaspoon vanilla extract
- 2 large eggs
- 1/4 cup unsweetened almond milk
- 1/4 cup unsalted butter, melted
- 1/2 teaspoon baking powder

- 1/2 cup powdered erythritol
- 1 cup blanched finely ground almond flour

Directions:

Mix the erythritol, almond flour, butter, baking powder, eggs, almond milk, and vanilla in a big bowl.

Halve the lime and strain the liquid into a little pot, then transfer it to the mixture.

Zest the lemon with a fine grinder and transfer 1 tbsp. of zest to the mixture and blend. Add the poppy seeds to your batter.

In the non-stick 6' circular cake tin, add your batter. Put the pan in the container of your air fryer.

Change the temperature and set the clock to about 300°F for around 14 minutes.

A wooden skewer inserted in the middle, if it comes out completely clean, means it's thoroughly fried. The cake will stop cooking and crisp up when it cools. At room temperature, serve.

9. "Banana" Nut Cake

Preparation time: 20 minutes

Cooking time: 30 minutes

Servings: 6-7 people

Ingredients:

- 1/4 cup of chopped walnuts
- 2 large eggs
- 1/4 cup of full-fat sour cream
- 1 teaspoon of vanilla extract
- 21/2 teaspoons of banana extract
- 1/4 cup of unsalted butter, melted
- 1/2 teaspoon of ground cinnamon
- 2 teaspoons of baking powder

- 2 tablespoons of ground golden flaxseed
- 1/2 cup of powdered erythritol
- 1 cup of blanched finely ground almond flour

Directions:

1. Mix the erythritol, almond flour, baking powder, flaxseed, and cinnamon in a big dish.
2. Add vanilla extract, banana extract, butter, and sour cream and mix well.
3. Add your eggs to the combination and whisk until they are fully mixed. Mix in your walnuts.
4. Pour into a 6-inch non-stick cake pan and put in the bowl of your air fryer.
5. Change the temperature and set the clock to about 300°F for around 25 minutes.
6. When fully baked, the cake will be lightly golden, and a toothpick inserted in the middle will come out clean. To prevent cracking, allow it to cool entirely.

10. Bacon Strips

Preparation time: 5 minutes

Cooking time: 12 minutes

Servings: 5 people

Ingredients:

- 10 slices sugar free bacon

Directions:

1. Put slices of bacon into the bucket of your air fryer.
2. Change the temperature and set the timer to about 400°F for around 12 minutes.
3. Turn the bacon after 6 minutes and proceed to cook. Serve hot.

11.Pumpkin Spice Muffins

Preparation time: 10 minutes

Cooking time: 15 minutes

Servings: 6 people

Ingredients:

- 2 large eggs
- 1 teaspoon vanilla extract
- 1/4 teaspoon ground nutmeg
- 1/2 teaspoon ground cinnamon
- 1/4 cup pure pumpkin purée
- 1/4 cup unsalted butter, softened
- 1/2 teaspoon baking powder

- 1/2 cup granular erythritol
- 1 cup blanched finely ground almond flour

Directions:

1. Mix the erythritol, almond flour, butter, baking powder, nutmeg, cinnamon, pumpkin purée, and vanilla in a big dish.
2. Stir in the eggs softly.
3. Add the batter into about six or more silicone muffin cups equally. Put muffin cups in the air fryer basket. If required, make them in groups.
4. Change the temperature and set the clock to about 300°F for around 15 minutes.
5. A wooden skewer inserted in the middle will come out completely clean if thoroughly cooked. Serve hot.

12. Veggie Frittata

Preparation time: minutes

Cooking time: minutes

Servings: people

Ingredients:

- 1/4 cup of chopped green bell pepper
- 1/4 cup of chopped yellow onion
- 1/2 cup of chopped broccoli
- 1/4 cup of heavy whipping cream
- 6 large eggs

Directions:

1. Whisk the heavy whipping cream and eggs in a big bowl. Add in the onion, broccoli, and bell pepper.
2. Load into a 6-inch circular baking dish that is oven-safe. Put the baking tray in the basket of an air fryer.
3. Switch the temperature to about 350 ° F and set the clock for around 12-minute.

4. When the frittata is finished, eggs must be solid and thoroughly cooked. Serve it hot.

13. Buffalo Egg Cups

Preparation time: 12 minutes

Cooking time: 12 minutes

Servings: 3 people

Ingredients:

- 1/2 cup of shredded sharp Cheddar cheese
- 2 tablespoons of buffalo sauce
- 2 ounces of full-fat cream cheese
- 4 large eggs

Directions:

1. In two (4') ramekins, add the eggs.
2. Mix the buffalo sauce, cream cheese, and cheddar in a little, microwave-safe container. For about 20 seconds, microwave and then mix. Put a spoonful on top of each egg within each ramekin.
3. Put the ramekins in the container of an air fryer.
4. Change the temperature and set the timer to about 320°F for around 15 minutes.
5. Serve it hot.

14. Crispy Southwestern Ham Egg Cups

Preparation time: 5 minutes

Cooking time: 14 minutes

Servings: 3 people

Ingredients:

- 1/2 cup of shredded medium Cheddar cheese
- 2 tablespoons of diced white onion
- 2 tablespoons of diced red bell pepper
- 1/4 cup diced of green bell pepper

- 2 tablespoons of full-fat sour cream
- 4 large eggs
- 4 (1-ounce) of slices deli ham

Directions:

1. Put a piece of ham at the bottom of four or more baking cups.
2. Whisk the eggs along with the sour cream in a big bowl. Add the red pepper, green pepper, and onion and mix well.
3. Add the mixture of eggs into baking cups that are ham-lined. Top them with some cheddar cheese. Put the cups in the container of your air fryer.
4. Set the clock for around 12 minutes or till the peaks are golden browned, cook at a temperature of about 320 ° F.
5. Serve it hot.

15. Jalapeño Popper Egg Cups

Preparation time: 10 minutes

Cooking time: 12 minutes

Servings: 3 people

Ingredients:

- 1/2 cup of shredded sharp Cheddar cheese
- 2 ounces of full-fat cream cheese
- 1/4 cup of chopped pickled jalapeños
- 4 large eggs

Directions:

1. Add the eggs to a medium container, and then dump them into 4 silicone muffin cups.
2. Place the cream cheese, jalapeños, and cheddar in a wide, microwave-safe dish. Heat in the microwave for about 30 seconds and mix well. Take a full spoon and put it in

the middle of one of the egg cups, around 1/4 of the paste. Repeat for the mixture left.

3. Put the egg cups in the container of your air fryer.
4. Change the temperature and set the clock for around 10 minutes to about 320 °F.
5. Serve it hot.

16. Crunchy Granola

Preparation time: 10 minutes

Cooking time: 5 minutes

Servings: 6 people

Ingredients:

- 1 teaspoon of ground cinnamon
- 2 tablespoons of unsalted butter
- 1/4 cup of granular erythritol
- 1/4 cup of low-carb, sugar free chocolate chips
- 1/4 cup of golden flaxseed
- 1/3 cup of sunflower seeds
- 1 cup of almond slivers
- 1 cup of unsweetened coconut flakes
- 2 cups of pecans, chopped

Directions:

1. Blend all the ingredients in a big bowl.
2. In a 4-cup circular baking tray, put the mixture into it.
3. Place the tray in the air-fryer container.
4. Change the temperature and set the clock to about 320°F for around 5 minutes.
5. Let it cool absolutely before serving.

CHAPTER 2: Air Fryer Chicken Main Dishes

1. Chicken Fajitas

Preparation time: 10 minutes

Cooking time: 15 minutes

Servings: 2 people

Ingredients:

- 1/2 medium red bell pepper, seeded and sliced
- 1/2 medium green bell pepper, seeded and sliced
- 1/4 medium onion, peeled and sliced
- 1/2 teaspoon garlic powder
- 1/2 teaspoon paprika
- 1/2 teaspoon cumin
- 1 tablespoon chili powder
- 2 tablespoons coconut oil, melted
- 10 ounces boneless, skinless chicken breast, sliced into 1/4" strips

Directions:

1. In a big bowl, mix the chicken and coconut oil and scatter with the paprika, cumin, chili powder, and garlic powder. Toss the chicken with spices until well mixed. Put the chicken in the basket of an air fryer.
2. Set the temperature and adjust the clock to about 350°F for around 15 minutes.
3. When your clock has 7 minutes left, throw in the peppers and onion into the fryer bucket.
4. When frying, flip the chicken at least two to three times. Veggies should be soft; when done, the chicken should be thoroughly cooked to at least 165°F internal temperature. Serve it hot.

2. Pepperoni and Chicken Pizza Bake

Preparation time: 10 minutes

Cooking time: 15 minutes

Servings: 4 people

Ingredients:

- 1/4 cup grated Parmesan cheese
- 1 cup shredded mozzarella cheese
- 1 cup low-carb, sugar-free pizza sauce
- 20 slices pepperoni
- 2 cups cubed cooked chicken

Directions:

1. Add the pepperoni, chicken, and pizza sauce into a 4-cup rectangular baking tray. Stir such that the beef is coated fully in the sauce.
2. Cover with grated mozzarella and parmesan. Put your dish in the air-fryer bucket.
3. Set the temperature and adjust the clock to about 375°F for around 15 minutes.
4. When served, the dish would be brown and bubbly. Instantly serve.

3. Almond-Crusted Chicken

Preparation time: 15 minutes

Cooking time: 25 minutes

Servings: 4 people

Ingredients:

- 1 tablespoon Dijon mustard
- 2 tablespoons full-fat mayonnaise
- 2 (6-ounce) boneless, skinless chicken breasts
- 1/4 cup slivered almonds

Directions:

1. In a food processor, pulse your almonds or cut until finely diced. Put the almonds equally and put them aside on a tray.
2. Completely split each chicken breast lengthwise in part.

3. In a shallow pot, combine the mustard and mayonnaise now, cover the entire chicken with the mixture.

4. Place each piece of chicken completely coated in the diced almonds. Transfer the chicken gently into the bucket of your air fryer.

5. Set the temperature and adjust the clock to about 350°F for around 25 minutes.

6. When it has hit an interior temperature of about 165 ° F or more, the chicken will be cooked. Serve it hot.

4. Southern "Fried" Chicken

Preparation time: 15 minutes

Cooking time: 25 minutes

Servings: 4 people

Ingredients:

- 2 ounces pork rinds, finely ground
- 1/4 teaspoon ground black pepper
- 1/4 teaspoon onion powder
- 1/2 teaspoon cumin

- 1 tablespoon chili powder
- 2 tablespoons hot sauce
- 2 (6-ounce) boneless, skinless chicken breasts

Directions:

1. Longitudinally, split each chicken breast in half. Put the chicken in a big pot and add some hot sauce to coat the chicken completely.

2. Mix the onion powder, cumin, chili powder, and pepper in a shallow container. Sprinkle the mix over your chicken.

3. In a wide bowl, put the seasoned pork rinds and dunk each chicken piece into the container, covering as much as necessary. Put the chicken in the bucket of an air fryer.

4. Set the temperature and adjust the clock to about 350°F for around 25 minutes.

5. Turn the chicken gently midway through the cooking process.

6. The internal temperature will be at most 165 ° F when finished, and the coating of the pork rind will be rich golden brown in color. Serve it hot.

5. Spinach and Feta-Stuffed Chicken Breast

Preparation time: 15 minutes

Cooking time: 25 minutes

Servings: 2 people

Ingredients:

- 1 tablespoon coconut oil
- 2 (6-ounce) boneless, skinless chicken breasts
- 1/4 cup crumbled feta
- 1/4 cup chopped yellow onion
- 1/2 teaspoon salt, divided
- 1/2 teaspoon garlic powder, divided
- 5 ounces frozen spinach, thawed and drained

- 1 tablespoon unsalted butter

Directions:

1. Add some butter to your pan and sauté the spinach for around 3 minutes in a medium-sized skillet over a medium-high flame. Sprinkle the spinach with 1/4 teaspoon salt, 1/4 teaspoon garlic powder now, add your onion to the plate.

2. Sauté for another 3 minutes, then turn off the flame and put it in a medium-sized dish. Fold the feta mixture into the spinach.

3. Lengthwise, carve a nearly 4' cut through the side of each chicken breast. Scoop half of the mix into each portion and seal with a pair of toothpicks shut. Dust with leftover salt and garlic powder outside of your chicken. Drizzle some coconut oil. Put the chicken breasts in the bucket of your air fryer.

4. Set the temperature and adjust the clock to about 350°F for around 25 minutes.

5. The chicken must be golden brown in color and have an internal temperature of at least 165 ° F when fully cooked. Cut and serve hot.

6. Blackened Cajun Chicken Tenders

Preparation time: 10 minutes

Cooking time: 17 minutes

Servings: 4 people

Ingredients:

- 1/4 cup full-fat ranch dressing
- 1 pound boneless, skinless chicken tenders
- 2 tablespoons coconut oil
- 1/8 teaspoon ground cayenne pepper
- 1/4 teaspoon onion powder
- 1/2 teaspoon dried thyme
- 1/2 teaspoon garlic powder
- 1 teaspoon chili powder

- 2 teaspoons paprika

Directions:

1. Mix all the seasonings in a shallow container.
2. Drizzle oil over chicken wings and then cover each tender thoroughly in the mixture of spices. Put tenders in the bucket of your air fryer.
3. Set the temperature and adjust the clock to about 375 °F for around 17 minutes.
4. Tenders, when completely baked, will have a temperature of 165 ° F centrally.
5. For dipping, use some ranch dressing and enjoy.

7. Chicken Pizza Crust

Preparation time: 10 minutes

Cooking time: 25 minutes

Servings: 4 people

Ingredients:

1 pound ground chicken thigh meat

1/4 cup grated Parmesan cheese

1/2 cup shredded mozzarella

Directions:

1. Combine all the ingredients in a wide bowl. Split equally into four portions.
2. Slice out four (6") parchment paper circles and push down the chicken mixture on each one of the circles. Put into the bucket of your air fryer, working as required in groups or individually.
3. Set the temperature and adjust the clock to about 375°F for around 25 minutes.
4. Midway into the cooking process, turn the crust.
5. You can cover it with some cheese and your choice of toppings until completely baked, and cook for 5 extra minutes. Or, you can place the crust in the fridge or freezer and top it later when you are ready to consume.

8. Chicken Enchiladas

Preparation time: 20 minutes

Cooking time: 10 minutes

Servings: 4 people

Ingredients:

- 1 medium avocado, peeled, pitted, and sliced
- Half cup full-fat sour cream
- 1 cup shredded medium Cheddar cheese
- Half cup of torn Monterey jack (MJ) cheese
- 1/2 pound medium-sliced deli chicken
- 1/3 cup low-carb enchilada sauce, divided
- 1 1/2 cups shredded cooked chicken

Directions:

1. Combine the shredded chicken and at least half of the enchilada sauce in a big dish. On a cutting surface, lay pieces of deli chicken and pour 2 teaspoons of shredded chicken mixture on each of your slices.

2. Sprinkle each roll with 2 teaspoons of cheddar cheese. Roll softly to close it completely.

3. Put each roll, seam side down, in a 4-cup circular baking tray. Over the rolls, pour the leftover sauce and top with the Monterey Jack. Put the dish in the air-fryer basket.

4. Set the temperature and adjust the clock to about 370 °F for around 10 minutes.

5. Enchiladas, when baked, would be golden on top and bubbling. With some sour cream and diced avocado, serve hot.

9. Jalapeño Popper Hassel back Chicken

Preparation time: 20 minutes

Cooking time: 20 minutes

Servings: 4 people

Ingredients:

- 2 (6-ounce) boneless, skinless chicken breasts
- 1/4 cup sliced pickled jalapeños
- 1/2 cup shredded sharp Cheddar cheese, divided
- 2 ounces full-fat cream cheese, softened
- 4 slices sugar-free bacon, cooked and crumbled

Directions:

1. Put the fried bacon in a medium-sized dish; add in half of the cheddar, cream cheese, and the jalapeño strips.

1. Using a sharp knife to build slits around 3/4 of the way across the chicken in each of the chicken thighs, being cautious not to go all the way through. You would typically get 6 to 8 per breast, cuts based on the chicken breast's length.

2. Spoon the premade cream cheese mix onto the chicken strips. Toss the leftover shredded cheese over your chicken breasts and put it in the air fryer basket.

3. Set the temperature and adjust the clock to about 350°F for around 20 minutes.

4. Serve it hot.

10. Chicken Cordon Bleu Casserole

Preparation time: 15 minutes

Cooking time: 15 minutes

Servings: 4 people

Ingredients:

- 1-ounce pork rinds, crushed
- 2 teaspoons Dijon mustard
- 2 tablespoons unsalted butter, melted
- 1 tablespoon heavy cream
- 4 ounces full-fat cream cheese, softened
- 2 ounces Swiss cheese, cubed
- 1/2 cup cubed cooked ham
- 2 cups cubed cooked chicken thigh meat

Directions:

1. Put the chicken and ham in a 6-inch circular baking pan and toss to blend the meat uniformly. Scatter on top of the meat some cheese cubes.

2. Add butter, heavy cream, cream cheese, and mustard in a big bowl and then spill the mix over your meat and cheese. Cover with rinds of pork. Put the pan in the bucket of your air fryer.

3. Set the temperature and adjust the clock to about 350°F for around 15 minutes.

4. When finished, the saucepan will be caramelized and bubbling. Serve hot.

11. Chicken Parmesan

Preparation time: 10 minutes

Cooking time: 25 minutes

Servings: 4 people

Ingredients:

- 1-ounce pork rinds, crushed
- 1 cup low-carb, no-sugar-added pasta sauce
- 1/2 cup grated Parmesan cheese, divided
- 2 (6-ounce) boneless, skinless chicken breasts
- 1 cup shredded mozzarella cheese, divided
- 4 tablespoons full-fat mayonnaise, divided
- 1/2 teaspoon dried parsley
- 1/4 teaspoon dried oregano
- 1/2 teaspoon garlic powder

Directions:

1. Cut each chicken breast longitudinally in half and hammer it to pound out a thickness of about 3/4". Sprinkle with parsley, garlic powder, and oregano.

2. On top of each slice of chicken, scatter 1 tablespoon of mayonnaise, then cover each piece with 1/4 cup of mozzarella.

3. Mix the shredded parmesan and pork rinds in a shallow bowl. Sprinkle the surface of the mozzarella with the paste.

4. In a 6' circular baking tray, transfer the sauce and put the chicken on top. Place the pan in the bucket of your air fryer.

5. Set the temperature and adjust the clock to about 320 ° F for around 25 minutes.

6. The cheese will be light browned, and when completely baked, the chicken's internal temperature will be at about 165 ° F. Serve hot.

12. Fajita-Stuffed Chicken Breast

Preparation time: 15 minutes

Cooking time: 25 minutes

Servings: 4 people

Ingredients:

- 1/2 teaspoon garlic powder
- 1 teaspoon ground cumin
- 2 teaspoons chili powder
- 1 tablespoon coconut oil
- 1 medium green bell pepper, seeded and sliced
- 1/4 medium white onion, peeled and sliced
- 2 (6-ounce) boneless, skinless chicken breasts

Directions:

1. "Slice each chicken breast into two equal parts entirely in half longitudinally. Hammer the chicken out until it is around 1/4" thick using a meat mallet.
2. Put out each chicken slice and arrange three onion pieces and four green pepper pieces on end nearest to you. Start to firmly roll the onions and peppers into the chicken. Both with toothpicks or a few strips of butcher's twine protect the roll.
3. Drizzle the chicken with coconut oil. Sprinkle with cumin, chili powder, and garlic powder on either side. Put all the rolls in the bucket of your air fryer.
4. Set the temperature and adjust the clock to about 350°F for around 25 minutes.
5. Serve it hot.

13. Lemon Pepper Drumsticks

Preparation time: 5 minutes

Cooking time: 22 minutes

Servings: 4 people

Ingredients:

- 1 tablespoon lemon pepper seasoning
- 4 tablespoons salted butter, melted
- 8 chicken drumsticks
- 1/2 teaspoon garlic powder
- 2 teaspoons baking powder

Directions:

1. Sprinkle some baking powder over the drumsticks along with some garlic powder and massage it into the chicken skin. Add your drumsticks into the bucket of your air fryer.

2. Set the temperature and adjust the clock to about 375°F for around 25 minutes.

3. Turn your drumsticks midway through the cooking process using tongs.

4. Take out from the fryer when the skin is golden in color, and the inside temperature is at a minimum of 165 ° F.

5. Put lemon pepper seasoning and some butter in a big dish. To the dish, add your fried drumsticks and turn until the chicken is coated. Serve it hot.

14. Cilantro Lime Chicken Thighs

Preparation time: 15 minutes

Cooking time: 22 minutes

Servings: 4 people

Ingredients:

- 1/4 cup chopped fresh cilantro
- 2 medium limes
- 1 teaspoon cumin
- 2 teaspoons chili powder
- 1/2 teaspoon garlic powder
- 1 teaspoon baking powder
- 4 bone-in, skin-on chicken thighs

Directions:

1. Toss some baking powder on your chicken thighs and rinse them.
2. Mix the chili powder, garlic powder, and cumin in a small bowl and sprinkle uniformly over the thighs, rubbing softly on and under the chicken's skin.
3. Halve one lime and squeeze the liquid across the thighs. Place the chicken in the bucket of an air fryer.
4. Set the temperature and adjust the clock to about 380°F for around 22-minute.
5. For serving, split the other lime into four slices and garnish the fried chicken with lemon wedges and some cilantro.

15. Lemon Thyme Roasted Chicken

Preparation time: 10 minutes

Cooking time: 60 minutes

Servings: 6 people

Ingredients:

- 2 tablespoons salted butter, melted
- 1 medium lemon
- 1 teaspoon baking powder
- 1/2 teaspoon onion powder 2 teaspoons dried parsley

- 1 teaspoon garlic powder
- 2 teaspoons dried thyme
- 1 (4-pound) chicken

Directions:

1. Rub the garlic powder, thyme, parsley, onion powder, and baking powder with the chicken.
2. Slice the lemon put four slices using a toothpick on top of the chicken, chest side up, and secure. Put the leftover slices inside your chicken.
3. Put the whole chicken in the bucket of your air fryer, chest side down.
4. Set the temperature and adjust the clock to about 350°F for around 60-minute.
5. Switch the sides of your chicken after 30 minutes, so its breast side is up.
6. The internal temperature should be at about 165 ° F when finished, and the skin should be golden in color and crispy. Pour the melted butter over the whole chicken before serving.

16. Teriyaki Wings

Preparation time: 60 minutes

Cooking time: 45 minutes

Servings: 4 people

Ingredients:

- 2 teaspoons baking powder
- 1/4 teaspoon ground ginger
- 2 teaspoons minced garlic
- 1/2 cup sugar-free teriyaki sauce
- 2 pounds chicken wings

Directions:

1. Put all of your ingredients in a big bowl or bag, excluding the baking powder and leave to marinate in the fridge for at least 1 hour.

2. Bring the wings into the bucket of your air fryer and dust with baking powder. Rub the wings softly.

3. Set the temperature and adjust the clock to about 400°F for around 25 minutes.

4. When frying, rotate the bucket two to three times.

5. Wings, when finished, should be crunchy and cooked internally to a minimum 165 ° F. Instantly serve.

17. Crispy Buffalo Chicken Tenders

Preparation time: 15 minutes

Cooking time: 20 minutes

Servings: 4 people

Ingredients:

- 1 teaspoon garlic powder
- 1 teaspoon chili powder
- 11/2 ounces pork rinds, finely ground
- 1/4 cup hot sauce
- 1 pound boneless, skinless chicken tenders

Directions:

1. Put the chicken tenders in a big bowl and pour them over with hot sauce. In the hot sauce, toss tender, rubbing uniformly.

2. Mix the ground pork rinds with chili powder and garlic powder in a separate, wide bowl.

3. Put each tender, fully coated, in the ground pork rinds. With some water, wet your hands and push down the rinds of pork onto the chicken.

4. Put the tenders in a single layer into the basket of the air fryer.

5. Set the temperature and adjust the clock to about 375°F for around 20 minutes.

6. Serve it hot.

CHAPTER 3: Air Fryer Side Dish Recipes

1. Pita-Style Chips

Preparation time: 10 minutes

Cooking time: 5 minutes

Servings: 4 people

Ingredients:

- 1 large egg
- 1/4 cup blanched finely ground almond flour
- 1/2 ounce pork rinds, finely ground
- 1 cup shredded mozzarella cheese

Directions:

1. Put mozzarella in a wide oven-safe dish and microwave for about 30 seconds or until melted. Add the rest of the ingredients and mix until largely smooth dough shapes into a ball quickly; if your dough is too hard, microwave for an additional 15 seconds.

2. Roll the dough into a wide rectangle among two parchment paper sheets and then use a sharp knife to make the triangle-shaped chips. Put the prepared chips in the bucket of your air fryer.

3. Set the temperature and adjust the clock to about 350°F for around 5 minutes.

4. Chips, when finished, would be golden in color and crunchy. When they cool down, they will become even crispier.

2. Avocado Fries

Preparation time: 15 minutes

Cooking time: 5 minutes

Servings: 4 people

Ingredients:

- 1-ounce pork rinds, finely ground
- 2 medium avocados

Directions:

1. Split each avocado in half. Now have the pit removed. Peel the outer gently and then split the flesh into 1/4'-thick strips.

2. Put the pork rinds in a medium-sized pot and drop each slice of avocado onto your pork rinds to cover it fully. Put the pieces of avocado in the bucket of your air fryer.

3. Set the temperature and adjust the clock to about 350°F for around 5 minutes.

4. Instantly serve.

3. Flatbread

Preparation time: 5 minutes

Cooking time: 7 minutes

Servings: 2 people

Ingredients:

- 1-ounce full-fat cream cheese softened
- 1/4 cup blanched finely ground almond flour
- 1 cup shredded mozzarella cheese

Directions:

1. Meltdown some mozzarella in your microwave for about 30 seconds in a wide oven-safe container. Mix in some almond flour to make it smooth, and add some cream cheese to the mix. Proceed to blend until dough shapes, slowly kneading using wet hands if needed.
2. Split the dough into two parts and roll between two pieces of parchment paper to a thickness of about 1/4". Cut an extra piece of parchment paper to fit in the container of your air fryer.
3. Put a small piece of flatbread; try working in two batches if necessary, on your parchment paper and into the air fryer.
4. Set the temperature and adjust the clock to about 320 ° F for around 7 minutes.
5. Rotate the flatbread midway through the cooking process. Serve it hot.

4. Radish Chips

Preparation time: 10 minutes

Cooking time: 5 minutes

Servings: 4 people

Ingredients:

- 2 tablespoons coconut oil, melted
- 1/2 teaspoon garlic powder
- 1/4 teaspoon paprika
- 1/4 teaspoon onion powder

- 1 pound radishes
- 2 cups water

Directions:

1. Put the water in a medium-sized saucepan and bring the water to a boil.

2. Cut the upper part and bottom of each radish, then cut each radish thinly and evenly using a mandolin. For this stage, you can use the cutting blade in your food processor.

3. For about 5 minutes or until transparent, put the radish pieces in hot water. To trap extra humidity, extract them from the boiling water and put them on a dry paper towel.

4. In a wide pot, combine the radish pieces and the rest of the ingredients until thoroughly covered in oil and seasoned. Put the radish chips in the basket of an air fryer.

5. Set the temperature and adjust the clock to about 320°F for around 5 minutes.

6. During the cooking process, rotate the basket at least two or three times. Serve it hot.

5. Coconut Flour Cheesy Garlic Biscuits

Preparation time: 10 minutes

Cooking time: 12 minutes

Servings: 4 people

Ingredients:

- 1 scallion, sliced
- 1/2 cup shredded sharp Cheddar cheese
- 1/4 cup unsalted butter, melted and divided
- 1 large egg
- 1/2 teaspoon garlic powder
- 1/2 teaspoon baking powder
- 1/3 cup coconut flour

Directions:

1. Combine the baking powder, coconut flour, and garlic powder in a wide dish.

2. Add half the melted butter, some cheddar cheese, egg, and the scallions and mix well. Pour the mixture into a rectangular 6-inch baking tray. Put it in the basket of your air fryer.

3. Set the temperature and adjust the clock to about 320 ° F for around a 12-minute timer.

4. Take out from the pan to enable it to cool thoroughly. Slice into four parts and add leftover melted butter on top of each piece.

6. Dinner Rolls

Preparation time: 10 minutes

Cooking time: 12 minutes

Servings: 6 people

Ingredients:

- 1 large egg
- 1/2 teaspoon baking powder
- 1/4 cup ground flaxseed
- 1 cup blanched finely ground almond flour
- 1-ounce full-fat cream cheese
- 1 cup shredded mozzarella cheese

Directions:

1. In a big oven-safe dish, put the cream cheese, mozzarella, and almond flour. Microwave for about 1 minute. Blend until smooth.

2. When thoroughly mixed and soft, add baking powder, flaxseed, and egg. Suppose the dough is too hard, microwave for an extra 15 seconds.

3. Split your dough into six portions and shape it into small balls. Put the balls into the bucket of your air fryer.

4. Set the temperature and adjust the clock to about 320 ° F for around a 12-minute timer.

5. Let the rolls cool fully before serving.

7. Cilantro Lime Roasted Cauliflower

Preparation time: 10 minutes

Cooking time: 7 minutes

Servings: 4 people

Ingredients:

- 2 tablespoons chopped cilantro
- 1 medium lime
- 1/2 teaspoon garlic powder
- 2 teaspoons chili powder
- 2 tablespoons coconut oil, melted
- 2 cups chopped cauliflower florets

Directions:

1. Toss your cauliflower with coconut oil in a big dish. Dust some garlic powder and chili powder. Put the prepared cauliflower in the bucket of your air fryer.

2. Set the temperature and adjust the clock to about 350°F for around 7 minutes.

3. At the sides, the cauliflower would be soft and starting to become golden. Put in the serving dish.

4. Slice the lime and squeeze the juice over your cauliflower. Garnish using cilantro.

8. Green Bean Casserole

Preparation time: 10 minutes

Cooking time: 15 minutes

Servings: 4 people

Ingredients:

- 1/2 ounce pork rinds, finely ground
- 1 pound fresh green beans, edges trimmed
- 1/4 teaspoon xanthan gum
- 1/2 cup chicken broth
- 1-ounce full-fat cream cheese
- 1/2 cup heavy whipping cream
- 1/2 cup chopped white mushrooms
- 1/4 cup diced yellow onion
- 4 tablespoons unsalted butter

Directions:

1. Melt some butter in a medium-sized skillet over medium flame. Sauté the mushrooms and onion for around 3-5 minutes before they become tender and fragrant.

2. Transfer the cream cheese, heavy whipped cream, and broth. Mix until thick. Bring it to a boil and decrease the flame to let it simmer. Sprinkle your xanthan into the pan and turn off the flame.

3. Cut the green beans into 2-inch pieces and put them in a circular 4-cup baking tray. Pour the combination of sauce over them and swirl until they are covered. Cover the dish with the rinds of ground pork. Place it in the bucket of your air fryer.

4. Set the temperature and adjust the clock to about 320°F for around 15 minutes.

5. When completely baked, the top will be golden brown, and green beans would be fork tender. Serve it hot.

9. Buffalo Cauliflower

Preparation time: 5 minutes

Cooking time: 5 minutes

Servings: 4 people

Ingredients:

- 1/4 cup buffalo sauce
- 1/2 (1-ounce) dry ranch seasoning packet
- 2 tablespoons salted butter, melted
- 4 cups cauliflower florets

Directions:

1. Toss the cauliflower with the butter and dry the ranch in a wide pot. Place it in the bucket of your air fryer.

2. Set the temperature and adjust the clock to about 400°F for around 5 minutes.

3. During frying, rotate the basket at least two to three times. Take out the cauliflower from the fryer basket when soft, and then toss in the buffalo sauce. Serve it hot.

10. Kale Chips

Preparation time: 5 minutes

Cooking time: 5 minutes

Servings: 4 people

Ingredients:

- 1/2 teaspoon salt
- 2 teaspoons avocado oil
- 4 cups stemmed kale

Directions:

1. Toss the kale in some avocado oil in a wide bowl and dust it with some salt. Put it in the bucket of your air fryer.
2. Set the temperature and adjust the clock to about 400°F for around 5 minutes.
3. Kale, when cooked completely, would be crisp. Instantly serve.

11. Roasted Garlic

Preparation time: 5 minutes

Cooking time: 20 minutes

Servings: 12 people

Ingredients:

- 2 teaspoons avocado oil
- 1 medium head garlic

Directions:

1. Remove the garlic from any remaining excess peel. However, keep the cloves protected. Slice 1/4 of the garlic head off, showing the tops of the cloves.
2. Add your avocado oil to it. In a small layer of aluminum foil, put the garlic head, tightly enclosing it. Put it in the bucket of your air fryer.
3. Set the temperature and adjust the clock to about 400 °F for around 20 minutes. Monitor it after about 15 minutes if the garlic head is a little shorter.
4. Garlic should be nicely browned when finished and very tender.

5. Cloves can pop out to eat and be scattered or sliced quickly. Up to 2 - 5 in an airtight jar store in the fridge. You can even freeze individual cloves on a baking tray, and then put them together in a fridge-safe storage bag when frozen completely.

12. Zucchini Parmesan Chips

Preparation time: 10 minutes

Cooking time: 10 minutes

Servings: 4 people

Ingredients:

- 1/2 cup grated Parmesan cheese
- 1 large egg
- 1-ounce pork rinds
- 2 medium zucchini

Directions:

1. "Cut zucchini into thick slices of about 1/4 ". To extract excess water, put on a dry kitchen towel or two paper towels for around 30 minutes.

2. Put pork rinds and process until finely ground in the food processor. Dump into a medium-sized bowl and blend with parmesan.

3. In a shallow bowl, beat your egg.

4. Add the egg into pork rind mixture; soak zucchini pieces in it, covering as thoroughly as possible. Put each piece gently in a thin layer in the air fryer bucket, working as required in groups or individually.

5. Set the temperature and adjust the clock to about 320 degrees F for around 10 minutes.

6. Midway through the cooking process, turn your chips. Serve hot.

13. Crispy Brussels sprouts

Preparation time: 5 minutes

Cooking time: 10 minutes

Servings: 4 people

Ingredients:

- 1 tablespoon unsalted butter, melted
- 1 tablespoon coconut oil
- 1 pound Brussels sprouts

Directions:

1. Please remove all of the loose leaves from the Brussels sprouts and break them in half.

2. Sprinkle the sprouts with some coconut oil and placed them in the bowl of your air fryer.

3. Set the temperature and adjust the clock to about 400 ° F and for around 10 minutes. Based on how they tend to cook, you might want to softly mix midway through the cooking period.

4. They should be soft with deeper caramelized spots when fully baked. Take out from the bucket of fryers and drizzle some melted butter. Serve instantly.

14. Cheesy Cauliflower Tots

Preparation time: 15 minutes

Cooking time: 12 minutes

Servings: 4 people

Ingredients:

- 1/8 teaspoon onion powder
- 1/4 teaspoon dried parsley
- 1/4 teaspoon garlic powder
- 1 large egg
- 1/2 cup grated Parmesan cheese
- 1 cup shredded mozzarella cheese
- 1 large head cauliflower

Directions:

1. Fill a big pot with 2 cups of water on the cooktop and put a steamer in the pot. Bring the water to a boil. Chop the cauliflower into florets and put it on a steamer bowl. Close the pot with a lid.

2. Enable cauliflower to steam for around 7 minutes before they are tender fork. Take out your cauliflower from the steamer basket and put it in a cheesecloth or dry kitchen towel, and leave it to cool down. Squeeze over the sink and extract as much extra moisture as necessary. If not all the moisture is extracted, the mixture would be too fragile to shape into tots. Crush to a smooth consistency using a fork.

3. Add in some parmesan, mozzarella, parsley, garlic powder, egg, and onion powder and place the cauliflower in a big mixing dish. Stir when thoroughly mixed. The paste should be sticky but hard to shape.

4. Roll into tot form by taking 2 teaspoons of the mix. Repeat for the remaining mixture. Put in the bucket of your air fryer.

5. Set the temperature and Adjust the clock to about 320 ° F for around 12-minute.

6. Switch tots midway through the cooking period. When fully baked, cauliflower tots should be crispy. Serve hot.

15. Sausage-Stuffed Mushroom Caps

Preparation time: 10 minutes

Cooking time: 8 minutes

Servings: 2 people

Ingredients:

- 1 teaspoon minced fresh garlic
- 1/4 cup grated Parmesan cheese
- 2 tablespoons blanched finely ground almond flour
- 1/4 cup chopped onion
- 1/2 pound Italian sausage
- 6 large Portobello mushroom caps

Directions:

1. Using a spoon, voiding scrapings, to hollow out each mushroom shell.

2. Brown the sausage for approximately 10 minutes or until thoroughly baked, and no red exists in a small-sized skillet over medium flame. Drain and then add some reserved mushroom scrapings, parmesan, almond flour, onion, and garlic. Fold ingredients softly together and proceed to cook for an extra minute, and then remove from flame.

3. Pour the mixture uniformly into mushroom caps and put the caps in a circular 6-inch pot. Put the pan in the bucket of your air fryer.

4. Set the temperature and adjust the clock to about 375 °F for around 8 minutes.

5. The tops would be browned and fizzing when it is cooked completely. Serve it hot.

16. Garlic Herb Butter Roasted Radishes

Preparation time: 10 minutes

Cooking time: 10 minutes

Servings: 4 people

Ingredients:

- black pepper
- 1/4 teaspoon ground
- 1/4 teaspoon dried oregano
- 1/2 teaspoon dried parsley
- 1/2 teaspoon garlic powder
- 2 tablespoons unsalted butter, melted
- 1 pound radishes

Directions:

1. Remove the radish roots and split them into quarters.
2. Put seasonings and butter in a shallow dish. In the herb butter, turn the radishes and put them in your air-fryer basket.
3. Set the temperature and adjust the clock to about 350°F for around 10 minutes.
4. Simply throw the radishes in the air fryer basket midway through the cooking time. Keep cooking until the edges start to turn dark brown.
5. Serve it hot.

17. Loaded Roasted Broccoli

Preparation time: 10 minutes

Cooking time: 10 minutes

Servings: 3 people

Ingredients:

- 1 scallion, sliced on the bias
- 4 slices sugar-free bacon, cooked and crumbled

- 1/4 cup full-fat sour cream
- 1/2 cup shredded sharp Cheddar cheese
- 1 tablespoon coconut oil
- 3 cups fresh broccoli florets

Directions:

1. In the air fryer basket, put the broccoli and drizzle with some coconut oil.
2. Set the temperature and adjust the clock to about 350°F for around 10 minutes.
3. During frying, turn the basket at least two to three times to prevent burning.
4. Remove from the fryer as the broccoli continues to crisp at the ends. Garnish with some scallion slices and finish with sour cream, melted cheese, and crumbled bacon.

CHAPTER 4: Air Fryer Snack and Appetizer Recipes

1. Bacon-Wrapped Brie

Preparation time: 5 minutes

Cooking time: 10 minutes

Servings: 8 people

Ingredients:

- 1 (8-ounce) round Brie
- 4 slices sugar-free bacon

Directions:

1. To shape an X, position two bacon strips. Put the third bacon strip over the middle of the X sideways. Position vertically over the X a fourth slice of bacon. On top of your X, it could appear like an addition sign (+). Position the Brie in the middle of the bacon.

2. Tie the bacon from around Brie, using several toothpicks to hold it. To suit your air-fryer container, take a piece of parchment paper and put your bacon-wrapped Brie on it. Put it in the container of your air fryer.

3. Set the temperature and set the clock to about 400°F for around 10 minutes.

4. When there are only 3 minutes left on the clock, rotate Brie gently.

5. The bacon will be crispy when grilled, and the cheese will be smooth and melted. Cut into eight pieces to serve.

2. Crust less Meat Pizza

Preparation time: 5 minutes

Cooking time: 5 minutes

Servings: 1 people

Ingredients:

- 2 tablespoons low-carb, sugar-free pizza sauce for dipping
- 1 tablespoon grated or cutup Parmesan cheese
- 2 slices sugar-free bacon, cooked and crumbled
- 1/4 cup cooked ground sausage
- 7 slices pepperoni
- 1/2 cup shredded mozzarella cheese

Directions:

1. Line the bottom of a mozzarella 6' cake tray. Put on top of your cheese some sausage, pepperoni, and bacon and cover with parmesan. Put the pan in the bowl of your air fryer.

2. Set the temperature and set the clock to about 400°F for around 5 minutes.

3. Remove from the flame once the cheese is fizzing and lightly golden. Serve hot with some pizza sauce as dipping.

3. Garlic Cheese Bread

Preparation time: 10 minutes

Cooking time: 10 minutes

Servings: 2 people

Ingredients:

- 1/2 teaspoon garlic powder
- 1 large egg1 large egg
- 1/4 cup grated Parmesan cheese
- 1 cup shredded mozzarella cheese1 cup shredded mozzarella cheese

Directions:

1. In a big bowl, combine all the ingredients. To fit your air fryer bowl cut a piece of parchment paper. Add the blend onto the parchment paper to form a circle and put it in the air fryer basket.

2. Set the temperature and adjust the timer to about 350°F for around 10 minutes.

3. Serve it hot.

4. Mozzarella Pizza Crust

Preparation time: 5 minutes

Cooking time: 10 minutes

Servings: 1 people

Ingredients:

- 1 large egg white
- 1 tablespoon full-fat cream cheese
- 2 tablespoons blanched finely ground almond flour
- 1/2 cup shredded whole-milk mozzarella cheese

Directions:

1. In a small oven-safe bowl, put almond flour, mozzarella, and cream cheese. Microwave for about 30 seconds. Mix until the mixture becomes a softball. Add egg white and mix until fluffy, circular dough forms.

2. Shape into 6 round crust pizza.

3. To suit your air fryer container, take a piece of parchment paper and put each crust on the parchment paper. Place it in the basket of your air fryer.

4. Set the temperature and adjust the clock to about 350°F for around 10 minutes.

5. Switch sides after 5 minutes and put any preferred toppings on your crust at this stage. Keep cooking until lightly golden. Immediately serve.

5. Spicy Spinach Artichoke Dip

Preparation time: 10 minutes

Cooking time: 10 minutes

Servings: 6 people

Ingredients:

- 1 cup shredded pepper jack cheese
- 1/4 cup grated Parmesan cheese
- 1/2 teaspoon garlic powder
- 1/4 cup full-fat sour cream
- 1/4 cup full-fat mayonnaise
- 8 ounces full-fat cream cheese, softened
- 1/4 cup chopped pickled jalapeños
- 1 (14-ounce) can artichoke hearts, drained and chopped
- 10 ounces frozen spinach, drained and thawed

Directions:

1. In a 4-cup baking dish, combine all your ingredients. Put it in the basket of your air fryer.

2. Set the temperature and adjust the timer for around 10 minutes to about 320 °F.

3. When dark brown and sizzling, remove from flame. Serve it hot.

6. Mini Sweet Pepper Poppers

Preparation time: 18 minutes

Cooking time: 8 minutes

Servings: 4 people

Ingredients:

- 1/4 cup shredded pepper jack cheese
- 4 slices sugar-free bacon, cooked and crumbled
- 4 ounces full-fat cream cheese, softened
- 8 mini sweet peppers

Directions:

1. Cut the tops of your peppers and lengthwise cut each one in the quarter. Remove the seeds and cut the membranes with a tiny knife.
2. Toss the bacon, cream cheese, and pepper jack in a tiny bowl.
3. Put each sweet pepper with 3 tsp. of the mixture and push down smoothly. Put it in the air fryer basket.
4. Set the temperature and adjust the clock to about 400°F for around 8 minutes.

5. Serve it hot.

7. Bacon-Wrapped Onion Rings

Preparation time: 5 minutes

Cooking time: 10 minutes

Servings: 4 people

Ingredients:

- 8 slices sugar-free bacon
- 1 tablespoon sriracha
- 1 large onion, peeled

Directions:

1. Cut your onion into large 1/4-inch pieces. Sprinkle the sriracha on the pieces of your onion. Take two pieces of onion and cover the circles with bacon. Redo with the rest of the onion and bacon. Put in the container of your air fryer.

2. Set the temperature and adjust the clock to about 350°F for around 10 minutes.

3. To rotate the onion rings midway through the frying period, use tongs. The bacon would be crispy once completely fried. Serve hot.

8. Mozzarella Sticks

Preparation time: 60 minutes

Cooking time: 10 minutes

Servings: 4 people

Ingredients:

- 2 big eggs
- 1 teaspoon dried parsley
- 1/2 ounce pork rinds, finely ground
- 1/2 cup of grated Parmesan or any other kind of cheese
- 6 (1-ounce) mozzarella string cheese sticks

Directions:

1. Put mozzarella sticks on a chopping board and slice in half. Freeze for about 45 minutes or till solid. Remove your frozen sticks after an hour if freezing overnight, then put them in a sealed zip-top plastic bag and put them back for potential usage in the freezer.

2. Mix the ground pork rinds, parmesan, and parsley in a wide dish.

3. Whisk the eggs together in a medium dish separately.

4. Soak a stick of frozen mozzarella into whisked eggs and then cover in Parmesan mixture. Repeat for the leftover sticks. Put the sticks of mozzarella in the basket of your air fryer.

5. Set the temperature to about 400 degrees F and adjust the clock for around 10 minutes or till it turns golden.

6. Serve it hot.

9. Pork Rind Tortillas

Preparation time: 10 minutes

Cooking time: 5 minutes

Servings: 4 people

Ingredients:

- 1 large egg
- 2 tablespoons full-fat cream cheese
- 3/4 cup shredded mozzarella cheese
- 1-ounce pork rinds

Directions:

1. Put pork rinds and pulses into the food processor pulse till finely ground.

2. Put mozzarella in a big oven-safe bowl. Cut the cream cheese into tiny bits and transfer them to the bowl. Microwave for about 30 seconds or so; all cheeses are molten and can be combined into a ball quickly. To the cheese mixture, add some ground pork rinds and eggs.

3. Keep mixing until the combination forms a ball. If it cools too fast and the cheese hardens, microwave for another 10 seconds.

4. Divide the dough into four tiny balls. Put each dough ball among 2 pieces of parchment paper and roll into a 1/4" flat layer.

5. Put the tortilla chips in a thin layer in your air fryer basket, operating in groups if required.

6. Set the temperature and adjust the clock to about 400°F for around 5 minutes.

7. Tortillas, when thoroughly baked, would be crispy and solid.

8. Instantly serve.

10. Bacon Cheeseburger Dip

Preparation time: 20 minutes

Cooking time: 10 minutes

Servings: 6 people

Ingredients:

- 2 large pickle spears, chopped
- 6 slices sugar-free bacon, cooked and crumbled
- 1/2 pound cooked 80/20 ground beef
- 11/4 cups shredded medium Cheddar cheese, divided
- 1 tablespoon Worcestershire sauce
- 1 teaspoon garlic powder
- 1/4 cup chopped onion
- 1/4 cup full-fat sour cream
- 1/4 cup full-fat mayonnaise
- 8 ounces full-fat cream cheese

Directions:

1. Put the cream cheese in a big, oven-safe dish and microwave for about 45 seconds. Add the Worcestershire sauce, sour cream, mayonnaise, garlic powder, onion, and

1 cup of Cheddar and mix well. Add fried ground beef and your bacon to it. Sprinkle the leftover Cheddar on top of the mixture.

2. Put in a 6-inch bowl and dump into the basket of your air fryer.

3. Set the temperature and adjust the clock to about 400°F for around 10 minutes.

4. When the surface is golden brown and bubbling, dipping is cooked. Scatter pickles over the dish. Serve hot.

11. Pizza Rolls

Preparation time: 18 minutes

Cooking time: 10 minutes

Servings: 8 people

Ingredients:

- 2 tablespoons grated Parmesan cheese
- 1/2 teaspoon dried parsley
- 1/4 teaspoon garlic powder
- 2 tablespoons unsalted butter, melted

- 8 (1-ounce) mozzarella string cheese sticks, cut into 3 pieces each
- 72 slices pepperoni
- 2 large eggs
- 1/2 cup almond flour
- 2 cups shredded mozzarella cheese

Directions:

1. Put almond flour and mozzarella in a big oven-safe bowl. Microwave for a minute. Withdraw the bowl and blend until a ball of dough forms. If required, microwave for an extra 30 seconds.

2. Crack the eggs into your bowl and blend until the ball becomes soft dough. Wet your hands with some water and gently knead your dough.

3. Rip off two wide pieces of parchment paper and brush with nonstick cooking spray on each side. Put your dough ball between the 2 pieces, facing dough with coated sides. To roll dough to a thickness of 1/4', use a rolling pin.

4. To cut into 24 rectangles, use a cutter. Put three pepperoni pieces and 1 strip of stringed cheese on each one of your rectangle.

5. Fold the rectangle in two, lining the filling with cheese and pepperoni. Ends closed by squeeze or roll. To suit your air-fryer bowl, take a piece of parchment paper and put it in the basket. On the parchment paper, place the rolls.

6. Set the temperature and adjust the clock to about 350°F for around 10 minutes.

7. Open your fryer after 5 minutes and rotate the rolls of pizza. Resume the fryer and proceed to cook until the rolls of pizza are golden brown.

8. Put the garlic powder, butter, and parsley in a tiny bowl. Brush the mix over the rolls of fried pizza and scatter the pizza with parmesan. Serve it hot.

12. Bacon Jalapeño Cheese Bread

Preparation time: 10 minutes

Cooking time: 18 minutes

Servings: 4 people

Ingredients:

- 4 slices sugar-free bacon, cooked and chopped
- 2 large eggs
- 1/4 cup chopped pickled jalapeños
- 1/4 cup of grated Parmesan cheese
- 2 cups shredded mozzarella cheese

Directions:

1. In a wide bowl, combine all your ingredients. Cut a slice of parchment to match the basket of your air fryer.
2. With a touch of water, dampen both of your hands and spread the mix out into a disk. Depending on the fryer's scale, you would need to split this into 2 small cheese bread.
3. Put the parchment paper and your cheese bread into the basket of the air fryer.
4. Set the temperature and adjust the clock to about 320°F for around 15 minutes.
5. Turn the bread gently once you have 5 minutes remaining.
6. The top would be golden brown when completely baked. Serve it hot.

13. Spicy Buffalo Chicken Dip

Preparation time: 10 minutes

Cooking time: 10 minutes

Servings: 4 people

Ingredients:

- 2 scallions, sliced on the bias
- 11/2 cups shredded medium Cheddar cheese, divided
- 1/3 cup chopped pickled jalapeños
- 1/3 cup full-fat ranch dressing
- 1/2 cup buffalo sauce

- 8 ounces full-fat cream cheese, softened
- 1 cup cooked, diced chicken breast

Directions:

1. Put the chicken in a spacious bowl. Add some ranch dressing, cream cheese, and buffalo sauce. Mix until the sauces are fully blended and completely soft. Fold the jalapeños along with 1 cup of Cheddar in it.

2. Transfer the mixture into a circular 4-cup baking dish and put the leftover Cheddar on top. Put the dish in your air-fryer basket.

3. Set the temperature and adjust the clock to about 350°F for around 10 minutes.

4. When cooked, it'll be brown at the top, and the dip will bubble. Serve it hot with some cut-up scallions on top.

14. Garlic Parmesan Chicken Wings

Preparation time: 4 minutes

Cooking time: 25 minutes

Servings: 4 people

Ingredients:

- 1/4 teaspoon dried parsley
- 1/3 cup grated Parmesan cheese
- 4 tablespoons unsalted butter, melted
- 1 tablespoon baking powder
- 1/2 teaspoon garlic powder
- 1 teaspoon pink Himalayan salt
- 2 pounds raw chicken wings

Directions:

1. Put the chicken wings, 1/2 teaspoon of garlic powder, salt, and baking powder in a wide bowl, then toss. Put the wings in the basket of your air fryer.

2. Set the temperature and adjust the clock to about 400°F for around 25 minutes.

3. During the cooking period, rotate the bowl two to three times to ensure even cooking.

4. Mix the parmesan, butter, and parsley in a shallow dish.

5. Please take out your wings from the fryer and put them in a big, clean dish. Over your wings, pour the butter mixture and toss until covered completely. Serve it hot.

15. Bacon-Wrapped Jalapeño Poppers

Preparation time: 16 minutes

Cooking time: 12 minutes

Servings: 5 people

Ingredients:

- 12 slices sugar-free bacon
- 1/4 teaspoon garlic powder
- 1/3 cup shredded medium Cheddar cheese
- 3 ounces full-fat cream cheese
- 6 jalapeños (about 4" long each)

Directions:

1. Slice off the tops of the jalapeños and cut lengthwise down the middle into two sections. Using a knife to gently detach the white membrane and seeds from the peppers.

2. Put the Cheddar, cream cheese, and garlic powder in a big, oven-proof dish. Stir in the microwave for about 30 seconds. Spoon the blend of cheese into your hollow jalapeño.

3. Place a bacon slice over each half of the jalapeño, totally covering the pepper. Place it in the basket of an air fryer.

4. Set the temperature and adjust the clock to about 400°F for around 12 minutes.

5. Flip the peppers halfway into the cooking period. Serve it hot.

16. Prosciutto-Wrapped Parmesan Asparagus

Preparation time: 10 minutes

Cooking time: 10 minutes

Servings: 4 people

Ingredients:

- 2 tablespoons salted butter, melted

- 1/3 cup grated Parmesan cheese

- 1/8 teaspoon red pepper flakes

- 2 teaspoons lemon juice

- 1 tablespoon coconut oil, melted

- 12 (0.5-ounce) slices prosciutto

- 1 pound asparagus

Directions:

1. Put an asparagus spear on top of a slice of prosciutto on a clean cutting board.

2. Drizzle with coconut oil and lemon juice. Sprinkle the asparagus with parmesan and red pepper flakes. Roll prosciutto across a spear of asparagus. Put it in the basket of your air fryer.

3. Set the temperature and adjust the clock to about 375 °F for around 10 minutes or so.

4. Dribble the asparagus roll with some butter before serving.

CHAPTER 5: Desserts

1. Mini Cheesecake

Preparation time: 10 minutes

Cooking time: 15-18 minutes

Servings: 2 people

Ingredients:

- 1/8 cup powdered erythritol
- 1/2 teaspoon vanilla extract
- 1 large egg
- 4 ounces full-fat cream cheese, softened
- 2 tablespoons granular erythritol
- 2 tablespoons salted butter
- 1/2 cup walnuts

Directions:

1. In a food mixer, put the butter, walnuts, and granular erythritol. Pulse until the items bind together to shape the dough.
2. Push the dough into a 4-inch spring form pan and put the pan in the bucket of your air fryer.
3. Set the temperature and adjust the clock to about 400°F for around 5 minutes.
4. Pick the crust when the timer dings, and let it cool.
5. Mix your cream cheese with the vanilla extract, egg, and powdered erythritol in a medium-sized bowl until creamy.

2. Pecan Brownies

Preparation time: 10 minutes

Cooking time: 20 minutes

Servings: 6 people

Ingredients:

- 1/4 cup low-carb, sugar-free chocolate chips
- 1/4 cup chopped pecans
- 1 large egg
- 1/4 cup unsalted butter, softened
- 1/2 teaspoon baking powder
- 2 tablespoons unsweetened cocoa powder
- 1/2 cup powdered erythritol
- 1/2 cup blanched finely ground almond flour

Directions:

1. Mix the almond flour, chocolate powder, erythritol, and baking powder in a big bowl. Stir in the egg and butter.

2. "Fold in the chocolate chips and pecans. Pour the mixture into a 6" circular baking tray. Place the pan in the bucket of your air fryer.

3. Set the temperature and adjust the clock to about 300°F for around 20 minutes.

4. A toothpick placed in the middle will fall out clean once completely fried. Please enable it to cool off entirely and firm up for about 20 minutes.

3. Cinnamon Sugar Pork Rinds

Preparation time: 5 minutes

Cooking time: 5 minutes

Servings: 2 people

Ingredients:

- 1/4 cup powdered erythritol
- 1/2 teaspoon ground cinnamon
- 2 tablespoons unsalted butter, melted
- 2 ounces pork rinds

Directions:

1. Toss the pork rinds and butter into a wide pan. Sprinkle some erythritol and cinnamon, and toss to cover uniformly.

2. Put the pork rinds into the bucket of your air fryer.

3. Set the temperature and adjust the clock to about 400°F for around 5 minutes.

4. Instantly serve.

4. Almond Butter Cookie Balls

Preparation time: 5 minutes

Cooking time: 10 minutes

Servings: 10 people

Ingredients:

- 1/2 teaspoon ground cinnamon
- 1/4 cup low-carb, sugar-free chocolate chips
- 1/4 cup shredded unsweetened coconut
- 1/4 cup powdered erythritol
- 1/4 cup low-carb protein powder
- 1 teaspoon vanilla extract
- 1 large egg
- 1 cup almond butter

Directions:

1. Mix the almond butter with the egg in a big pot. Add protein powder, vanilla, and erythritol to it.

2. Fold in the coconut, chocolate chips, and cinnamon. Roll into 1" spheres. Put the balls in a 6' circular baking tray and place them in the bucket of your air fryer.

3. Set the temperature and adjust the clock to about 10 minutes to around 320 °F.

4. Please enable it to cool fully. Up to 4 days in an airtight jar placed in the fridge.

Conclusion

These times, air frying is one of the most common cooking techniques and air fryers have become one of the chef's most impressive devices. In no time, air fryers can help you prepare nutritious and tasty meals! To prepare unique dishes for you and your family members, you do not need to be a master in the kitchen!

Everything you have to do is buy an air fryer and this wonderful cookbook for air fryers! Soon, you can make the greatest dishes ever and inspire those around you.

Cooked meals at home with you! Believe us! Get your hands on an air fryer and this handy set of recipes for air fryers and begin your new cooking experience! Have fun!

CPSIA information can be obtained
at www.ICGtesting.com
Printed in the USA
LVHW020355160621
690356LV00014B/1476